1991

The
Responsible
Administrator

Terry L. Cooper

The
Responsible
Administrator

An Approach to Ethics
for the
Administrative Role
Third Edition

Jossey-Bass Publishers

San Francisco • Oxford • 1990

THE RESPONSIBLE ADMINISTRATOR
An Approach to Ethics for the Administrative Role, Third Edition
by Terry L. Cooper

Copyright © 1990 by: Jossey-Bass Inc., Publishers
350 Sansome Street
San Francisco, California 94104
&
Jossey-Bass Limited
Headington Hill Hall
Oxford OX3 0BW

Library of Congress Cataloging-in-Publication Data

Cooper, Terry L., date.
    The responsible administrator : an approach to ethics for the
administrative role / Terry L. Cooper. — 3rd ed.
        p.   cm.—(The Jossey-Bass public administration series)
    Includes bibliographical references (p.   ) and index.
    ISBN 1-55542-290-X (alk. paper)
    1. Civil service ethics—United States.   2. Government executives—
Professional ethics—United States.   I. Title.   II. Series.
JK468.E7C66   1990
172'.2—dc20   90-5042
                                                                 CIP

Manufactured in the United States of America

The paper in this book meets the guidelines for
permanence and durability of the Committee on
Production Guidelines for Book Longevity of the
Council on Library Resources.

JACKET DESIGN BY WILLI BAUM

FIRST EDITION

Code 9093

The Jossey-Bass
Public Administration
Series

Contents

Preface

The Responsible Administrator was written for students and practitioners of public administration who want to develop their ethical as well as technical competence. It is for men and women in public service, or preparing for it, who sometimes worry what is the right thing to do, but who either have not taken the time to read books on ethical theory or suspect that such treatises would not be helpful at the practical level.

The education, training, and day-to-day practice of public administrators tends to be dominated by the practical problems of getting the job done. Concerns about *what* should be done and *why* it should be done get swept aside by the pressures of schedule and work load. Modern society is preoccupied with action, to the exclusion of reflection about values and principles. Theory is diminished to theories that concern means—"how to" crowds out "toward what end?"

Ethical theory, in particular, tends to suffer under the sway of this modern mentality. Because ethics involves substantive reasoning about obligations, consequences, and ultimate ends, its immediate utility for a producing/consuming society is suspect. Principles and values, "goods" and "oughts," seem pretty wispy stuff compared to cost-benefit ratios, GNP, tensile strength, organizational structures, assembly lines, budgets, and deadlines. The payoff for dealing formally with ethics is unclear for individual administrators and for organizations as well.

The result is a tendency either to totally ignore the study of ethics or to deal with it superficially. A study conducted by the Hastings Center two years before the first edition of this book was published revealed that "few higher-education institutions offer courses in ethics" (Watkins, 1980, p. 10). The researchers attributed this neglect primarily to the controversial nature of the teaching of ethics. Academicians apparently had difficulty agreeing on who should teach these courses, as well as some apprehension about "the dangers of indoctrination" (p. 10).

Since 1980 interest in administrative ethics seems to have mushroomed. The demand for in-service training sessions has increased substantially, more articles on ethics have appeared in the professional literature, sessions on ethics have grown in number and attendance at the annual conference of the American Society for Public Administration (ASPA), and in 1989 ASPA conducted its first national conference on governmental ethics, with seven hundred participants, including both practitioners and scholars.

However, April Hejka-Ekins (1988) recently surveyed 139 of the more than 200 schools that belong to the National Association of Schools of Public Affairs and Administration (NASPAA) and found that only 66 (31.4 percent) had offered an ethics course during 1985–86 or 1986–87. It appears that academe has responded weakly to the new interest; there is a disturbing lag in developing courses as part of the core curriculum of public administration education.

The underlying assumption behind this uneasiness with the formal study of ethics seems to be one of relativity and subjectivity. In a pluralistic society, where no one religious or cultural tradition is dominant, ethics tends to be viewed as a private, individual matter, not susceptible to the canons of rational inquiry. Openly to address the study of ethics in an academic setting is to run the risk of either creating unresolvable conflicts among those who hold differing ethical perspectives or unfairly propagandizing for one particular point of view.

The upshot of this reluctance to teach ethics is that once students leave universities, they are ill equipped to think about the ethical problems they face regularly on the job. We should not be surprised, then, to see expedience and technical considerations dominate decision making. Even when ethical issues are recognized, they are considered hopelessly frustrating and beyond the domain of rational analysis. We can predict that decisions involving value conflicts will not be engaged as systematically, or as seriously, or as openly as matters of economics, politics, and organizational survival.

Purpose of the Book

The Responsible Administrator is one attempt to respond to this state of affairs, especially as it is manifested in public bureaucracies. It is important to identify the particular contribution that is intended here. The focus of the book is the *role* of the public administrator in an organizational setting; the key concept used in dealing with that role is *responsibility*. Both these terms are peculiarly modern in connotation. Both suggest a world view in which the power of tradition is broken and human beings are left to construct a world of their own making. Roles must be devised and responsibility defined as ways of reestablishing obligations in our modern, pluralistic, technological society. Technology is applied not only to production, but also to society itself.

Gibson Winter (1966, pp. 254–255) has observed: "Responsibility is a relatively new term in the ethical vocabulary, appearing in the nineteenth century with a somewhat ambiguous meaning. The term evaluates action and attributes it to an agent; it does so in lieu of cosmic or natural structures of obligation. The historical awareness of the nineteenth century, the scientific and technological revolutions, and the collapse of metaphysical systems had undermined fixed notions of obligations. The term 'responsibility' was a way of filling this gap by defining the scope of accountability and obligation in contexts of law and common culture."

Similarly, Richard McKeon's study of the emergence of the term in Western thought reveals that responsibility first appeared in English and French in 1787. It was used initially in reference to the political institutions arising out of the American and French revolutions, but its use continued through the nineteenth century. When "constitutional government was vastly extended, in scope of operation and in spread among nations, as a result of contacts of cultures and peoples," the concept of responsibility became increasingly significant as a way of defining a common set of values among people of divergent cultures and traditions (1957, p. 23).

The concept of *role* then becomes a convenient way to package expectations and obligations associated with the modern world. As we cease to view social functions as received intact from the past, but as something to be manipulated and created anew, we take upon ourselves bounded obligation in the form of various roles. People exercise responsibility and are held responsible in society by accepting and carrying out an array of more or less well-defined roles: "employee," "parent," "citizen," and "group member." The most problematic roles are those that are not clearly defined, usually because there is little agreement about the boundaries of responsibility associated with them. What does it mean to be a responsible parent in the last decade of the twentieth century? Or a responsible spouse? A responsible citizen? A responsible politician? Or a responsible public administrator?

The problem is that although administrators are held responsible for certain duties (duties that constitute the professional role), they sometimes *believe* they are obligated to act otherwise. This is because administrators, along with everyone else in modern society, maintain an array of roles related to family, community, and society, each carrying a set of obligations and vested with certain personal interest. The quite common result is conflict among roles as these competing forces push and pull in opposite directions. The effects of these conflicts are compounded by the range of discretion administrators must exercise. Legislation frequently provides only broad language about its intent, leaving the specifics to administrators. Consequently, ethical standards and sensitivity are crucial to the responsible use of this discretion.

Organization of This Book

The first and most basic task of this book is to illuminate the ethical decision-making process. Chapter One begins with some basic concepts for understanding the different levels of deliberation at which ethical problems are addressed. This is followed by a model for analyzing and resolving these problems. The model is partly linear, involving a sequence of steps, and partly nonlinear, requiring a search for integration of several key elements, including moral rules, ethical principles, self-image, and the norms of the political community. It also combines reasoning, emotion, and beliefs.

Chapter Two develops the social context within which the public administrator must work and discusses the problem of defining and maintaining the administrator's role in the diverse and relativistic environment of modern society. Without the guidance of a coherent tradition, in modern societies the administrative role is just one more set of obligations and interests that must be managed amid an array of other competing roles. One significant implication of this social context is the inescapably political nature of public administration.

Chapter Three addresses the dual nature of administrative responsibility in modern society: objective responsibility (in which one is held accountable by superiors, the public, and legislation) and subjective responsibility (in which one feels and believes oneself to be responsible). Conflict between these two forms of responsibility seems to be the most common form in which ethical dilemmas emerge.

Chapter Four further develops the conflict between subjective and objective responsibility. Conflicts of authority, role, and interest are reviewed. It is not that these three forms of conflicting responsibility require distinctly different forms of analysis to be resolved. Rather, understanding the different ways we experience conflicts helps us clarify the key actors and relationships that must be examined and dealt with if we are to achieve resolution.

Chapter Five presents two general approaches to maintaining, from a management perspective, responsible conduct in public organizations—internal and external controls. External controls include instruments imposed from outside the individual, such as codes of ethics and ethics legislation; internal controls involve the professional values and standards that public servants have internalized through the socialization process, both personal and professional.

Continuing the management perspective from Chapter Five, Chapter Six focuses on the importance of establishing congruence among the various internal and external controls. Two examples illustrate what happens when this is not done. Four components of responsible conduct are then discussed: individual attributes, organization structure, organization culture, and societal expectations.

Chapter Seven shifts the perspective to an individual attempting to act ethically in the face of management that has become corrupt or lost sight of its mandated mission in the public interest. The problem is one of conflicting loyalties—to superiors on the one hand and to the public on the other. Whistle blowing is recognized as one response to this kind of conflict. Sources of organizational pressure on individual employees are outlined, organizational remedies are discussed, and the ultimate necessity for individual responsibility is asserted. The chapter closes with a treatment of the components required for individual ethical autonomy.

The concluding chapter summarizes the argument developed through the previous seven chapters and presents a model of responsible administration that brings together the components of responsible conduct from Chapter Six and the components of individual ethical autonomy from Chapter Seven.

The case material in the book is derived from actual situations; they are real cases, fictionalized only slightly to protect those who wrote them. They are intended primarily as illustration, but also to stimulate thinking about the ethical problems they portray. For both reasons, the situations are left unresolved. To indicate an outcome would diminish the experience of dilemma they are calculated to evoke; it would also short-circuit the reader's own reflections. For the same reason, the case narratives are a bit longer and more detailed than usual. Again, the ultimate purpose of *The Responsible Administrator* is to illuminate the ethical situation of the public administrator and cultivate imaginative reflection about it—not to prescribe a particular set of public service values.

This book is largely descriptive and analytical; it is only

secondarily prescriptive, and even then only in a particular sense. It prescribes techniques that individual administrators can use in analyzing ethical dilemmas they confront, and it outlines the desirable combination of components for fostering responsible administration. However, there is no attempt to develop a substantive ethic for public administrators. That is a necessary and important undertaking, but it is dealt with in another volume on citizenship and public administration (Cooper, 1991). For the purposes of this book, a public service ethic is assumed.

Acknowledgments

Intellectual honesty and humility require admitting that writing a book is not a task for which an author ought to take sole credit. The more I write and reflect, the clearer it becomes that scholarship is truly a collective enterprise. I wish to express my deepest appreciation to the women and men at all levels of American public service who have shared their struggles, insights, and creativity. Their cases and ensuing discussions in ethics workshops I have conducted since 1975 are the empirical basis for this book and a major source of any knowledge I may be able to pass along. I have been deeply impressed by their intention to do the right thing in the face of formidable impediments.

I also wish to thank my colleagues around the nation who are teaching and engaging in research on administrative ethics. Our numbers have grown substantially since 1982 when *The Responsible Administrator* first appeared. Through sessions at the annual conferences of ASPA, the establishment of the Ethics Network and its *Ethnet* newsletter by Bayard Catron, and the annual symposia of the Theory Network, a genuine community of scholars and practitioners is emerging around the nation who are committed to the development of public administrative ethics.

My thanks also go to the reviewers who carefully examined the previous edition of this book and gave me their constructive advice, and to Alan Shrader at Jossey-Bass, whose competent editorial guidance has been invaluable.

To Lucy Samuels, Marie Smith, and Artimese Porter, who prepared the manuscript for publication, I owe appreciation for helping me through the trials of word processing, last-minute re-visions, and races to the post office.

And finally, I wish to express again my gratitude to my dear-est and best colleague—my wife, Megan—whose inspiration, insights, writing skill, knowledge of the field of public admin-istration, and personal support were freely and warmly given at every stage of this project.

All these people and more have helped to broaden and sharpen my thoughts. I deeply appreciate their gifts to me, but what I have done with them in these pages is my responsibility, not theirs.

Los Angeles, California   Terry L. Cooper
September 1990

The Author

Terry L. Cooper is associate professor of public administration at the School of Public Administration, University of Southern California. He received his B.A. degree (1960) from the University of California at Los Angeles in history, his M.Th. degree (1964) from the School of Theology at Claremont, and his Ph.D. degree (1973) from the University of Southern California in social ethics.

Cooper's research interests have included administrative ethics, citizen participation, and citizenship in the American tradition. His publications include *An Ethic of Citizenship for Public Administration* (1991) and numerous journal articles.

Cooper served on the Committee on Professional Standards and Ethics of the American Society for Public Administration from 1976 to 1982 and was involved in the writing of its *Applying Professional Standards and Ethics in the Eighties: A Workbook and Study Guide for Public Administrators*. During 1988–89 he was a Fulbright Professor at the Chinese University of Hong Kong, where he lectured and conducted research on the anticipatory responses of Hong Kong senior civil servants to the transfer of sovereignty to the People's Republic of China in 1997.

Chapter One

Understanding
Ethical Decision Making

James A. Michener's novel *Chesapeake* (1978) portrays the history of two families who settled near each other on the shores of Chesapeake Bay during the American Colonial era. As Quakers, the Paxmores tended to espouse values quite different, in both religion and politics, from those of the Steeds, devout Roman Catholics. However, in spite of their divergent doctrines and frequent conflicts, the two families managed to live as neighbors with a kind of grudging respect and a willingness to work things out.

In the closing pages, there is a scene involving the family patriarchs of the mid-1970s, Pusey Paxmore and Owen Steed. The two men are sitting on the porch of the Paxmore house, looking out over the Chesapeake and reflecting on the events of Watergate. Pusey had been a high-level appointee in the Nixon White House, and Owen was one of the oil company executives who had covertly, and illegally, raised money for CREEP, the Committee to Re-elect the President. Both men's careers were seriously damaged by the

1

scandals, and both have returned home to retire and to think. During this particular conversation, there is this insightful and pithy exchange:

Steed: How do you explain the corruption, the near-treason?

Paxmore: Men without character slip from one position to the next. And never comprehend the awful downward course they're on.

Steed: Couldn't Nixon have stopped it?

Paxmore: Woodrow Wilson could have. Or Teddy Roosevelt. And does thee know why? Because they had accumulated through years of apprenticeship a theory of government. A theory of democracy, if thee will. And they would have detected the rot the minute it started.

Steed: Why didn't the Californians?

Paxmore: For a simple reason. They were deficient in education. They'd gone to those chrome-and-mirror schools where procedures are taught, not principles. I doubt if any one of them had ever contemplated a real moral problem, in the abstract where character is formed.

This bit of dialogue (p. 1049) suggests the underlying assumption of this book: Ethical public administration requires a *theoretical* perspective on the role of the public administrator. Moreover, this theoretical perspective must be developed by practicing administrators through a combination of experience, contemplation, and study, whether in a structured course or through self-motivated inquiry.

The theories of others, including scholars from various disciplines and historical periods, are essential ingredients in a professional ethic, but a fundamental assumption of this book is that knowing the thoughts of others is only the beginning. Administrators must also develop skill in *thinking about* ethical problems, toward the end of creating a working professional ethic of their own. Without cultivating this ability to theorize and generalize from experience, no public administrator can transcend the boundaries of particular events to comprehend and assess them. Without the illumination born of the marriage of abstract thought and practical experience, it is impossible to see where we are going. Choice is constrained and freedom is ultimately stunted by the unforeseen consequences of our actions.

This chapter presents a sequence of steps you might employ in thinking about ethical issues you confront. The goal is not only to develop skills in resolving particular situations, but to help you cultivate a habit of using such instances as opportunities to develop and refine a working "theory" of ethical conduct. Case material (based on actual situations, but partially fictionalized to protect the persons involved) is introduced here and throughout the book to illustrate the treatment of concrete administrative problems. To stimulate your thinking, they are generally left unresolved.

Ethical Problems

You were recently hired as the manager of a municipal department of parks and recreation. Soon after you assumed your duties you discovered that the payroll clerk was falsifying the payroll account by continuing to carry the names of laid-off employees. When the clerk picked up the payroll at City Hall, he would pull out those checks, endorse and cash them, and keep the proceeds.

Most administrators would have no difficulty recognizing that this clerk is not only involved in unethical conduct but is also clearly violating the law. Both moral and legal sanctions against stealing are well established and generally accepted. You are immediately aware that this behavior is unacceptable and must be stopped, although you would probably pause to think carefully about the best course of action. Your responsibility for the image of the organization may suggest firing the clerk quietly, involving as few other people as possible. However, your responsibility for maintaining the public trust may lead you to consider formal charges and prosecution. Sometimes, as in this case, the ethical situation is quite clear but the demands of administrative responsibility for resolving it are much less so. More often, however, both the ethical issue and its implications for administrative responsibility are complex and ambiguous.

Consider another situation. You are the director of a unit

within a federal regulatory agency that is charged with monitoring the use of potentially harmful commercial chemicals. Linda, a junior project manager under your supervision, is responsible for studying a broad-spectrum insecticide used in agriculture by small grain farmers, large truck gardeners, and cotton farmers and in the livestock industry as an animal spray. She has been assigned to determine whether this product should be removed from the market.

At a party Linda met a man named George, who she later learned was the Washington representative for the insecticide manufacturer. After several dates with George she became rather fond of him and wanted to pursue the relationship. However, Linda realized that their professional roles created a potential conflict of interest for her and she decided to tell you about the situation. She intended to continue seeing George, she said; she considered herself mature enough to maintain a separation between her professional and private lives. Linda insisted that her feelings for George would not influence her judgment in any way; in fact, she and George had never even discussed the chemical in question.

In this case the ethical situation is much less clear. Has Linda done anything that represents a breach of professional ethics? Because of her relationship with George, it might well be difficult for her to maintain objectivity in discharging her duties. But perhaps not. People differ in their ability to manage tensions of this kind. And what is your responsibility? Is it more important to avoid even the appearance of unethical conduct within your organization, or to support an employee's right to freedom in her private life? Should Linda be trusted until her behavior demonstrates otherwise? What are your alternatives?

Consider yet another situation. A soil bacterium common to warm climates can sometimes be found in ground waters of such areas. It seldom causes disease in humans, but when it does the infection is very severe. The bacterium enters the body through an open wound and produces infections resulting in a mortality rate of 75 percent.

You are a department manager for a public utility district that produces electricity through steam-driven turbines. The department has constructed a lake for this purpose, which is also open to the public for recreational use. Recently a man was injured in a boating accident that severely lacerated his legs. He developed gangrene and, after a double amputation, eventually died.

A technician in your department suspected that the man may have contracted the bacterial infection, and decided to run tests. He reported that the bacterium is indeed in evidence throughout the lake and, although no one can be certain without an autopsy, he believes it was the cause of death. Has the department committed an unethical act by not monitoring the quality of the water more carefully? Does it have a moral obligation to inform the public health authorities? The victim's family? The general public? What is your responsibility to your organization in the face of possible litigation and public outcry? What is your responsibility to those who have used the lake for recreation and those who may use it in the future?

Here you are dealing not simply with the questionable or clearly immoral actions of a particular individual, but rather a matter of organizational policy. How should the department define its obligations to society? Does it owe something to the deceased man's family and to others who may use the lake? Should it merely try to rid the lake of the bacterium and leave it open to use?

Ethics as an Active Process

As these three cases demonstrate, ethical issues arise in many different forms for administrators, but they nearly always raise difficult questions of administrative responsibility. The answers we give to these questions over time amount to a de facto administrative ethic. The central thesis of this book is that it is through this process of defining professional responsibility in specific, concrete administrative situations that an operational ethic is developed. Every administrator has such an ethic by virtue of having made decisions about ethical issues, even if the decision is to ignore the problem. A decision to take no action is, in fact, a decision about personal responsibility.

This operational ethic, hammered out in actual decision making, is the basic concern here. Many professional associations, business firms, and governmental organizations have adopted codes of ethics. They amount to officially espoused statements of appro-

priate conduct that reflect noble but often general and abstract principles. Formal codes of this kind do serve a useful function, but
without the support of other techniques involving day-to-day decision making, they tend to be ineffective as a way of achieving desired conduct.

The focus of this book is ethics as an active process—an
ongoing process that occurs whenever circumstances force us to deal
with conflict, tension, uncertainty, and risk. As administrators define the boundaries and content of their responsibility in resolving
specific ethical dilemmas, both great and small, they create for
themselves an "ethical identity." Often this is done without consistent, intentional, and systematic reflection, but that need not be the
case. Skill in addressing ethical issues can be learned and cultivated,
if we recognize the importance of doing so. As an initial step, we
must have a framework for understanding ethics in dynamic rather
than static terms.

To be consistent with this approach, I must advance an operational definition of ethics. This requires more than the usual
brief textbook or dictionary definitions, where ethics is considered
"the attempt to state and evaluate principles by which ethical problems may be solved" (Jones, Sontag, Becker, and Fogelin, 1969,
p. 1), or "the normative standards of conduct derived from the philosophical and religious traditions of society" (Means, 1970, p. 52),
or "the task of careful reflection several steps removed from the
actual conduct of men" concerning "the assumptions and presup-
positions of the moral life" (Gustafson, 1965, p. 113).

Gibson Winter (1966) defines ethics by describing the functions it serves in the social world. As an active enterprise, he says,
"Ethics seeks to clarify the logic and adequacy of the values that
shape the world; it assesses the moral possibilities which are projected and betrayed in the social give-and-take" (p. 218). Anyone
engaged in ethical reflection takes on the task of analyzing and
evaluating the principles embodied in various alternatives for conduct and social order. Ethics is, according to Winter, "a science of
human intentionality" (p. 219). Doing ethics, then, involves thinking more systematically about the values that are embedded in the
choices we otherwise would make on practical or political grounds
alone. As we reflect on these implicit values, we ask ourselves how

they are consistent with our obligations and toward what ends they lead. Keeping in mind the obligations and goals of the role we occupy, we seek to rank-order them for a particular ethical decision we confront.

Levels of Ethical Reflection

Henry David Aiken (1962) has constructed a framework for explaining the fluid nature of ethical argument that we can adapt for understanding the process of ordering our values and making decisions about ethical dilemmas. Aiken assumes that in a broad sense ethics has to do with concepts such as *good, right,* and *ought,* but that in the arena of everyday life, considering the practical meanings of these abstract concepts causes us to deal with them at different levels of seriousness and systematic reflection. Often we simply express emotion about what is "good" or what someone "ought" to do. At other, less frequent, times we face ethical questions that force us to reflect long and hard about our fundamental world view—even the meaning of life itself.

From this perspective it is possible to identify four distinctive levels at which we deal with ethical concerns.

The Expressive Level. Many times every day we find ourselves simply venting our feelings about something. When you learned about the misdeeds of the payroll clerk in your department, or Linda's involvement with George, or the presence of the bacterium in the lake water, you may well have responded first at this level: "That stupid clerk should have known better!" "Linda, this relationship disturbs me deeply." "We must have a bunch of incompetents managing the lake operation!" These spontaneous, unreflective expressions of emotion are perhaps the most common form of value judgment. They neither invite a reply nor attempt to persuade others. They provide neither evidence nor detailed descriptions of a state of affairs. However, depending on who utters them, and how intensely, they may be followed by a more rational and systematic treatment of the problem.

The Level of Moral Rules. This is the first level at which serious questions are raised and serious answers given. We address the problem of appropriate conduct and begin to assess alternatives and consequences. We consider these courses of action and their anticipated outcomes in the light of certain rules, maxims, and proverbs that we hold as moral guides:

> "Always be a good team player."
> "Loyalty to your clients comes first."
> "If you're not part of the solution, you are part of the problem."
> "Honesty is the best policy."
> "Truth will win out."
> "My country, right or wrong."
> "Never fight a battle you can't win."
> "Take care of number one."
> "The public should be trusted."
> "Love your neighbor as yourself."
> "Do unto others as you would have them do unto you."
> "Don't air the dirty linen outside the organization."

Some of the more colorful moral rules emerge around particular roles and reflect the informal moral code of those roles and the organizational culture in which they are enacted. For instance, here are a few from the field of law enforcement:

> "It is better to be tried by twelve than carried by six."
> "You can't make an omelette without breaking a few eggs."
> "What goes around comes around."
> "Don't embarrass the bureau."
> "Don't rat on a fellow officer."

These are examples of moral rules we acquire through the socialization process from our families, religious affiliations, education, and professional experiences. For better or worse, they provide rules of thumb for appraising a situation and deciding what ought to be done.

For example, the problem of Linda and George. After your initial emotional reaction, you have to think about how to handle this highly sensitive state of affairs. Some alternatives immediately come to mind:

> Order Linda to stop seeing George.
> Transfer her to another task.
> Discuss the matter with your supervisor.
> Trust her to do the job without being biased by the relationship.

Then you consider the possible consequences:

> Linda may resign.
> Progress on investigating the chemical may be delayed.
> The media may pick up the story.
> A biased decision may be reached about the chemical, with serious consequences for the public.
> You may be blamed for irresponsible conduct if your superior discovers the relationship without being informed.

As you evaluate the alternatives and their possible consequences, various moral rules and maxims come to mind as reference points for arriving at a decision:

- "You should be fair with subordinates under your supervision." Would I handle this situation differently if it involved a male member of my staff?
- "Avoid even the appearance of evil." Even if Linda performs in an objective professional manner, will the credibility of my organization be eroded if this situation is picked up by the press?
- "Honesty is the best policy." If I take any action that Linda perceives as punishment or distrust, am I discouraging honest communication from my staff? Should I tell my boss, or should I maintain Linda's confidence and accept responsibility for dealing with the situation myself?

Most of the time, the problem is resolved at this level. As we review the facts of the case, the alternatives for action, and their likely consequences on the one hand, and associate them with our stock of relevant moral rules on the other, the field of alternatives begins to narrow, and one or two rules emerge as crucial. We move toward a decision, with the practical consequences and the moral justification related in some way that is acceptable to us.

Not that our decisions are necessarily consistent from case to case. At the level of moral rules, which is where most practical administrative decisions are made, rationality and systematic reflection are involved but only in a limited, piecemeal fashion. Most of the time we are ad hoc problem solvers, not comprehensive moral philosophers. However, on occasion we are driven to the next level of generality and abstraction, usually because we are unable to reach a decision by applying our available repertoire of practical moral rules.

The Level of Ethical Analysis. When the available moral rules prove ineffective in a particular case, or when the actions they seem to prescribe do not feel right, a fundamental reconsideration of our moral code may be required. In the normal routine of the administrative role, we do not usually undertake this kind of basic reassessment. However, sometimes an issue is so unique, so complex, or so profound in the consequences of its resolution that we have no choice but to reexamine the ethical principles that are implicit in our routine norms for conduct.

A brief, but adequate, definition of *principle* is "a general law or rule that provides a guide for action." An ethical principle is a statement concerning the conduct or state of being that is required for the fulfillment of a value; it explicitly links a value with a general mode of action. For example, "justice" may be considered a significant value, but the term itself does not tell us what rule for conduct, or state of society, would follow if we include justice in our value system. We would need a *principle* of justice to show us what pattern of action would reflect justice as a value. A common form of the justice principle is "Treat equals equally and unequals unequally." We might interpret this principle as meaning that if all adult citizens are politically equal, they should all have the same political rights and obligations. If one has the vote, all must have it.

Or, if we look at another value, "truth," we might start with a general principle to indicate its meaning for conduct and then develop more specific statements for particular conditions. Generally, we might support this principle: "Always tell the truth." But when faced with a particular situation, we might revise the principle to "Always tell the truth unless innocent third parties would be seriously harmed."

Defining the ethical dimensions of a problem may require us to tease out not only the values that are in conflict, but also the unarticulated principles that indicate the mutually exclusive kinds of conduct those values dictate. Otherwise, values are far too vague to have much meaning in ethical analysis. If we say we believe in "freedom" or "liberty," that conveys meaning of only the most general sort. If, however, we identify and elaborate principles about liberty, the meaning becomes more specific and ethically useful. We might, for example, indicate that liberty means we ought not to interfere, without special justification, in the chosen course of any rational being or impose on him conditions that will prevent him from pursuing his chosen courses of action. Although this statement does not prescribe precisely what should be done in every situation, it does provide some conditions and qualifications for the range of conduct that falls under "liberty."

There are several ways to train people to clarify this distinction between values and principles and cultivate the skill of thinking in a principled fashion. One way would be to give participants a list of values, or have them make up their own, and then develop these values into statements of principle, varying from brief and general to highly elaborate and more specific. Another would be to spend time developing principles as part of the exercise in defining ethical issues discussed later in this chapter. First, have the participants identify the contending values in a case, then ask them to write statements of principle for each. Finally, when time and interest permit, readings on specific ethical principles might be assigned, such as Sissela Bok on secrecy and truthfulness or John Rawls on justice.

To illustrate the use of principle at the level of ethical analysis, let us refer back to the contaminated lake. If you discover that eight other people have developed symptoms suspiciously similar to those associated with the bacterium, the problem will have changed significantly. Now the fate of human lives may clearly and directly depend on what you do; expeditious action is required. Because the consequences for the department will be serious indeed, you go to your supervisor without delay.

However, you are met with an unexpectedly cool and cautious response. He listens and asks a few questions, but seems not to share your sense of urgency. After a lengthy discussion, during which you become increasingly angry, he finally informs you that he has known about the bacterium for some time. When the lake was built, more than two years ago, the bacterium was detected through routine water analyses. Since there was no practical way of ridding the water of this bacterium, and since the utility district had needed public support for the project, he had decided to keep the entire matter quiet. He had been advised that at existing levels of contamination, the risk of human infection was low.

The administrator orders you to take no action, but instead to leave the problem entirely in his hands. He tells you that there is little likelihood that any of the eight people could be treated effectively at this point and that any action would jeopardize the future of this facility and precipitate serious damage to both the department's public image and its financial well-being.

What do you do? None of your well-worn precepts about loyalty to the organization or social responsibility help here. You are not satisfied to keep quiet and leave it to the boss, but you have no hope of changing his mind. He seems firmly committed to waiting the situation out, hoping it will blow over. On the other hand, if you go to the public or the local elected officials with the story you will lose your job and probably have great difficulty finding another one.

Confronted with this kind of dilemma, you begin to reflect about the things you value most. You ask yourself what you are willing to risk and what you want to preserve at all costs. More specifically, you think about your personal integrity, professional reputation, financial security, the well-being of your family, the importance of your career, and the extent of your obligation to the organization, its employees, and management. You wonder what you owe the public; you consider your duty to the local elected officials. Furthermore, you begin to imagine the future consequences of allowing this kind of managerial conduct to continue.

As you engage in this inventory and evaluation of your fundamental principles, a kind of rough hierarchy begins to emerge.

This particular dilemma causes you to clarify and reorder your priorities. You realize that if you are to continue in your position, you must maintain your obligation to a central principle—the public interest. You took an oath to uphold the public interest when you accepted the position. All other commitments and values must be viewed in relation to that responsibility to a basic principle. The potential negative consequences for the people of the area are great, and their right to know the risk must be upheld. Ultimately, the principle of democracy and the integrity of democratic government are also at stake. If managers like your division chief are allowed to continue, self-government will be subverted; people need to know what is going on in public agencies if they are to truly participate in governing. Information about matters of public safety and welfare should not be withheld from the people and their elected representatives.

However, when you took your job you also accepted another principle: loyalty to the organizational hierarchy of your department. The orderly conduct of the public's business requires that subordinates work through superiors if accountability and efficiency are to be maintained. But this loyalty is not an end in itself; it exists for the ultimate benefit of the citizenry, for the public interest.

Another concern is the service provided by the department. Strong public resistance to building a dam had been overcome by promising the lake as a recreational facility. Closing the lake in the wake of disclosures about bacterial contamination might well result in demands to cancel the department's operating license. If the generating plant were closed down precipitously, electrical service would be severely curtailed. Without electricity, industrial firms would have to cut back production and lay off workers. Hospital services might be jeopardized. High-rise office buildings and schools might be unable to function. The public interest would be seriously and extensively damaged.

If the public interest is your fundamental controlling principle, you must weigh the probable public impact for each alternative. Ultimately the health of the citizenry must be protected, but your sense of due process requires that you act in a measured and prudent fashion. You decide on the following sequence of steps:

First, you will approach the general manager of the department, your boss's boss, thus maintaining loyalty to those above you who are responsible for the proper operation of the organization. This provides for the orderly management of the problem without unduly alarming the public.

Then, if the general manager does not act to remedy the situation, you will take your information to the mayor and city council. In this way you prevent the political process from being circumvented when serious public concerns are at stake, although orderly procedure may be sacrificed.

Finally, if the elected officials fail to take action, you will inform the local media. Orderly and efficient resolution of the problem will likely be lost altogether, but the ultimate right of a democratic citizenry to control the governmental bodies established for its benefit will be preserved.

If you are unable to arrive at this kind of ordering of principles and alternatives, it may be necessary to move to the next level.

The Postethical Level. This final point is exemplified by the question "Why should I be moral?" Most administrators seldom reach this most fundamental philosophical level of reflection. Only when pushed by a particularly persistent or cynical adversary, or under the sway of a deeply disillusioning experience, or confronting a profound personal crisis, are we likely to function at this level. Here the struggle is to find some basis for valuing those things that were identified at the level of ethical analysis. Why is integrity important? Or truth? Or security? Or loyalty? Or the well-being of others? At this level we begin to question our world view—our views of human nature, how we know anything to be true, and the meaning of life.

Resolution at this level is achieved only when practical indecision has been removed. It may require developing, or confirming, a world view grounded in philosophical or religious perspectives. When we have discovered an adequate motive to allow ourselves to "play the moral game," this level is resolved.

A Dynamic Process. This four-tiered framework should be viewed in highly dynamic terms. Only in books or scholarly papers do people move logically through these decision-making steps. In real life we move up and down through the levels as we grapple with what is good or what we ought to do. We may first engage a problem expressively as we react spontaneously with our immediate feelings, but then move rather quickly to problem solving at the level of moral rules. As we get new information and the situation becomes more complex, we may move back again to the expressive level. Then, having vented our irritation and frustration, we may move back again to the search for appropriate moral rules.

If the issue proves unsusceptible to any of our practical maxims and rules, we may move briefly back to an expression of feelings and then to the level of ethical analysis. After a process of evaluating our basic priorities, we may finally be able to reach an action decision by applying rules that now appear to be consistent with the newly established priorities. Or we may find ourselves in such a profound quandary that we move to the postethical level and ponder why we are so concerned with morality anyway.

This movement among the various levels is usually not a matter of conscious choice, although it may be. The transitions occur because we need to solve a problem, not necessarily because we consciously think about which level is appropriate. In a concrete situation as we attempt to integrate known facts, unknown but possible consequences of action, feelings, and values we find ourselves moving through these stages with varying degrees of rational reflection and abstraction. In day-to-day administrative decision making we manage this process without giving it much reflective thought. However, a basic assumption of this book is that the more we consciously address and systematically process the ethical dimensions of decision making when we confront significant issues, the more responsive we become in our work as administrators.

Uses of the Framework. It is important to be aware not only of where *we* are in this framework at any given moment, but also where our colleagues are operating as we discuss issues with them. Often confusion is generated within a staff because some are venting emotion, while others are articulating various moral rules, and still others are reflecting on basic principles. Sometimes everyone is presenting moral rules, but the rules are in conflict, and someone needs to move to the level of ethical analysis. Fundamental values, principles, goals, and objectives need to be clarified and ordered, both for the individuals and the organization, before an acceptable rule for action can be identified.

This framework helps us focus our attention on the stages in ethical decision making. It suggests that if we want to become more systematic in handling ethical issues, we need to examine more carefully what takes place at the two levels where rational reflection is most critical: the levels of moral rules and ethical analysis. This is where skill in decision making can be cultivated. Here we attempt to think about what we should do; there is intentionality and some degree of systematic treatment of the problem. At the expressive level, only emotion is involved. At the postethical level, the considerations are too abstract, too personal, and, in modern pluralistic societies, too varied to be susceptible to any generalized approach. People holding radically different philosophies and theologies are not likely to reach agreement at this level, although they may do so at levels two and three. Also, public accountability in this kind of heterogeneous society requires reasoned application of moral rules and ethical principles, rather than metaphysical assertions.

It is at the levels of moral rules and ethical analysis, then, that we are most likely to be able to account for our conduct publicly in terms that can be evaluated by political officials and the citizenry. If we proceed with reasoned justification, linking the consequences of our decisions with a tradition of moral rules, ethical principles, or some combination of the two, then our conduct is reviewable by members of the political community, and our deliberations and deeds are accessible for public debate and logical assessment. The higher we move up the ladder of public organizational leadership, the more important it becomes for us to be able to be accountable for our actions in this way. Therefore, in the remainder of this book we are concerned with applying systematic reflection at the levels of moral rules and ethical analysis.

A Decision-Making Model

In addressing any ethical issue we want to move from a problem to a course of action that will resolve it. This movement involves both *description* and *prescription*. That is, we describe to ourselves, and sometimes to others, an objective state of affairs, and then attempt to prescribe what specific steps should be taken to change the situation. Between these two steps, we do the kind of reflection involved at the levels of moral rules and ethical analysis. It is far more important that we comprehend these steps for ourselves and develop the required skills than it is to simply read someone else's prescriptions.

Books and articles that attempt to prescribe for administrators may be inspiring or thought provoking, but they are usually so general as to provide little guidance for specific decisions. Although they offer value orientations that readers may find appealing, the link between a value system and a concrete situation is missing. We often refer to this dilemma as the problem of application. We may want to apply a set of values that seem compatible with our view of the administrative role, but how to move from general to specific prescription is not clear.

This reflective link between description and prescription involves several important steps, and they are represented in the model shown in Figure 1.

The Descriptive Task. When a problem comes to our attention, it is usually presented in a fragmentary or distorted fashion, often with judgmental language and inflections. Perhaps, in the case of the payroll clerk discussed at the beginning of this chapter, you learn about his conduct from a secretary in the office whom he has treated rudely. Having discovered several suspicious names on the payroll list, she eagerly retaliates by concluding that he is involved in illegal activities. The secretary's report to you includes considerable embellishment of what she actually knows to be true, along with a derogatory appraisal of his character.

Any experienced administrator would know that such a report does not represent an adequate description of the clerk's activities. The names may appear suspicious to the secretary because she does not know them, but there may be a reasonable explanation. Maybe he has, indeed, been sexist in his dealings with her but scrupulously honest in his handling of the payroll. Sexism is a problem to be dealt with, but it must not be confused with the payroll issue. It is clear that you must gather more factual information and sift out

Figure 1. Ethical Decision-Making Model.

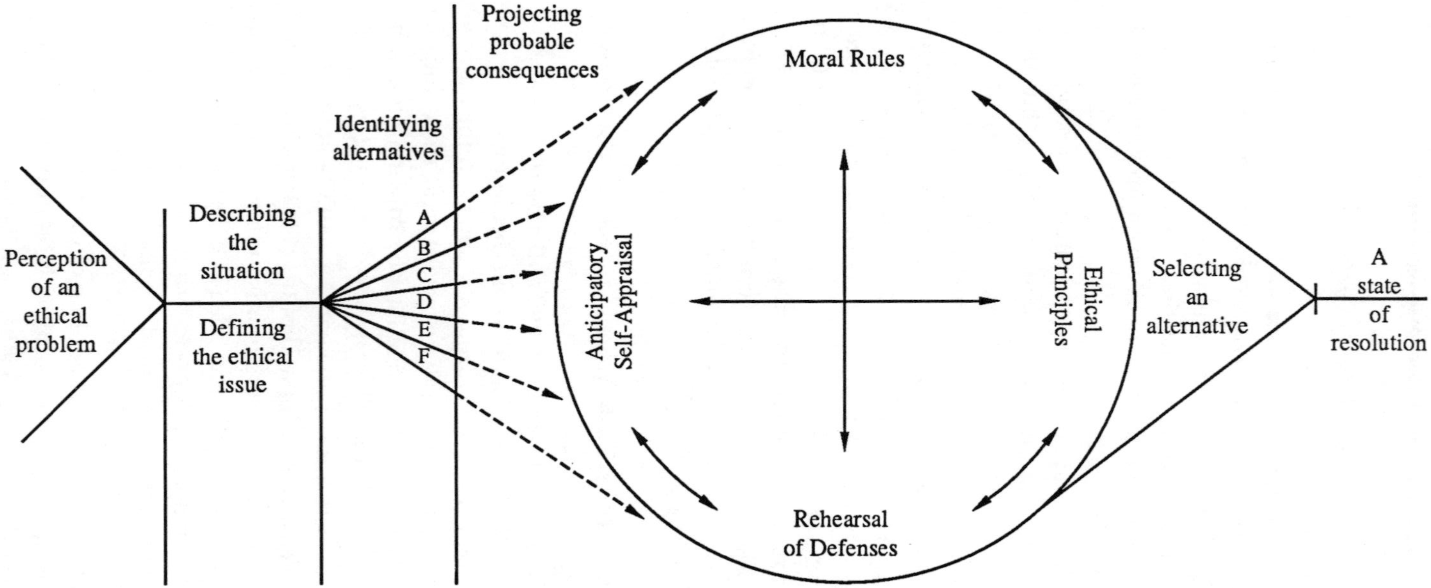

unfounded judgments before you have a full and objective description. Without this you dare not proceed to any kind of prescription.

In this example it is obvious that the descriptive task is critical, but there are many situations where it is equally important but much less obviously so. If the report comes not from a secretary but from someone above us in the organizational hierarchy, we are much more likely to accept it as an accurate description of events. Howard Becker refers to this tendency as the "hierarchy of credibility." He suggests that "from the point of view of a well socialized participant in the system, any tale told by those at the top intrinsically deserves to be regarded as the most credible account obtainable of the organization's workings" (1973, p. 7).

Admittedly, under the pressure of life in most organizations we seldom have the time or resources to conduct a full investigation. However, we must always attempt to describe as objectively as possible the facts of a situation. This might include identifying the key actors, the viewpoints of each, the issues, the sequence of events, and the risks involved.

Although it is impossible to avoid value-laden language altogether, it *is* possible to resist using words and phrases that blatantly create a cast of good guys and bad guys. This is a useful skill to cultivate in dealing with ethical problems since it helps to push us beyond the expressive level. Whether we are struggling with a decision alone or discussing it with someone else (a staff person, a supervisor), we must force ourselves to describe the situation with more than the influence of our gut reactions. If we are to deal with real people involved in real events, we must first face what has actually happened.

Defining the Ethical Issue. With the necessary details before us, the next step is to define the ethical issue involved. Experience with workshops on ethics indicates that public administrators seem to have the greatest difficulty with this second step. It is not that they are unable to recognize an ethically problematic situation; their sensitivity to such matters is encouragingly keen. They know when they are confronted with expectations, demands, opportunities, and conflicting interests that have ethical significance. But many have difficulty in articulating which values and principles are at stake.

The tendency is to define the problem in practical rather than ethical terms.

For example, consider an administrator who is asked by a superior to provide confidential information about a colleague being considered for promotion, someone who is a close personal friend and is not qualified for the job. Workshop participants usually define the problem as keeping the boss happy but not hurting or offending the friend. This is a definition of the practical dilemma, but behind these practical considerations are some conflicting values and principles which need to be identified.

"Conflicting loyalties" would be the most general statement of the ethical issue involved here. However, we could go further and consider obligations. On the one hand there are the obligations to a friend: to preserve confidentiality, honesty, and trustworthiness. On the other hand, the obligations to a superior: to provide honest and objective information about co-workers being considered for greater responsibility. These obligations contribute to the best interests of the organization. Also, there is an obligation to the citizenry to uphold the public interest. Thus, the problem could be defined as conflicting loyalties or conflicting obligations, depending on the details of the case and our own ethical priorities.

Unless we can focus the analysis on underlying ethical issues of this kind, we may resolve the matter on purely practical grounds. We may make a decision without ever really engaging the important values and principles that are pulling us in different directions. Ethical analysis skills, ethical autonomy, and ultimately our ethical identity are developed through engagement of this kind. Without it the practical demands and exigencies of a situation are likely to whip us around in a manner destructive of ethical judgment and antithetical to personal integrity.

Because this step of defining ethical issues is so difficult, those who conduct training sessions or classroom instruction must spend considerable time working on it in a variety of ways before moving on to the full range of steps leading to final resolution. Some lecturing to illustrate the distinction between the practical and ethical dimensions of a problem is probably necessary at the outset.

The next step ought to involve the participants, under the

instructor's leadership, working through the definitional problem in a case or two. Then it seems helpful to divide the participants into groups of three or four, each group with a different case situation, and ask them to define the ethical issue on their own. During the report-back session, all the participants are then exposed to several different definitional problems.

Identifying Alternative Courses of Action. With an adequate definition of the ethical issue before us, we are ready to move on to identifying alternative courses of action. After describing the situation as objectively as possible, and defining the ethical issue, the most difficult requirement is resisting the inclination to view the alternatives in dichotomous terms: *Either* you do this *or* you do that. Either you tell Linda to stop seeing George, or you trust her to handle the relationship in a professional manner. This either-or view is the most common trap in the ethical process. Rarely does an ethical issue have only two or even three possible solutions, but there appears to be a force within us, as pervasive as gravity, that impedes the spinning out of alternatives.

Use whatever methods or techniques are necessary to remove the blocks, because until at least the most significant alternatives are acknowledged, we risk overlooking the best solution. A simple grid form can help decision-making groups broaden their perspective. Down the left side, group members list all the alternatives they can think of; on the right side, they write the probable consequences, both positive and negative. First they brainstorm alternatives for ten to fifteen minutes, without evaluating any of them; if an alternative is conceivable, they are required to list it. This may sound like a simple procedure, but experience with a large number of groups indicates that some people have an almost irresistible tendency to reject an alternative as soon as it is uttered.

Projecting the Probable Consequences. Once the range of alternative solutions has been widened, the positive and negative anticipated consequences of each possible course of action need to be projected. If you tell Linda to stop seeing George, what is likely to be the outcome? What if you transfer her to another position? Ask another member of the staff to work along with her? Tighten your supervision of her work? What chain of events will likely unfold, and toward what end?

Projecting the consequences of alternatives is a key dynamic in our natural, informal decision making. As we consider what we should do, we usually run out a movie in our minds. For each alternative we construct a scenario with actors, interaction, and consequences. Here we are attempting to raise this informal process to a more formal, conscious and systematic level. We begin by intentionally pushing out the boundaries of our range of considered alternatives, and then attempting to be more imaginative in our creation of these projections into the future.

John Dewey described this process as one of "deliberation" in which we experiment with "a dramatic rehearsal," in our imagination, of "various competing possible lines of action" (1922, p. 190; see also Schutz, 1970). A reasonable choice of a course of conduct requires us to consider the full range of alternatives, rather than only the one or two that dominate our feelings and imagination.

The skill involved here is *moral imagination,* the ability to produce a "movie in our minds" with realistic characters, a believable script, and clear imagery. The "movies" we create tend to be more like slide shows, or jerky, black-and-white, silent melodramas rather than epic productions in color with stereophonic sound and complex plots. The more imaginative we can be in projecting the probable consequences of an alternative, the more our ethical decision making is enhanced.

Writing out scenarios for each alternative may help you develop this skill. Although no administrator has the time to do this with every issue, it may be a worthwhile exercise for particularly complex problems. Groups can use the grid form described above. After listing possible alternatives down the left side and the probable consequences for each along the right side, the group then talks through a scenario for each one, attempting to refine the projected consequences.

Finding a Fit. The remainder of the process is no longer linear in nature. Achieving resolution involves a search for a "fit" among the four elements in the circle in Figure 1, and that search is not simply a matter of reasoning from one thing to the next. This basis for such a "fit" is more like the logic of esthetics; it requires proportion and balance among the four elements.

The first consideration is the *moral rules* that can be adduced to support each alternative and the projected consequences. Identifying these will tend to happen quite naturally in a group setting as individuals are allowed to opt for a particular decision alternative and defend it. However, anyone engaged in this process alone or leading a group session must be sure that all alternatives are addressed and none dismissed too easily or quickly.

The next consideration is a *rehearsal of defenses*. Here we systematically consider each alternative by asking ourselves, "How would I defend this particular option, if required to do so?" This is the test of how well a particular alternative will fit with the accepted norms of the wider professional and political communities of which we are a part. Once again, moral imagination is a critical skill as we try to picture ourselves, as vividly as possible, explaining to a superior, or subordinates, or professional peers, or the press, or a court of law, why each possible course of action was chosen. In group situations, this exercise is most useful as the field narrows toward one or two alternatives.

Harlan Cleveland (1972, p. 104) advocates an approach of this kind by suggesting that an administrator ask himself or herself the following key question before getting committed to any particular course of conduct: "If this action is held up to public scrutiny, will I still feel that it is what I should have done, and how I should have done it?" Cleveland insists that if those involved in well-known cases of corruption had seriously asked themselves this question and answered it honestly, most of these instances of betrayal of public trust would never have happened.

In this process of rehearsing defenses, which ethicists sometimes call "the test of publicity," we may find it necessary to move from the discovery and application of moral rules to the third consideration—an attempt to discern the implicit *ethical principles* at stake. This occurs when the available moral rules are not sufficiently satisfying to permit resolution. One alternative may tend to maximize the security of the individual or organization, while another may promote social justice, or yet another may enhance democracy. As we consider the hierarchy of basic principles, we again rehearse the justification for each option: "How could I justify giving higher priority to social justice than organizational security in this instance?"

As we engage in this process of arraying alternatives, drawing out the probable consequences in the most realistic terms, and rehearsing the application of rules and principles, both a rational and an emotional search for resolution is underway. But what constitutes resolution?

Resolution is reached when we discover an alternative that satisfies our need to have sound reasons for our conduct and our need to feel satisfied with the decision. Since a supremely rational alternative that provides complete emotional satisfaction is rarely available, resolution is ordinarily an approximate state. What we achieve represents the best combination of reasons and affective comfort. It should be emphasized, however, that the assumption here is that both the reasons and the feelings involved in this resolution should include the obligations of the public service role. This decision-making process must be informed by education, training, and guided socialization into a public service ethic if the public interest is to be approximated. Here we are describing and systematizing the process that needs to be informed by such an ethic.

Sorting through and selecting adequate reasons occur through the process described above. Arriving at a feeling of satisfaction with a decision happens during the same process, but involves a set of dynamics not yet described. It is time to consider the fourth element in the circle, *anticipatory self-appraisal.* This is the test of how well a course of action fits with our own self-image. As we imagine ourselves undertaking various courses of action, we may experience self-disapproval in connection with certain alternatives. According to Janis and Mann (1977), these anticipations can arouse guilt, remorse, and self-reproach. When we see ourselves, in our mind's eye, carrying out a decision that is inconsistent with our core values, we do not like the self we envision. When we project ourselves into the future and look back on the act as though it had been completed, we are dissatisfied with ourselves. We anticipate not feeling good on the morning after. We experience, in advance, a kind of ethical hangover.

In the same way, other decision alternatives create self-approval. The movie in our minds portrays us acting in a way that makes us feel proud and draws praise, or at least approval, from people whose opinions we value. We are drawn toward these options by the reenforcing power of anticipatory feelings of satisfaction.

These anticipatory feelings are usually not appraised systematically, but they create inclinations either to reject alternatives that seem incongruent with our values or the norms of significant reference groups, or to choose congruent ones. To the extent that we are able to relate this emotional process to the rational process, we gain ethical autonomy. We can intentionally and systematically assess decision alternatives in terms of the soundness of our reasons for selecting each one and how we can expect to feel about choosing it. We may also be able to identify the sources of those positive or negative feelings. Are we anticipating approval or disapproval from our colleagues in the local chapter of the American Society for Public Administration? From the boss? Or are long-held personal values involved? How important is the source of those feelings? Are there other persons or groups whose evaluation of the decision is equally, or more, important?

In brief, these are the steps in a fully systematic and self-conscious ethical decision-making process. Obviously, no practicing administrator could be expected to apply this model to every ethical issue. However, the assumption here is that if this model is used with the more significant problems, administrators will cultivate over time something like an intuitive decision-making skill that will serve them well when there is no time for such explicit and formal exercises. Daniel Isenberg's research on senior managers indicates that the most effective ones systematically develop such intuitive decision models that make possible "the smooth automatic performance of learned behavior sequences" (1984, p. 85). Isenberg maintains that this "is not arbitrary or irrational, but is based on years of painstaking practice and hands-on experience that builds skills" (p. 85). When these skills are used under the pressure of limited time for reflection "we compress years of experience and learning into split seconds. This compression is one of the bases of what we call intuition as well as the art of management" (p. 83).

However, by using the model we achieve a greater degree of ethical autonomy through this process because we become more aware of both our own values and the external obligations under which we act. Even when we develop intuitive skill, it is possible to raise the grounds for our conduct to conscious consideration when necessary. Janis and Mann (1977) observe that authorities sometimes attempt to elicit obedience by creating the illusion that subordinates have no choice but to follow orders. The power of this manipulation of the perceived range of real choices is vividly portrayed in the experiments on obedience to authority conducted by Stanley Milgram (1974), which are discussed at greater length in Chapter Seven. These studies demonstrated that more than half of a random sample of American citizens were willing to comply with orders that appeared to result in serious harm to another person. One of the critical factors in their decision to follow distasteful instructions was the scientist's repeated statement "You have no other choice. The experiment requires that you continue." Defining the situation in such constrained terms leaves a decision maker feeling helpless before a single unacceptable option; ethical autonomy is reduced to zero. Consciousness of alternative choices is foreclosed.

Although it is easier to conceive of this kind of ethical tunnel vision in cases where we are being manipulated by an authority, it occurs more pervasively. We develop blinders that allow us to see only one alternative, or at most a very few. Until we take the initiative to systematically and aggressively widen the range of conceivable options, and assess how they fit both rationally and emotionally with our value system, we are at the mercy of the most obvious courses of action. Developing moral imagination requires discipline and practice as demanding as any other intellectual and creative activity, but its rewards are greater measures of self-awareness, self-control, and decision-making flexibility.

Summary

In this initial chapter we began by examining some typical public administrative cases in which an ethical dilemma could be discerned. We then defined ethics as an active process involving the ordering of our values with respect to a particular decision. Next, we considered the four levels of reflection at which this process occurs. The chapter concluded with a review of a decision-making model that may be used to systematically and self-consciously move from the description of an ethical problem to a prescribed course of action.

In the next chapter we step back from particular ethical decisions to look at the social and political setting in which public administrators make ethical decisions. This setting imposes certain conditions that significantly shape the nature of the problems that public administrators encounter.

Part One

Ethics for Individual Administrators

Chapter Two

**Public Administration
in Modern Society:
The Context of
Administrative Ethics**

For purposes of examining the ethical dimensions of administration, it is helpful to understand the administrative role in relation to the social and cultural context in which it functions. This perspective is crucial both for adequately describing ethical situations and for developing realistic prescriptions for dealing with them. The key concept in a sociocultural perspective on the administrative role is moderization.

Modernization is a global term for describing the social, cultural, and economic attributes associated with urban industrial society. Berger, Berger, and Kellner (1973) argue that the key phenomena of modernity are bureaucracy and technological production. In fact, they contend that these are the carriers of modern consciousness. As we become involved with bureaucratic organization and the process of technological production, a distinctively modern way of thinking about the world and our place in it begins to emerge.

Characteristics of Modernization

This modern world view is characterized by the following traits:

The Attempt to Apply Scientific Principles to Much of Life. The thought of the late nineteenth and early twentieth centuries was heavily influenced by a belief that science could be introduced into more and more areas of human life (Nelson, 1982). This led quite naturally to an emphasis on instrumental rationality. It was thought that science could provide better methods for everything, from conducting our personal affairs to managing a family to running a factory to providing public goods and services. The tendency was to look to science for one best way of doing things that was consistent with generic scientific principles. Thus, we began to think about the need to order and standardize society as well as our own lives.

Under the sway of this scientific approach to life, efficiency of interaction and production becomes a concern, along with predictability of the behavior of others. In modern society tradition no longer provides stability, order, and consistency of conduct; these things have to be thought about and worked out through organizations, rules, laws, and policies based on scientific principles.

Multiplicity and Differentiation of Roles. Social relationships and personal identity become more complex. People no longer identify themselves with one role, or even a few. Our lives become an intricate network of interrelated roles. We move through these roles without thinking very explicitly about the changes in behavior they require. During the course of one day we may assume a broad array of roles—parent, spouse, neighbor, administrator, church member, investor, citizen, rowing partner—each with its own behavior pattern.

Separation of Work and Private Life. Work no longer blends easily into our private lives. It is separated in time and space from home, family, and neighborhood. In traditional society the farmer or herdsman lived at his place of work and made no precise temporal distinctions between work and nonwork. The same was typical for physicians, artists, lawyers, shopkeepers, and craftsmen. However, in modern society work is done in a particular place and during defined hours. Deviations from this norm are viewed as intrusions of work into our private life, or vice versa.

Relativism. Neither roles nor values are viewed as absolute. Roles are acquired and given up, and they vary in importance from time to time. Consequently, they are often maintained with considerable role distance. That is to say, they are not allowed to comprehend our identity. Roles are relative to particular times and places; they are not inherent in our most essential selves.

Similarly, values within society exhibit enormous diversity. Some people believe one thing and some another. We are not shocked to discover this fact in modern society; instead we tend to acknowledge and emphasize the relativity of values.

Pluralization of Society. The significant dynamic behind all four of these characteristics is the pluralization of modern society. As people from diverse cultures have moved with great rapidity into urban commercial and industrial centers during the last two hundred years, they have found it necessary to confront one another's differences. The homogeneity of traditional society, with its unifying and stabilizing cultural bonds, has been broken. Very little can be assumed or taken for granted. New forms of organization have developed and new ways of coping with a broad spectrum of life-styles, diets, preferences, political philosophies, and modes of exchange have evolved. This "pluralization of life worlds" has led to the segmentation of individual lives as people have attempted to relate themselves to "severely discrepant worlds of meaning and experience" (Berger, Berger, and Kellner, 1973, p. 64).

The early stages of this pluralizing process are vividly illustrated in the musical *Fiddler on the Roof*. In a little Russian village named Anatemka an orthodox Jewish community lives out a predictable and stable existence through the highly integrated web of tradition, which encompasses daily routines as well as major events such as birth, marriage, and death. The leading figure, Tevye, constantly reminds himself and the audience that tradition is how he knows who he is and what God expects of him. "Without our tradition," he says, "we are as shaky as a fiddler on the roof" (Stein, 1971, p. 64).

And, indeed, in the course of the play we see the integrity and absoluteness of Anatemka's traditions challenged by the arrival of the czar's troops. Familiar traditions governing courtship, marriage, and family roles are confronted with different traditions from an alien society—and robbed of their power. Although in this case it was a matter of modern society invading a traditional community, rather than the migration of rural villagers to an urban area, the process of pluralization is essentially the same.

In 1927, in *The Public and Its Problems*, John Dewey described how this emerging heterogeneity gave rise to a multiplicity of "publics." From Dewey's perspective there is no such thing as a unitary public in modern society. As people pursue their various self-interests through social interaction, there are certain unintended indirect consequences, which may be viewed positively or negatively. Entrepreneurs who establish steel mills to make a profit indirectly create air pollution. However, they may also, without planning to do so, create a market for smaller businesses in the surrounding area. Publics either diminish or enhance these indirect consequences by calling for the appointment of public officials and the passage of laws.

Thus, governmental organizations have served an increasingly pluralized public during the last one hundred years. These publics, according to Dewey's thesis, are generated by the heterogeneous composition of modern industrial society. As we attempt to realize our own interests we invariably find ourselves linked interdependently with others who are different. We are sometimes inhibited in achieving our goals by the activities of others and sometimes helped, but whatever the case, we begin to realize that our fate is bound up with the decisions and behavior of other people whose values differ, more or less, from our own.

Implications for Public Administration

It appears that modernization has three major implications for public administration.

The Political Nature of Public Administration. An initial impact of modernization on public administration was the attempt to separate politics from administration in order to develop a science of administration, a science that was expected to lead to a more efficient delivery of public goods and services. To the progressive reformers of the late nineteenth and early twentieth centuries, this seemed to offer an advance beyond the highly politicized public administration that had existed under the urban political machines of the nineteenth century and in traditional societies for most of human history. However, the paradox was that although modern thinking emphasized the application of scientific rationality to government, other characteristics of modern society made this no more possible in twentieth-century America than it had been in the traditional societies of the past.

The separation of politics from administration may have existed in the minds of Max Weber (1946), Woodrow Wilson (1887), Leonard White (1926), Frank Goodnow (1900), and a generation of other scholars, but almost nowhere else. The notion that politicians make policy decisions involving substantive rationality while administrators simply apply their best scientific instrumental reasoning toward implementation has been sufficiently attacked to require no extensive treatment here (Gaus, 1936; Waldo, 1948). Administrators in the modern world are at least involved in politics with a small *p*, and often indirectly in capital-*P* partisan political activity. Modernization creates pressures and dynamics that compel administrators to be involved in decisions about goals and policies, and to compete with others for power and resources (Benveniste, 1977; Wamsley and Zald, 1973).

The multiplication and differentiation of roles are the critical phenomena in the politics of the public administrative role. Each of these roles may be understood as a bundle of obligations and interests that any public administrator might have acquired in the course of becoming an adult in modern society. That is, each role is constituted by a set of obligations, well or poorly defined, that administrators must carry out to maintain the role, and a set of interests—income, social status, and job satisfaction—that they derive from the role. We must bear the obligations to secure the interests.

Some of these roles belong exclusively to the private life of home, family, and community; some have to do with the world of work; and some overlap the two realms. Together they represent the complex multifaceted identity of a modern administrator (Downie, 1971; Means, 1970).

From time to time these differentiated roles come into conflict with each other; the interests and obligations associated with them compete for our time, attention, and energy. We must manage this conflict effectively to prevent one role from destroying another. For example, the role of investor may create tension with the role of administrator in a public organization if an attractive investment opportunity arises that involves association with organizations being regulated by that public agency. Potential conflicts of interest could detract from the administrator's objective judgment, or at least could be perceived that way by the citizenry.

The conflict between these roles arises from antithetical attractions: personal economic interests and the obligation to protect the public interest. The tension between them may be compounded if the administrator facing the investment opportunity has significant financial needs to maintain the roles of spouse and parent. And if this hypothetical administrator belongs to a professional association with a strong position against this type of conduct, the conflict is deepened and the tension increased.

The politics of the administrative role is rooted in this kind of tension (Tullock, 1965; Crozier, 1973; Wamsley and Zald, 1973). Since values in modern society are not universally accepted, there are no absolutes to define precisely what ought to be done when roles conflict. Values are ordered and priorities established among roles through negotiation with ourselves and others in each situation, generally along the lines described in the first chapter. It is in trading off our own varied interests for the interests of the organization we work for, and vice versa, that the political dynamics of the administrative role emerge.

Sheldon Wolin (1960) has provided the basis for a further explanation of organizational politics. His focus is the evolution of communities through the modernizing process. Wolin argues that during the nineteenth and twentieth centuries, the "organic," integrated, tradition-based communities of the preindustrial and preurban era began to crumble in the face of migration to urban and industrial areas. People began to look to organizations to fulfill the needs previously satisfied by their communities. They sought stability, identity, belonging, security, purpose, and power in organizations of all kinds: religious, industrial, labor, reform, political, scientific, commercial, and governmental.

In this process the "natural" networks of relationships of the older organic communities were broken up. They were transformed by the rationality and intentionality of organization builders into instruments for achieving particular goals. They were designed to refine steel, manufacture automobiles, provide water, reform government, operate transit facilities, and enforce building and safety regulations.

However, contrary to Weber's ideal type, people refused to participate in these organizations in a partial fashion. Although modernization tends to fragment identity among an array of roles and separate work from home, individuals tend to resist. They tend to want to participate in organizations as wholes; they try to spill over the boundaries of roles in a drive to recreate "natural communities." These unintended communities, described by Selznick (1966), subvert the goals of organizations and divert their resources toward satisfying the personal needs of their members.

This overlay of two sets of conflicting goals creates the motivation to engage in political activity both within and beyond the organization. Members of the organization bring with them the often unarticulated goal of self-fulfillment through social relationships and interaction, but the organization is established to achieve certain specific goals for a public, or for the owners of the organization. Negotiating the tension between these goals requires continual political transaction within the organizations and among external forces.

Furthermore, the opportunity to engage in political behavior is heightened by the latitude of discretion granted to public administrators (Nachmias and Rosenbloom, 1980; Rohr, 1989). The growing complexity and technical nature of problems addressed by government have created a tendency in legislators to delegate enormous powers to administrators, who are presumed to have specialized knowledge of particular policy areas. Thus, the implementation of legislation becomes, in fact, an exercise in substantive policy making. Broad legislative "shells," debated publicly and approved by elected officials, are then filled with a multitude of administrative decisions which are far less visible and far more difficult to monitor. These circumstances are highly conducive to political transactions (Lieberman, 1973; Davis, 1969; Lowi, 1979; Benveniste, 1977).

If the administrative role in modern society is inevitably political, and heavily discretionary in nature, significant ethical considerations must be acknowledged. For example, using the two broad categories of internal and external political transactions, we can identify three types of ethical concerns associated with each: corruption, loss of efficiency, and abuse of power. If we look at some typical external political transactions we find these ethical concerns manifest in the following ways:

1. Agency-Political Party

In transactions between a public agency and a political party, the ethical concern is usually for corruption of the agency's legally mandated mission. The party may use its influence with agency employees to circumvent established procedure for the benefit of the party or certain of its members. This corrupts the public interest that all public servants are obligated to uphold.

2. Agency-Agency

When two public agencies become involved in political transactions, the concern is for loss of efficiency. This kind of situation typically involves competition for resources and jurisdiction, that is, a struggle for power. The time and effort expended amount to a waste of the citizens' money as well as a breach of their good faith. Poor stewardship of public resources is ultimately the equivalent of stealing from those who have entrusted you with their property.

3. Agency-Constitutional Branch of Government

Political interaction between an agency and members of the executive, legislative, or judicial branches of government produces a concern for abuse of power and for corruption. Abuse of power may occur when members of these branches attempt to use an administrative agency for their own advantage. For example, if a president tries to use the powers of the Internal Revenue Service or the FBI against political opponents, he is going beyond the appropriate use of his executive power. On the other hand, if an agency becomes involved in using its resources in unusual ways to influence public officials, that may also be a matter of corruption. When, for example, a planning department cooperates in bribing members of a city council to gain favors for a developer, that agency's maintenance of the public trust has become corrupted.

4. Agency-Interest Groups

Corruption is also the concern when interest groups become involved in efforts to influence a public agency. When labor unions, chambers of commerce, community improvement associations, professional associations, industrial associations, taxpayers organizations, and lobbies of various kinds move beyond persuasion and begin to offer favors, corruption is imminent. The agency may find itself "on the take." Its charge to serve the public interest is then corrupted by the rewards of special interests.

When we turn to the internal politics of public organizations the primary concern is with loss of efficiency. When individual members or subunits of an agency begin to compete for resources and jurisdiction, or build coalitions with others, the resources provided by the citizenry to accomplish a legally established mission are siphoned off. The political gamesmanship of the members of the organization diverts time, money, and effort away from the provision of public goods and services. The taxpayers are deprived of some portion of what government rightfully owes them.

The politics of public administration, then, raises some potentially serious concerns for the ethical performance of administrators. As we all know, politics is unavoidable. Given the dynamics of modern society and the overlay of personal and organizational goals that result from these dynamics, the notion of clearly separating politics from administration is not valid. However, it is possible to identify a spectrum of administrative politics ranging from minimal to pervasive. It is also possible to conceive of approaches to reducing, or minimizing, the clearly unethical manifestations of political conduct. (These will be discussed further in Chapters Five and Six.) The significant question is not how to remove politics entirely from administration, but how to constrain it, and under what circumstances.

Separation of the Public Administrative and Citizen Roles. The second impact of modern society on public administration is that there is a tendency to separate the role of public administrator and the role of citizen. The administrator as both employee of the citizenry and member of the citizenry occupies an unusual position in modern society, although it is not unique. Elected officials, appointed officials, and other public employees find themselves in a similar situation. All who work for a government bear a dual obligation: they are responsible to serve the public and they are members of the public they are supposed to serve.

These dual roles sometimes create conflicting obligations: a public administrator is not simply a "servant at large" of the people, but rather a public servant within a particular organization. This role as employee of a specific organization, although theoretically only an expression of a larger public servanthood, is far more powerful and concrete in its sanctions and incentives. The role of public servant quite easily becomes limited to, and defined by, the particular organization. When this occurs, loyalty to the organization may become confused with duty to uphold the public interest. This, in turn, often gets translated into an assumption that carrying out the orders of superiors is tantamount to fulfilling the duty as a public servant.

The tendencies to separate roles and to create a demarcation between work and private life encourage this shrinking of obligation to the narrow limits of the work role within an organization. Both of these characteristics of modernization make it possible to remove the tension that ought to exist between the dual roles of the public administrator. We can settle into a schizophrenic pattern of expressing concern about civic virtue, and exercising the rights and duties of citizenship away from the office, while thinking only of our personal advantage, and that of the organization, when involved in the world of work. The building and safety administrator who is paid off regularly by building contractors can be a faithful informed voter, an active member of a church, a doting parent, and a supporter of his neighborhood burglary prevention group.

Weber's (1946) emphasis on functional rationality for administrators, which is also a reflection of modernization, further encourages the bifurcation of these two critical roles. We think substantively about the goals and ends of government only in the private sphere of citizenship. In the role of public administrator, on the other hand, we are encouraged to think only of the best means to accomplish the goals predetermined by superiors or elected officials.

The dichotomization of citizen and administrative roles is seldom complete; however, the pressure to move in this direction is strong in modern society, and the outcome amounts to an unknown number of public administrators who have given up some measure of their citizenship at the workplace. It is only by devising ways of encouraging public administrators to maintain a linkage between these two roles that we can sustain a broader view of the role of public servant than simply loyalty to a governmental organization. The tension provided by the citizenship role stretches the boundaries of the administrative role to include the hierarchy of law and the democratic tradition.

The ethical significance of these dual role characteristics should be clear, at least in broad outline. One of the reasons civil service positions are generally available only to citizens is the assumption that they will carry into public organizations a primary loyalty to the people. This loyalty, which should precede loyalties to any particular agency or government official, will enhance the trustworthiness of their service (Stahl, 1976). Since public service is a fiduciary role, anyone who accepts such employment is ultimately bound by an obligation to the public of that jurisdiction. This bond of trust is maintained only if one acts within a public organization as a citizen with certain added responsibilities—as a citizen first, and secondarily as one citizen among others who agrees to do work on behalf of all. Paul Appleby (1965, p. 335) has characterized the occupants of this dual role as "the especially responsible citizens who are officials."

This is particularly critical for those who assume administrative roles, for they take upon themselves even greater fiduciary responsibilities. They agree not only to perform work on behalf of the people of a governmental jurisdiction, but also to assist in structuring, coordinating, supporting, supervising, and evaluating the work of others who have chosen to serve the collective weal. In the words of Michael Walzer (1970, p. 216), "They are citizens in lieu of the rest of us; the common good is, so to speak, their specialty." They bear responsibility not only for their own use of public resources, but also for achieving the most efficient and effective expenditure of those resources by others.

This compound fiduciary responsibility of public administrators suggests that it is of critical importance that those who occupy these roles maintain a lively awareness of the primacy of their obligations as citizens. Whenever an employing organization is found to be carrying out its mission in a fashion not in the best interests of the citizenry, all public administrators, and indeed all public employees, should feel duty bound to take action on behalf of their fellow citizens. The failure to do so represents a breach of trust and a denial of the responsibilities of citizenship. This is an ethical concern of the most fundamental sort.

The responsibility associated with the role of the citizen is admittedly problematic. For most of us, there is no formal statement of what that responsibility entails, since only naturalized citizens are required to take an oath to uphold the U.S. Constitution. However, it seems reasonable to argue that what is required for those seeking citizenship is implied for those who are citizens by birth.

Another kind of problem is raised by Walzer, who suggests that some people seriously question the moral priority of citizenship in the mid-twentieth century because of the alienation and powerlessness felt by many. He argues that "they experience a kind of moral uneasiness; their citizenship is a source of anxiety as well as of security and pride" (1970, p. 204).

Nevertheless, Walzer and other citizenship theorists assert the importance of the concept and the functions it suggests. The actual state of the citizenship role may be one of disarray: Dennis Thompson (1970) argues that normative citizenship theory functions as an ideal and pictures a desirable state of affairs that is not yet realized. We might argue that rehabilitation and enhancement of the meaning of citizenship are of crucial importance in the modern democratic administrative state. If democratic citizenship continues to wane in meaning and diminish in reality, democratic administration would seem to be impossible. The responsibility of the public administrator must be grounded in an understanding of the responsibility of the citizen.

Although not all the citizenship literature projects the same ideal, two threads seem to run through those theories that are democratic in orientation. One of these is, of course, participation of some kind in the making of political decisions. The other, which is more directly relevant here, is an obligation to consider the opinions and wishes of other members of the citizenry along with one's own. In Pranger's words: "Incumbent upon the good member, the virtuous citizen, is the ability to make political decisions which at once protect his own integrity and take cognizance of the integrity of others" (1968, p. 102).

Similarly, Walzer maintains that unless citizens have "a sense of the whole over and above their sense of themselves as particular persons," they will have little interest in participating in politics. He concludes that "it is upon some such sense of the whole that the ideal of citizenship rests" (1970, p. 215). As we will see in Chapter Three, the position taken here is that the notion of the public interest, which public administrators are charged to uphold, involves this concern for inclusiveness, a fundamental obligation of citizenship in a democracy.

Does this primary obligation to the citizenship role suggest that public administrators should run to the press, or an elected official, or a prosecutor every time something occurs that is not totally consistent with the legislative mandate for their organization? Certainly not! It is important to assess the seriousness of a situation, consider the full range of values at stake, and then act in proportion to these circumstances. There is nothing to be gained and much to be lost by overreacting to a perceived problem. A press conference is hardly warranted the first time the boss asks you to hire a friend who does not rank as highly as other candidates for a position. A talk with the boss to express your disapproval of the request might be more appropriate. George Graham (n.d., p. 2) proposes a series of steps that are generally consistent with this "proportional" approach. His prescriptions are founded on the concept of due process, which requires "all administrators in exercising the power and discretionary authority with which they are entrusted to be informed, to be fair, to be rational, and to be reasonable."

Maintaining a citizenship role while serving as an administrator of the public's business requires a healthy sense of critical perspective about an agency's conduct, but it does not necessitate disproportionate responses to misdeeds that may do more harm to the organization than good. The organization itself is a piece of the public's property. Attention to the double obligations of being a citizen-administrator implies the careful adjustment, repair, or on occasion the major overhaul of the public's machinery. Moral imagination is the requisite skill and ethical autonomy is the quality of character necessary for such stewardship.

Managers of Diversity. The third implication of modernization is that public administrators must be managers of diverse interests. This necessity grows out of the relativity of values and the pluralization of society. In the absence of any unitary value system with absolute authority in society, both the political and the administrative processes of government become the focus of diverse interests. The administrative arm of government becomes significantly involved in managing these interests because, even with the complex political representation provided by the federal government, people still do not feel that their preferences, needs, and problems are cared for adequately. They tend to organize in groups with others who have similar interests. These voluntary associations can be seen asserting their proposals and demands at every point in the policy-making process, from electoral politics to the legislative process to the implementation stage. Kenneth Meier (1979) points out that most of these groups have long since learned that administrative agencies are key leverage points since most legislative proposals originate there and are shaped by these agencies in significant ways during implementation. (See also Lowi, 1979.)

Interest-group theorists such as Calhoun (1953), Bentley (1949), and Truman (1951) have argued that these citizen organizations are essential for democratic representation in the modern state. The formal machinery of government could not possibly be designed to represent the changing spectrum of interests in a pluralistic mass society like the United States with sufficient particularity. It is far more efficient and effective to allow these groups to form themselves and project their own demands into the governmental process (Ornstein and Elder, 1978).

However, Parenti (1970) has identified a serious problem with this theoretical perspective: It assumes that all significant interests can be represented in this fashion. In his case study of efforts to organize a low-income community in New Jersey, Parenti concludes that only those with the necessary economic resources can make themselves heard effectively by government through interest-group activity. The impediments that citizens must surmount in order to influence public decision making have been conceptualized as "participation costs" by a number of scholars including Buchanan and Tullock (1962), Warren and Weschler (1975), and myself (Cooper, 1979).

The greatest leverage for reducing or subsidizing these costs lies with public administrators. They and their organizations deal with a defined set of public services. Administrators have great potential for influencing policy developments about these services, and often considerable discretion in their actual delivery. Administrative initiative in managing the plural interests of modern society is essential for effective government. Representation of interests in this kind of society, particularly at the scale of contemporary industrial urban society, necessitates active involvement of public administrators. They can provide a link between citizens and elected officials that is vital in the national, state, county, and even city governments whose populations have expanded substantially during the last fifty years.

However, the tendency of public administration during the first three-quarters of this century was to place a high value on standardized services and respond to the pluralization of society with reluctance (Caro, 1975). From Weber to Wilson to Goodnow to White to Gulick and Urwick, we find a rather consistent development of the notion that the chief task of public administrators is to implement policy efficiently by applying generic scientific principles. This perspective eschewed notions that social and cultural variation might significantly affect administrative principles. A generic approach to administration, combined with an emphasis on efficiency, gave rise to a tendency to standardize public services. Something like an assembly-line concept of economies of scale seemed to be operative: "If you can determine the one best way to educate children, then the more children you can educate within a single administrative structure, the more efficiently public education can be provided." This hypothetical statement exemplifies the kind of thinking that characterized public administration's approach to the provision of public services. Centralization, of course, has been one of the logical concomitants of standardization, particularly during the New Deal, World War II, and the postwar years.

Another factor contributing to the tendency to standardize services is the bureaucratic assumption that equality is the equivalent of equity (Cooper, 1979). If everyone is treated the same, then everyone will be treated fairly. This assumption appears to have gained dominance through the American Progressive movement of the late nineteenth and early twentieth centuries. Reacting against the special favors, patronage, and nepotism of corrupt machine governments, the Progressives called for equal treatment of all citizens and government employees. "Without fear or favor" was the way public administrators were to perform their duties. Good government was understood as standardized government, which would, in turn, yield efficient government.

Only recently have we begun to realize that this approach is unworkable and impractical. A more systemic view of the relationship between public agencies and the citizenry is required. If administrative agencies of government are to remain effective and viable, they must view themselves as open systems in turbulent environments. The citizenry, the most important component of the environment, must not be ignored, nor even yielded to reluctantly under the pressure of interest groups. Rather, those who direct and manage these systems must act with initiative to be certain that input from the societal environment is being sought out and encouraged; that participation costs are reduced or subsidized as much as possible.

The result of this kind of dynamic interaction with the social environment may be a trading off of some measure of production efficiency for a varied array of service types and delivery modes. It may even lead to the devolution of service provision or delivery to lower levels of scale such as neighborhoods. All this may look less orderly and therefore less efficient in the short run, but may represent a more effective adaptation to the pluralistic environment of modern society. It may be a matter of giving up a limited kind of efficiency, which suboptimizes the production at the level of single agencies, for the sake of the broader efficiency of the entire democratic governmental system (Bennis, 1966).

The ethical concern related to this third proposition is for social equity. The assumption that equal treatment is fair treatment needs to be reexamined. If, in fact, members of a population are not the same, but quite varied in their tastes, needs, preferences, and backgrounds, then treating them as though they were the same is not fair.

Inequity has often been institutionalized in the practices of public agencies under the banner of standardization. This is because the standards adopted have tended to be the key attributes of one population group—often those of the majority. Consequently, so-called standardized civil service exams have often assumed the attributes of white, Anglo-Saxon, Protestant males as the norms. Public education has been built around curricular assumptions that favor the offspring of middle-class English-speaking nuclear families. Housing codes have been standardized around ideal, newly built structures and contain a bias against the varying conditions and needs of older neighborhoods.

Achieving social equity requires a response from public agencies that seeks to approximate the needs, preferences, and demands of the citizenry. Since everyone is not the same in these respects, public administrators need a set of techniques for generating citizen input into organizational decision making, and the skills to use them, to maintain an accurate assessment of the social environment. This kind of intelligence would make it possible, then, to consider the array of services and means of service delivery congruent with that organization's constituent groups.

This is not simply a pragmatic attempt to achieve greater client satisfaction. Although it is concerned with providing public services in a more satisfying fashion, it is more fundamentally a matter of equitable treatment of the citizenry. Furthermore, from one perspective, in a modern industrial society the full realization of citizenship involves the ability to consume public services. According to Warren and Weschler (1975), citizenship in such a society requires more than the legal constitutional rights normally assumed to be the privileges of citizenship. They argue that people are deprived of their full citizenship if services are provided in such a way that they are too costly to consume.

"Consumption costs" are defined by Warren and Weschler as increments of time, effort, and money that must be added by a citizen-consumer to a public good or service to make it consumable. If one has to walk or drive three miles to reach the nearest bus stop, those travel costs must be added to the fare to ascertain the true cost of consuming bus service. Thus, if services are standardized the costs of consuming public services will be distributed disproportionately to resources. Justice in the distribution of public services will not be achieved, or even approximated.

A parallel ethical concern has to do with the distribution of the "participation costs." If public administrators are to develop a more accurate assessment of citizens' needs, preferences, and demands, it has been argued that active pursuit of citizen input is necessary. To achieve that goal, participation costs must be low enough to allow the full population spectrum to participate. Again, this is not only a matter of practical necessity, but it is also an ethical consideration. Citizens should not be deprived of the right to participate in public decision making because it requires a greater expenditure of time, effort, money than they can afford, or than the anticipated benefits seem to warrant.

Public administrators in modern society need to be effective managers of diverse interests. As both Ostrom (1974) and Waldo (1965) have argued, public administrators must abandon their almost exclusive preoccupation with the costs of producing public goods and services, and begin to balance these costs against those which must be borne by citizens, if democratic administration is to take place. Waldo states the case thus: "It has long seemed to me that our approach to administration is far too much 'producer oriented,' far too little 'consumer oriented.' . . . But if we value not only efficiency and productivity, but also seek to increase human equality and the values of participation, do we give these the attention they deserve in and relating to the administrative process?" (p. 45).

Political Theory and Administrative Ethics

Since the first edition of this book it has become increasingly clear that an adequate normative theory of the public administrative role, including a normative ethical theory, must be developed within the context of a larger political theory of public administration. Such a theory lies beyond the scope of this volume, but it seems appropriate to indicate at this point some of the ethical issues that will need to be dealt with in such a theory.

The diversity of modern society, the tendency to separate the administrative role from the citizenship role, and the demise of the modern notion of separating politics and administration, with its ensuing recognition of the unavoidability of administrative discretion—all these forces pose some serious problems for a definition of the administrative role. It is now clear that public administrators make political judgments that range from timing of policy proposals, to budget strategies, to extensive rules and regulations for laws that legislators intentionally made vague. Public administrators exercise discretion, and they do so politically with both legislators and clientele groups. Administrators seem to be firmly ensconced within the policy "iron triangle" as key participants in the political process of public policy formation and adoption. However, although we acknowledge this fact, and find no dearth of descriptive analyses of the dynamics involved, we have nothing approaching an adequate prescriptive political theory of the administrative role that would define the obligations of the administrator in the politics of the policy process (Fleishman, 1981).

From this lack of normative clarity, ethical issues emerge around three related aspects of the democratic public policy process: representation, education, and implementation.

Representation. In modern democracies it is assumed that the people maintain political sovereignty, but that their interests, demands, and preferences are reflected in the public policies that are adopted. This has been understood as occurring through the process of representation, which, until recent years, has been assigned entirely to the political role. However, if we have now discovered that administrators also act in politically significant ways in the policy process, then it is unclear whether in so doing they also incur obligations for representation. It seems plausible to argue that in a democratic polity, representation of popular preferences, demands, and interests must operate in some fashion whenever substantive policy decisions are being made. If this proposition is valid, public administrators bear an obligation to represent the citizenry whenever they are influencing or determining the substantive content of policies (Chandler, 1984).

Should we accept the representative obligations of public administrators, there are only more questions to be answered. We must then ask to what extent and in what ways are administrators so obligated? How must their exercise of discretion be informed by the people? Is some kind of regular and systematic accounting to the public required, analogous to the electoral process, or is accountability maintained through elected officials? In other words, should administrative representation involve a direct relationship with the people, or one that is indirect? If it is direct, systematic and regular citizen participation seems an essential function for the administrator. If indirect, then elected officials and administrators bear responsibility for discovering ways of acknowledging and carrying out a shared obligation.

Furthermore, if public administrators are obligated to represent the citizenry in some fashion, the classic debate over "trustee" versus "delegate" definitions of representational obligation must be addressed once more, this time in the administrative context. Are public administrators trustees of such normative goals as the public interest, social equity, or regime values? Should it be their responsibility to advocate such values and principles, even if the people do not clearly support them?

Or, on the other hand, are administrators more like delegates of the people, whose primary concern should be discerning public preferences and demands and responding to the public will? How are professional judgment and popular sovereignty reconciled with each other? If they are irreconcilable, which should receive priority? (Grunebaum, 1981). Of course, the very nature of professionalism for public administrators turns on the answer to these questions. Is professional judgment fundamentally oriented toward technical expertise, or popular will? Which takes priority?

We might be tempted to conclude too quickly that the trustee definition is more appropriate for the administrator, since that is a nonelective role. It might appear that representation through delegation occurs only through a specific overt act, such as election. We might assume that unless the people engage in an act of choosing some individual to represent them, delegation of political responsibility cannot occur. This is not necessarily the case, however. Delegation of authority and responsibility to organizations and categories of personnel also occurs through legislation, including the normal process and in some states the initiative of citizens. These are acts of general delegation. Presumably, persons who then accept positions within those designated organizations are agreeing to bear responsibility for carrying out the public will expressed in the law. If that will is not clearly defined in law, we might conclude that there is an implied obligation to discern it, through whatever means possible.

Of course, the problem with carrying out the delegative role in many such cases is that all too often the legislation, of necessity, does not spell out the public's will with great clarity. Thus, the administrator is left with a delegation of public authority and responsibility that does not specify in much detail what is expected. Political conflicts avoided and technical questions unaddressed in the legislative process are passed along to administrators for resolution.

The quandary over delegate versus trustee obligations is embedded in these characteristics of much of our legislation. On the one hand, unresolved political issues call for administrators to act as responsive delegates in arriving at some publicly acceptable actions. On the other hand, technical considerations seem to require trustees who exercise the best professional judgment in getting the job done while serving the broad normative goals of the polity. Consequently, the question still remains: Which of these aspects of public policy should take precedence? Should the public administrator be obligated to represent the citizenry primarily as a delegate, or as a trustee? Is the answer variable, and if so under what conditions should one or the other become dominant?

Education. It is generally assumed in democratic theory that not only do the sovereign people vote, but they cast a more or less informed ballot. One justification for political debate is its educational value. When points of view are exchanged, reason is put to the test of opposing ideas, perception is broadened, information is acquired, and self-interest is tempered by the interests of others. It is through this process of talking to one another and to their political leaders that a public is formed and public opinion is transformed into public judgment (Yankelovich, 1981).

In the classic democratic formulation the key actors in this educational process of debate and deliberation are the citizenry and their elected representatives. However, in the modern administrative state the role of the career public administrator must be accounted for in some way. Since administrators are close to the problems, possess specialized knowledge and technical expertise, have ongoing relationships with their clientele groups, and tend to maintain longer tenure in government than most politicians, they appear to be essential participants in the democratic educational process. Their contributions seem to be necessary for the full development of public judgment.

However, the obligations of this aspect of the administrative role—teaching and learning through public deliberation—are neither clearly defined nor generally acknowledged. For example, one can read the entire winter 1985 issue of the *Kettering Review* (devoted to exploring how the public learns the public's business, with articles by thoughtful individuals such as Derek Bok, Daniel Yankelovich, Robert MacNeil, Geraldine Ferraro, and David Mathews) and be left with the impression that public administrators have no role to play in this process. This journal—generally insightful, sophisticated, and "dedicated to improving the quality of public life in the American democracy"—makes no mention of public administrators as significant participants in the public dialogue. The classical assumptions, focusing exclusively on the citizens and their political leaders, seem not to have been revised here for the modern administrative state. The media and the university are acknowledged, but not the bureaucrats who run our governments on a day-to-day, year-to-year basis.

However, if the obligation of public administrators for a key educational role in the public policy process is to be established, there are difficult questions to be answered and issues to be resolved. The obligation for informing and educating elected officials "behind the scenes" is generally accepted. Analyzing data, conducting research, preparing briefing papers, providing evaluation studies, and developing cost estimates for elected officials upon request are all well within the classical view of public administrators as nonpolitical instruments in the hands of politicians. However, once we move away from that view, how do we redefine the obligations and responsibilities of administrators for educating politicians and learning from them? How should we understand the educational relationship between administrators and politicians in the policy process?

For example, is there an obligation to go beyond the reactive mode, providing information only when requested? Should the administrator role include preparing and disseminating information not requested? Should an agency administrator feel obligated to plan and conduct a systematic educational process, formal or informal, for politicians? Should this include a deliberate challenge of political positions that do not appear to be well grounded in factual knowledge, or values and principles that are inconsistent with the American political tradition, or proposals that rest on faulty methods? Public administrators use these approaches from time to time, but should we now include them among the defined professional obligations?

Furthermore, should we sometimes expect administrators to carry on this educational process, not "behind the scenes" but out on "center stage" in full public view? If politics and administration cannot be neatly separated, does it make sense to think in terms of the total subordination of the administrative role to the political one? Or should we understand administrative obligation as including the chastening of political whims and passions with information, expertise, and experience? If public administrators are "citizens in lieu of the rest of us" should we not hold them responsible for publicly asking the hard questions and articulating the counterarguments that expand and balance political debate so that their fiduciary obligations are visibly executed?

On the other hand, how should we understand the obligation of the public administrator to learn from elected officials? The professional perspectives of the administrator, rooted in specialized knowledge, technical expertise, and clientele relationships, may need to be leavened with political knowledge of particular constituencies and the ways of legislative bodies. Administrative specialists can become narrow and isolated from the texture of the political community. They may be overly influenced by client groups and too firmly convinced of the "one best way" of getting the job done. They may forget the importance of political support, not only in adopting policy but also in carrying it out. Legislative proposals, administrative rules and regulations, and agency implementation plans may need to be informed regularly by political realities.

In addition to a mutual obligation for mutually educative interaction between administrators and elected officials, we must also think through a similar relationship between citizens and public administrators. Perhaps administrators who cultivate the kind of relationship with politicians outlined above should be prepared to offer two kinds of knowledge to the citizenry. The first is their own substantive knowledge of particular policy arenas and issues, and the second is procedural knowledge about how government works. If public administrators are, indeed, "the especially responsible citizens who are officials," should not teaching their fellow citizens these things be among their central responsibilities? If the rest of us are to be able to carry out our citizenship obligations, is it not essential that citizen administrators provide us with their best technical information and judgments, in an understandable form, as well as a more effective understanding of how both the bureaucracy and the legislative process work?

Communicating substantive information to the public is essential if self-government is to be even approximated. Should not public administrators understand this as an ongoing primary role obligation that cannot be set aside or curtailed in order to "get on with the job"? Is that not the most fundamental job, apart from which administrative efficiency is short-sighted and doomed to failure?

Should we not also agree that career public administrators are likely to be the best "civics" teachers available to the citizenry? Experience with students, especially undergraduates, suggests that one of the weakest links in our democratic process is teaching our young people how their government really works. Somehow they arrive at the university with a wooden, oversimplifed conception of the way public policy is formed and implemented. This caricature, acquired in textbooks, is carried over into adult life. Quite reasonably, then, most of our citizens either have little or no interest in government, since it appears to be boring in the extreme, or they become quickly disillusioned over the gap between "the world as it is and the world as they would like it to be." In either case they remain aloof and disengaged from activities that appear to be either dull or beyond their powers.

Administrators engaged with the governmental process on a daily basis may be the best sources of a richer and more interesting knowledge of its practical workings. How can we best conceptualize a public educational obligation for administrators? Might it call for an expanded understanding of how administrators are involved in policy making, perhaps as procedural "coaches" or "tutors" for the citizens, as well as substance experts?

Now let us turn to the reciprocal aspect of the educative obligation between administrators and citizens. Is there not the responsibility to learn from citizens as well as teach them? If administrators stand in a representative relationship to the citizens, is it not essential that they understand the perspectives, problems, perceived needs, and priorities of citizens? Since administrators control focused public resources, are they not obliged to reach out beyond their clientele groups and political allies to help cultivate a "public conversation"? David Mathews (1985) argues persuasively that a democratic public cannot form and act on its own behalf without such ongoing "conversation." It cannot move beyond public *opinion* to public *knowledge*, and finally to public *judgment*, without this communication. Mathews insists that "a democratic community begins with—in fact, is—a conversation of people talking to one another. If the public is not talking, there is no democratic state" (p. 60). Unfortunately, Mathews's assumption seems to be that only elected officials and the media bear the responsibility for this communicative process. Does that not amount to the omission of an enormous set of actors with knowledge, experience, and resources? Should we not agree that the administrative role also carries with it a central obligation to stimulate this conversation among citizens and to learn from it?

Implementation. Finally, the third aspect of the policy process that gives rise to ethical issues about the administrative role in a political environment is implementation. In the classical paradigm this was the administrative area of responsibility. It was assumed that administrators receive policy decisions adopted by the politicians and then apply their best functional rationality to putting them into practice. Administrators were expected to use their professional judgment about the most efficient means for achieving the purposes defined by the legislative process.

However, once we acknowledge the inescapably political nature of the public administrative role, the obligations of the administrator in implementation are no longer so clear. For example, since legislative proposals often originate through administrative initiative, what obligation should the administrator bear for specifying at the outset how a proposed policy would likely be implemented? Should tentative rules, regulations, standards, and time schedules be considered along with the policy statement during legislative debate, rather than left until later for administrators to handle, as is typically the case now? Would this serve the purpose of making administrative action more visible and, therefore, more politically accountable?

Also, we face again a problem raised in the earlier discussion of the representational obligations of the public administrator. How should we expect administrators to balance professional expertise with representation of the citizen during the implementation phase? Aside from whatever is currently required by law for citizen participation in the implementing of policies, should public administrators bear an ethical obligation for representing the interests, preferences, and demands of the people throughout this process? If so, is the trustee or the delegate perspective more appropriate here at the implementation stage? Should we understand the administrators' best professional judgment as tantamount to the trustee approach to representation, and therefore sufficient? Or should we expect administrators, in implementing policies, to think of themselves as delegates in need of regular instructions from the people? Is there an appropriate shift, from delegative representation in the adoption stage, as policy is first being formed, to a trustee perspective in implementation, since technical judgments are most prominent at that point? Or, again, is the appropriate perspective variable from policy to policy, depending on complexity, specificity, scope, significance of probable impact, and other factors?

From these three aspects of the public policy process—representation, education, and implementation—a plethora of ethical issues emerges concerning the proper definitions of the administrative role in an unavoidably political context. No answers have been provided, but the questions raised begin to sketch out an agenda for normative theory development.

These attributes of the administrative role in modern society and the ethical concerns that emerge from them lead quite naturally to a consideration of administrative responsibility. The next chapter begins this consideration with a discussion of the origins of the term *responsibility* and two ways of conceptualizing it.

Chapter Three

Administrative Responsibility: The Key to Administrative Ethics

Responsibility is the key concept in developing an ethic for the administrative role. Frederick Mosher (1968, p. 7) once observed, "Responsibility may well be the most important word in all the vocabulary of administration, public and private." Two major aspects of that concept are used here: subjective and objective responsibility.

When you are confronted with a problem over what you ought to do in a given situation, you are experiencing the need to define your responsibility in the administrative role. For example, assume that you are an administrator in a federal agency that allocates funds to state agencies for highway construction. Your organization's mission is to review proposed highway routes for their anticipated environmental impact. Highway projects that significantly affect the environment require an environmental impact statement (EIS); others do not. One section of a federal law mandates that highways constructed with federal money may not impact or use public park land, unless it has been determined that there is no feasible and desirable alternative—a question that is normally determined in the EIS.

A member of your staff comes to you with a problem. She has recently met with officials from a certain state to discuss a proposed highway improvement. The existing highway is narrow, with no shoulders, and is heavily used by elementary school students on bicycles and on foot. It is extremely unsafe, as the number of accidents clearly indicates. The school board, the parents association, the local newspaper, the council of churches, and state highway officials are all calling for immediate action to widen the highway and alleviate these hazardous conditions. The problem is that, according to the state highway planners, widening the road sufficiently would require taking a strip of land five feet wide by one hundred feet long from a fifty-acre municipal park. This can be done within the law, but an EIS must be prepared to identify and justify the environmental impact. This process typically takes two years to complete.

You are responsible for complying with the law under which your organization operates, but you also believe your responsibility is to help reduce the hazardous road condition as quickly as possible. Two types of responsibility can be identified in this case. They are sometimes referred to as objective and subjective responsibility (Mosher, 1968; Winter, 1966). Objective responsibility has to do with expectations imposed from outside ourselves, while subjective responsibility concerns those things for which we feel a responsibility. As we shall see, this is not to be understood as a difference between real and unreal; subjective responsibility, as an expression of our beliefs, personal and professional values, and character traits, is just as real as the more tangible manifestations of objective responsibility. These concepts will be the main focus of this chapter since they seem to represent the most common ways in which administrators actually experience problems in defining their responsibility in concrete situations.

Objective Responsibility

The specific forms of objective responsibility discussed here include two dimensions: accountability and imposed obligation. All objective responsibility involves responsibility *to* someone, or some collective body, and responsibility *for* certain tasks, subordinate personnel, and goal achievement. The former is accountability and the latter is obligation. Accountability and obligation, responsibility *to* someone else *for* something—these are the dual dimensions of objective administrative responsibility.

In terms of relative importance, obligation is the more fundamental; accountability is the means for ensuring the fulfillment of obligation in a hierarchical structure. Accountability implies superior-subordinate relationships and the exercise of authority from the top down to maintain the flow of work toward the achievement of mandated goals.

If we explicate these two aspects of objective responsibility in the organizational and political contexts of the public administrative role, we can clarify the relationship of responsibility among the key actors in the policy process. These will be ordered from more to less proximate relationships of accountability, and from less to more fundamental relationships of obligation.

First, public administrators are most immediately responsible to their organizational superiors for carrying out their directives, or mutually agreed-upon goals, and for the conduct of their subordinates. They must be able to explain their conduct, and allocation of time and other resources, as consistent with the work plan and objectives of the organization, whether these result from orders originated in a strict hierarchical fashion, or from some collaborative decision-making process. This is the most proximate relationship of accountability, involving a regular reporting process. However, the relationship of obligation here is the least fundamental. The organization's work plan, specific objectives, and task assignments are simply instrumental in nature. They are pursuant to policies established in the political arena.

Objective responsibility also for the actions of subordinates is essential to the Weberian bureaucratic ideal type. Superiors must direct the activities of those under their supervision, provide resources for accomplishing the work, delegate adequate authority for assigned duties, and monitor performance. They in turn are held accountable for how their subordinates use the resources provided and exercise delegated authority toward the fulfillment of an assignment. This assumes, of course, that superiors are also accountable for clearly defining the assigned duties in the first place and, wherever discretion is allowed, delineating its boundaries. Subordinates are instructed to refer to their superiors any decisions that exceed the stipulated bounds of discretion, and thus the superiors maintain ultimate responsibility.

Second, public administrators are responsible to elected officials for carrying out their wishes as embodied in public policies. Such policies are collectively determined for legislative acts, or singly determined for executive orders. As we have seen previously, this obligation includes both preparing policy proposals and implementing legislation and executive orders. Administrators must be able to explain their actions and use of resources as consistent with legislative intent, or the intent of executive orders. This relationship of legal accountability is less proximate than the first, since it involves relatively infrequent reporting, but it is a more fundamental obligation. Since public policy is the basis for the organizational mandate and mission, obligations to those who establish policy supersede obligations to organizational superiors.

Finally, public administrators are responsible to the citizenry for discerning, understanding, and weighing their preferences, demands, and other interests. They may respond by changing programs within existing law, or by recommending new legislation to elected officials. Administrators must be able to explain their conduct to the citizenry as consistent with either the wishes of the citizenry, or the larger public interest. This is the least proximate relationship of accountability, with only very infrequent and often indirect reporting of conduct and achievements. It is, however, the most fundamental relationship of obligation, since the citizenry are sovereign and public administrators are their fiduciaries. Sharing representative and fiduciary functions with elected officials in modern democratic society means that this relationship of obligation is also shared. For both groups, this is the source of role ambiguity and conflict.

One final word about the nature of accountability in all three relationships is in order. Accountability may be understood in both practical and ethical terms. The responsible administrator must be prepared to answer for conduct from both perspectives, but ethical accountability must finally prevail. Generally, we should assume that an administrator will be expected to explain actions from a practical perspective in terms such as cost effectiveness, efficiency, economy, feasibility, and productivity, and from an ethical perspective according to values and principles such as equity, equality, freedom, truthfulness, beneficence, human dignity, privacy, and democracy. The practicality of conduct is never sufficient in and of itself. Unless a course of action can be adequately explained on ethical grounds, it is not a responsible act. The full meaning of responsibility requires ethical as well as practical accountability.

To illustrate these concepts, think back to the federal highway case described above.

Responsibility to Elected Officials Through Support for the Law.
Your responsibility to elected officials through compliance with the law is a matter of objective responsibility. You are expected to behave according to the wishes of those set in authority over you. Here the expectations are those of duly elected legislators expressed in a legally codified statement. That legislation prescribes how you shall conduct yourself when the construction of highways affects public park land, apart from your own feelings about the matter.

Objective responsibility involves accountability to someone else and obligation for a particular standard or category of performance. It is objective in that the source of accountability and obligation lie outside yourself. Objective responsibility is not the result of a series of decisions you made about what ought to be done. Rather it flows from the decisions of others about what someone occupying your administrative position ought to do. Your decision to accept the position is understood to be tantamount to accepting these expectations and constraints. Objective responsibility projects generalized obligations for all who fill this type of position without any attempt to acknowledge the individual needs, limitations, preferences, or predilections of a particular incumbent. It is through these external generalized obligations that the role is structured, given its distinctive content, and maintained through changing times, incumbents, and situations. It is through hierarchical arrangements that accountability is maintained. The stability and continuity of the role are rooted in these two aspects of objective responsibility.

Responsibility to the laws governing your organization and your conduct within it is one form of objective responsibility for your role as a public administrator. Ultimately, of course, legal responsibility includes an obligation to uphold the Constitution. Through the Constitution and specific pieces of legislation consistent with it, the intentions of the citizenry for those employed in the public service are presumed to be formally expressed. Inherent in the fiduciary nature of the public administrative role is the objective responsibility to the law. Legal mandates for public agencies are a manifestation of primary obligation to serve the public's interests, not those of the people employed by the agencies. Responsibility to the law is a constant reminder that public organizations and their administrators exist on behalf of the public.

Thus, in the highway-widening case you are held accountable for acting consistently with your obligations under the law that governs the use of park land. Your own personal opinion about the relative importance of highway safety versus park space is not the controlling factor, but rather the course of action that the law requires of you as an agent of the public. In accounting for your conduct and justifying your decision, it will not be sufficient to explain that you "have loved that park since you were a kid and just couldn't stand to see it whittled away for a highway." This would likely be viewed as irresponsible conduct.

Responsibility to Superiors and for Subordinates. In addition to law, there are numerous other objective sources of responsibility for public administrators: organizational rules and policies, official job descriptions, and professional standards. However, alongside law, the most prominently experienced objective responsibility is to the hierarchical accountability structure of the organization for which you work—your responsibility to organizational superiors and your responsibility for the conduct of subordinates.

Paul Appleby (1952) has argued that hierarchy is "the formal structure and instrument of responsibility" (p. 340). The chain of command, with its successive delegations of responsibility, is the means by which the generalized intentions of the law are approximated in concrete programs and services. Successive approximations of general legal intent are achieved by specifying accountability for particular aspects of the total task. Particular organizations and individuals are held responsible for implementing specific portions of the legal mandate or providing support for others in fulfilling their responsibility.

Whatever individuals working within the hierarchies of governmental organizations may feel about them, they are the formally accountable means of maintaining conduct that is consistent with the wishes of the citizenry. Appleby insists that only through "loyalty upward disciplined by the sanctions of hierarchy" (p. 228) can the public be maintained at the highest level in democratic decision making. Public servants may very well feel constrained and limited in their range of discretion by the chain of command, but that is one of the intended functions of organizational structure. The personal preferences of individual public employees must be subjugated to the popular will, presumably as communicated through the organizational chain of command.

From Appleby's perspective, this is accomplished by making officials at the top of the hierarchy responsible for the conduct of those below. Then, as diverse public preferences and demands are introduced at various subordinate levels of the organizational structure, they are pushed upward for resolution. Those with greater objective responsibility for conformity to law and popular will are held accountable for reconciling these multiple, often conflicting, demands. According to Bailey (1965, p. 283), this view of the objective responsibility of hierarchies assumes that "the basic morality of the system is in its forcing of unitary claims into the mill of pluralistic considerations," as they move upward.

Once again, the case of the highway and the park exemplifies this process. The member of your staff who laid the problem before you recognized that there were conflicting public demands that she was not competent to resolve at her level of responsibility. The law, expressing the presumed intent of the citizenry of the nation, clearly required an EIS, but the local public, as represented by the newspaper, churches, school board, parent associations, and state highway officials, were primarily concerned about the expeditious widening of the road. Her only responsible option was to carry the problem up the chain of command to the next level.

Authority and *politics* are the key concepts for understanding this upward movement. The pressure of political conflict, combined with insufficient authority to resolve it at any given level in the hierarchy, creates the necessity for moving the problem up the ladder of responsibility. When it reaches an organizational level at which there is both responsibility for resolving the conflict and authority to do so, then a decision can and should be made. If, for example, you have been delegated the authority to make exceptions to the legal requirement for an EIS, then you are obligated to decide whether to do so in this case. However, if you have not been authorized by your superiors to grant exceptions, the problem will need to be pushed upward until it reaches someone with that authority and obligation.

Or, if you have the authority to resolve the issue and attempt to do so, but some significant actors in the political arena are not satisfied with the outcome, they may appeal to those higher in the chain of command to review and override your decision. In matters of serious consequence this movement up the hierarchy may reach the top of the organizational pyramid without being settled and eventually find its way into the judicial system for resolution.

One of the pathologies of bureaucratic organizations is a failure to exercise responsibility when you are, in fact, authorized and obligated to make a given decision (Barnard, 1952). Passing the buck up the chain of command because you do not want to bear your obligation for deciding is just as irresponsible as acting when you are not authorized to do so or allowing subordinates to engage in misconduct. This reluctance to accept the share of the responsibility delegated to you results in superiors being inundated with decisions they should not have to make, thus leaving subordinates without adequate direction. It distorts the organizational structure and impedes the flow of work.

However, the objective responsibility that an administrator experiences from the organizational hierarchy must not be viewed as the rigid one-way process exemplified by the strictest interpretation of the Weberian ideal type (Weber, 1946). Carl Friedrich has criticized Weber's model precisely at this point; it does not sufficiently acknowledge the possibility of consultation and cooperation between levels of the organization (Friedrich, 1952). The exercise of objective responsibility to the hierarchy should not involve a simple flow of directives from top to bottom; it should be far more complex and dynamic. The apparently fixed subordinate-superior relationships should be more fluid because of the need for consultation and sharing information up and down the hierarchy. Superiors in any bureaucratic organization are highly dependent on the specialized knowledge and experience of subordinates. Subordinates, in turn, need to consult regularly with those above them about legal requirements, clarification of agency regulations, and political considerations. Appleby's normative view of this process has been described by Egger (1965, p. 307) as "the structuring of a network of intelligence and communication which provides a matrix of abundantly diverse and catholic values and influences for the decisions of a pluralistic society."

Hugh Heclo (1975) has described the responsibility of individual public administrators in terms that are generally consistent with those of Appleby. It was Appleby's belief that, far from being the docile submissive implementer, "the function of an administrator was to complicate the lives of his political masters at least to the extent of assuring that they did not resolve complex issues on the basis of disingenuously simple criteria" (Egger, 1965, p. 307). Heclo referred to this active, even aggressive, role of the administrator as one of exercising "neutral competence." By that he meant not the conduct of a docile and simply compliant automaton but "a strange amalgam of loyalty that argues back, partisanship that shifts with the changing partisans, independence that depends on others" (p. 82). Both Appleby and Heclo were describing the responsibility of the top levels of administration to political officials; however, the mode of conduct they suggest seems generally appropriate for all levels of the administrative hierarchy.

The objective responsibility of any public administrator to the chain of command does not imply a passive acceptance of directives from above, or the unilateral issuance of orders to those below. It includes the systematic filtering upward of information that will complicate the lives of superiors in the sense of providing a more accurate representation of issues, and the regular clarification downward of acceptable norms for conduct. If democratic government is to be maintained in a modern pluralistic society, those with authority and responsibility for making decisions should do so with full knowledge of relevant technical information, public opinion trends, positions of interest groups, interpretations of the law, past practice, the views of interested elected officials, the perspectives of other governmental agencies, and the best informed judgment of subordinates, both practical and ethical. Those in subordinate positions should act with clear directives from above about the publicly mandated mission of the organization, and these directives should be based on full knowledge of all relevant factors.

When your staff member came to you with the problem of the highway and the park she was acting responsibly, from the perspectives of Appleby and Heclo, if she complicated your life with relevant information about a decision she did not have authority to make. If, for example, she informed you that, in addition to support of the project from the churches, school board, parent association, newspaper and state highway officials, there was also opposition from other quarters, she would be carrying out her objective responsibility. She might have told you that the state environmental agency, the municipal parks and recreation commission, the local chapter of the Sierra Club, a homeowners' association in the area surrounding the park, and a city council member from that district were strongly opposing the highway project, and threatening litigation. Also, she should have apprised you of the possibility of a more expensive alternative course of action that would involve a realignment of the highway but would permit the use of industrial property on the opposite side of the roadway instead of the park land.

The objective responsibility of public administrators to the hierarchy of an organization includes not only taking decisions up the chain of command when their authority has been transcended by the magnitude of an issue, but also passing along as much information as needs to be considered in arriving at a decision. This is not only a matter of individual responsibility, but when summed throughout an entire organization, or an entire government, it amounts to the responsible conduct of the public's business. Wilensky (1967) has demonstrated that the flow of intelligence through an organization is essential not only for the organization's survival but, more important, for achieving democratic values.

The dysfunctions of this hierarchical system, are, of course, well documented (Merton, 1952). With particular concern for the flow of information, both Tullock (1965) and Perrow (1972) identify two different types of problems. Tullock describes the tendency for subordinates to withhold or distort information, while Perrow argues that superiors often receive appropriate information but are unwilling to use it. The common motivation in both cases is the desire to protect self-interests. Subordinates tend to filter out information that may upset the boss and create problems for themselves, while those higher in the chain of command tend to suppress information that is not favorable to their positions.

The difficulty here is centered in a lack of congruence between subjective and objective responsibility. We will return to the problem of incongruity between these forms of responsibility in Chapters Four and Five. For now, suffice it to say that the assumption here is that it is not necessarily bureaucratic organization, per se, that gives rise to these problems. Based on years of experience in applied research on hierarchical organizations, Elliott Jaques (1976, p. 2) argues that bureaucracies are "dependent institutions, social instruments, taking their initial objectives and characteristics from the associations which employ them." Jaques insists that bureaucratic organizations can be effective and humane tools for a democratic society. We will return to his prescription for "requisite" organizations in Chapter Six.

Responsibility to the Citizenry. A third form of objective responsibility is an obligation to serve the public interest. Whether by formal oath, governmental code of ethics, or legislative mandate, all public administrators are ultimately responsible to measure their conduct in terms of the public interest. However, it is impossible to identify any definition of "the public interest" that would receive widespread support, among either scholars or practitioners. The result is that public administrators are confronted with an array of alternatives for conceptualizing the public interest, left to fend for themselves, and expected to serve this confusing idea even though it is a far less specific and concrete form of objective responsibility than either the will of elected officials embodied in law or the organizational chain of command (Held, 1970).

　　The confounding paradox is that it is assumed that an indefinite concept of this kind should guide our judgment in responding to these two far more definite and proximate sources of obligation. It is not surprising then that as a practical matter we either treat it as the object of lip service, along with the flag, motherhood, and apple pie, or we reduce it to balancing power in a political struggle along the lines of the pluralist tradition, with its interest-group theory, as discussed in Chapter Two. In the former case we may have been exposed to abstract philosophical treatises that have convinced us that the public interest is impossible to define, and has little to do with the realities of life in a governmental agency (Friedrich, 1962). In the latter instance we may have internalized the pluralist notion that balancing organized interests is the way democracy in a mass society approximates the general well-being of the citizenry (Harmon, 1969).

　　The public interest is clearly a problematic concept. None of the attempts at defining it has been very useful in providing guidance for the practicing administrator. And yet it remains in our political tradition, in our legislation, in our official codes of ethics, in our political debates, in our campaign rhetoric, and in our deepest reflections during times of profound crisis such as Watergate and the Vietnam War. It remains a part of our thinking about the ends of public policy and the responsibility of public servants—and rightly so.

　　The function served by the concept of public interest is not so much one of defining specifically what we ought to do, or even providing operational criteria for particular decision-making problems. Rather, it stands as a kind of question mark before all official decisions and conduct. The primary obligation to serve the public interest as a member of the citizenry should cause the administrator to ask whether all relevant interests have been considered, whether "the interests and welfare of more inclusive populations than self, family, clan, or tribe" are accounted for in the decision (Waldo, 1974, p. 267).

　　Has the range of viewpoints represented in the development of your policy recommendations, program implementation plans, or service-delivery guidelines been too restricted? Are you and your staff listening to opinions that run contrary to your own, or to those that would not benefit the organization politically? Have you seriously considered the gains and losses of those not represented in the hearing room, or the advice of experts, or the lobbying process?

The obligation to serve the public interest should always cause administrators and elected officials to feel a little uneasy, not quite sure that everyone worth hearing has been heard. That is its most practical function. The fulfillment of this objective responsibility is to be found neither in adopting a Benthamite utilitarian formula, nor in a universal blueprint for society, but in a mind-set. It is a matter of carrying out your duties as though you might be required to stand before the assembled populace and explain your conduct.

Walter Lippman's oft-quoted words are appropriate here. He observed that the public interest is "what men would choose if they saw clearly, thought rationally, acted disinterestedly and benevolently" (Held, 1970, p. 205). Admittedly, this is an extremely general statement with a very significant *if* in the middle. However, it does suggest an attitude in dealing with the public's business that is more than rhetoric. It is not unlike the conditions stipulated by John Rawls (1971) as the necessary prerequisites for arriving at principles of justice that could be defined as "fair."

Rawls insists that anyone who attempts to reflect on this problem should do so from the "original position," that is, without consideration for one's own social, cultural, economic, or biological circumstances. We should attempt to reason about the requirements of justice as though we did not know our own social class, natural assets and abilities, intelligence, strength, or even the political and economic characteristics of our society. He terms this perspective "the veil of ignorance." One of the basic conclusions Rawls reaches by reasoning from this assumed vantage point is this: "All social primary goods—liberty and opportunity, income and wealth, and the bases of self-respect—are to be distributed equally *unless an unequal distribution of any or all of these goods is to the advantage of the least favored*" (p. 19, emphasis added). In other words, if none of us actually knew what our situation in society might be, according to Rawls, we would all think it just to distribute these goods equally unless we could increase the advantages of those who turn out to be among the least favored. We would do so because from behind "the veil of ignorance" it would be in our interest to do so; none of us would want to run the risk of winding up among the disadvantaged without these provisions.

This very limited treatment of the complex and carefully reasoned philosophy of John Rawls is included only to suggest the attitude required of administrators in serving the public interest, an attitude built on rationality and benevolence, both inclusive and projected over the long run. It is an attitude that attempts to eschew short-run personal gains and resists immediate pressures. It is a frame of mind that struggles to maintain a commitment to an evolving social system, a vision of the distant future, and a sense of equity that excludes none. It assumes that public servants can realize that they are primarily members of the public, whose fortunes will rise or fall with the concern and fairness exercised in the conduct of the public's business.

Subjective Responsibility

Externally imposed obligations are only one dimension of responsibility. Alongside these are our own *feelings* of, and *beliefs* about, responsibility. Objective responsibility arises from legal, organizational, and societal demands on our role as public administrator, but subjective responsibility is rooted in our own beliefs about loyalty, conscience, and identification. Subjective responsibility reflects the kind of professional ethic developed through personal experience that was discussed at the beginning of Chapter One. We believe in being legal, and so we are compelled by our conscience to act in a particular way, not because we are required to do so by a supervisor or the law, but because of an inner drive composed of beliefs, values, and predispositions to act in a certain way.

Faced with the highway problem, for example, although you may have no specific objective responsibility for reducing hazardous conditions, nevertheless you may have an intense concern for the safety of children. All the law requires of you is to prepare an environmental impact statement when park land is involved. That is also what the hierarchy of your agency expects of you. The one source of objective responsibility that may require more of you is the obligation to serve the public interest. However, that is such an abstract and elusive notion that it may not serve even the purpose of expanding the perspective of the decision maker, unless there is a strong sense of subjective responsibility. Sometimes subjective responsibility reenforces a person's objective responsibilities, sometimes not. Sometimes it moves the public-interest obligation to the forefront, other times it obscures it altogether.

Our feelings and beliefs about responsibility to someone or for something emerge from the socialization process. They are manifestations of values, attitudes, and beliefs we acquire from family, public schools, religious affiliations, friends, professional training, and organizational involvement. Through these experiences we begin to perceive patterns in physical nature and in the behavior of others that become a part of our cognitive system.

According to Rokeach (1970, pp. 112–113), these beliefs may be descriptive ("I believe rain is a form of water"), evaluative ("I believe rain is good for the earth"), or prescriptive ("I believe experiments to increase rainfall should be encouraged"). These beliefs, Rokeach explains, are organized into attitudes as they become oriented around types of situations. They are relatively enduring and create within us a predisposition to respond in a consistent fashion to these situations. Values are types of beliefs more basic than other beliefs we may hold; they are central to our belief systems and thus to our attitudes. They are beliefs about how we ought to behave and about the desirability of certain end states. If we can imagine three concentric circles, values are located in the innermost circle, indicating their fundamental relationship to the more specific beliefs one holds, beliefs lie in the middle ring, and attitudes are placed in the outer circle to suggest that they are generalized composites of values and beliefs (see also Wright, 1971).

Values are powerful influences in human experience. Although we have referred to subjective responsibility as involving feelings, it is important to note that the values from which this kind of responsibility emerges are not simply emotional expressions. They have three components, which affect the way we live: cognitive, affective, and behavioral. Values not only emerge from our cognitive interaction with our environment, but they also, in turn, shape our perceptions as we continue to experience the world. Values also evoke emotional responses to what we perceive; we have positive and negative feelings associated with what we believe about what we perceive (Drews and Lipson, 1971). This combination of cognitive and affective responses to the physical and social environment creates predispositions within us toward certain kinds of behavior. In other words, what we believe and how we feel about that belief affect our character, which in turn shapes our conduct. A value functions as a powerful imperative to action; it is "a standard or yardstick to guide actions" (Rokeach, 1970, p. 160).

As a federal administrator considering the hazardous highway, you may have formed an *attitude* of support for any effort that proposes to alter highways for the sake of increased safety for children. This attitude may be composed of a number of *beliefs* about the accident rate on narrow highways, the best means for reducing that rate, the vulnerability of pedestrians and bicycle riders, the special vulnerability of children traveling by these means, and the desirability of walking and riding bicycles instead of driving motor vehicles. At a deeper and more determinative level in your cognitive system there may be some fundamental values about preserving the dignity of human life and the particular importance of protecting children. These values motivate you to feel responsible for expediting the widening of the highway. They cause you to want to take action in that direction.

These sources of subjective responsibility may be rooted in one or more of our other roles, such as member of a professional association, citizen, parent, or member of a religious organization. For example, our membership and involvement in the American Society for Public Administration (ASPA) may create, through the experiences it provides, a sense of subjective responsibility that influences our conduct in our work roles. This may arise from ASPA's de facto ethical standards expressed through the informal norms of its culture. We acquire these through participation in its activities. Note that these may be more or less consistent with ASPA's espoused ethics set forth explicitly in its code of ethics.

Subjective responsibility is rooted in these basic determinative beliefs that we refer to as values, which become more or less elaborated as principles. These principles connect values to broad criteria for conduct. As we confront problems and issues, our values, and the principles associated with them, give rise to feelings and inclinations to behave in a certain way, or to seek the fulfillment of a particular goal.

Chester Barnard in *Functions of the Executive* (1964) has argued that these values and principles are organized into various constellations, which he terms private "codes" governing the conduct of an individual (p. 262). His notion of codes suggests that values and principles are not merely ranked hierarchically, but also are structured into subsystems. These normative subsystems are functionally related to the various types of activities in which we are involved. They serve as unwritten, internal codes of conduct for particular aspects of our lives. Although Barnard does not relate these internal codes specifically to the roles we occupy, it is generally consistent with his conceptual scheme to do so. Identifying internal codes with roles helps to clarify both how they are organized and how they are linked to behavior. Values that are appropriate for defining and structuring a given role function as a subsystem of our total value system, functionally oriented around conduct in a particular role, but related also to other value subsystems for other roles.

Roles were described generally in Chapter Two as bundles of obligations and interests. Now the description needs to be elaborated in a more complex fashion. There are two components involved in the enactment of a role: the objective and the subjective. The objective component consists of those external obligations that were discussed under objective responsibility. They give to the role a structure, stability, predictability, and continuity that approximate the will of the citizenry. The subjective component consists of a subsystem of values and principles that we construct in the process of responding to those objective obligations and expectations. As we assume the role, and begin to act it out in making particular decisions, we organize a set of values and principles that guide our specific, personal, individual responses to the generalized objective definition of the role.

In other words, we develop a structure of subjective responsibility that is the counterpart of the objective responsibility imposed from outside ourselves. This is the way we mesh our own needs and idiosyncratic perspectives with the demands of the role. A role evokes within us a need to create a value subsystem, a code for living out its objective responsibilities in a way that is compatible with our own inner inclinations.

This inner code may or may not be significantly informed by some professional consensus about the responsibility of public administrators. Sometimes, when an administrator has not been socialized by a professional community, idiosyncratic personal values derived from other roles provide the only source for subjective responsibility; no identifiable public-service ethical norms shape the conduct of the administrator. In these cases, the public role is carried out on the basis of personal values that may or may not be consistent with public expectations. Inconsistency may be discovered only when some significant action by the administrator is found by superiors, political officials, or the public to be at odds with public-service norms.

Barnard (1964) also makes a useful distinction between "moral status" and "responsibility." Moral status has to do with the attributes of the inner code for a particular role: "simple or complex, high or low, comprehensive or narrow." Responsibility, on the other hand, is "the power of a particular private code of morals to control the conduct of the individual in the presence of strong contrary desires or impulses" (p. 263). Thus, we may have a clearly worked out code for any given role, but may not behave consistently in a manner that is congruent with the code. To the extent that our codes do not consistently control our behavior, we may be described as irresponsible. A responsible person's conduct is not at odds with his or her code for that role.

Sometimes we say that those whose actions are in conflict with what they believe are lacking in integrity. They cannot be trusted because their inner controls are so weak that their behavior is unpredictable. Maintaining a high degree of subjective responsibility is important not only for the sake of our sense of wholeness, self-esteem, and identity—essential as these are to mental health— but also for the fulfillment of our objective responsibility. As Srivastva and Cooperrider (1988) suggest, integrity involves wholeness, not only with ourselves but in our relationships. They maintain that integrity is not a single character trait and not limited to particular roles, but rather "a sophisticated state of processing experience in the world that encompasses moral judgment, creativity, and intuitive capability, as well as rational-analytic powers." They further assert that executives who have this kind of integrity "invite trust from others" because they are "consistent in word and deed" (p. 5). More essentially than organization charts and procedures, it is this trust that actually integrates the organization.

Egger (1965, p. 303) cautions us to be suspicious of the notion that an administrator can function "as a sort of ethical automaton." He argues, in effect, that the need for logic and consistency in our administrative behavior requires a developed subjective responsibility. The range of administrative discretion that the objective sources of responsibility allow must be structured by "possession of some of the impediments of reflective morality." An administrator needs "some bench marks for relating the various and frequently conflicting claims of competing values which enter into his official actions." These will not be provided by the law, the courts, or delegated authority; they are too general in nature. According to Egger (1965, p. 304), sources of subjective responsibility are the means for "the maintenance of a consistent and perhaps corrective ethical continuum in the administrative process."

Consequently, subjective responsibility is not only an unavoidable fact of human experience, growing out of our socialization and our other roles, but its conscious and systematic development is essential for carrying out objective responsibility in a consistent, rational, and dependable fashion. Consistent and powerful internal controls allow administrators to exercise discretion in a pattern that is relatively predictable and therefore engenders trust among associates. The ethical process is the means by which these internal sources of responsibility are related to external demands. Moral imagination is the requisite skill for meshing the two without a loss of integrity. The reflective decision-making approach discussed in Chapter One outlines the steps for maintaining congruence between values and external obligations associated with the administrative role.

Now let us turn to another case situation and attempt to apply some of these concepts and distinctions related to subjective and objective responsibility.

"What to Do About Mrs. Carmichael"

The Municipal Redevelopment Agency (MRA) is involved in a project in Victoria, one of the older communities in Urbopolis. Since most of the turn-of-the-century housing is in a seriously dilapidated state, the Urbopolis City Council has declared Victoria an appropriate area for redevelopment.

You have been appointed assistant project director, with primary responsibility for determining which of the houses should be rehabilitated and which must be demolished. You have a staff that includes two specialists in municipal building codes and housing construction. You have assigned them to conduct on-site inspections of the residences in the first project area and prepare a draft report with their recommendations. They are nearing the completion of their field work; another two or three weeks should do it.

Harmon, one of the two specialists, buzzes you on the intercom to say that he and Franklin, the other specialist, need to talk with you as soon as possible. They want to talk about Mrs. Carmichael, who lives in project area one; in fact, she has lived there for thirty years. Mrs. Carmichael is now eighty-two years old, her husband is deceased, and her income has been so battered by inflation that it barely meets her basic living expenses. The mortgage has been paid off, but there have been taxes and maintenance costs. Some time ago Mrs. Carmichael began to neglect repairs on her home as her money shrank in value, year by year. "Now," Harmon says, "her house is in pretty bad shape." He sums up the condition of the house by admitting that according to the standards they have been applying elsewhere in the first project area, Mrs. Carmichael's home should be demolished.

However, Harmon cannot bring himself to recommend the destruction of the old woman's home. This is his fourth redevelopment project and he has seen it happen before. "Elderly people, whose homes cannot justify rehabilitation loans, are relocated into apartments, or board and care homes, only to lapse into senility and sometimes death." Harmon never felt very good about it before, but he just cannot stand to do it again. He tells you that he knows what the law requires and what the MRA project guidelines specify, but it seems wrong. He argues that "the government has no business treating decent people who have worked hard all their lives as though they were disposable trash."

You feel moved by Harmon's concern for Mrs. Carmichael, but you are unsure about what it means for you and the project. It occurs to you that Franklin has said nothing so you ask if he agrees with Harmon.

No, Franklin does not agree. He feels as strongly as Harmon but not in the same way. "It is too bad about Mrs. Carmichael, and all the Mrs. Carmichaels who get caught in her predicament, but there is nothing *we* can do about it," says Franklin. He tells you that the MRA's job is to rehabilitate when it can and demolish when it cannot, and there are laws and rules and standards that must govern those decisions.

Franklin insists that you cannot go around making exceptions; you have to be fair with everyone and that means treating everyone equally. There must be no special favors or the entire project will be jeopardized. Everyone will demand an exception and nothing will get done. The only way to deal with this case is to go by the book. "Let the relocation unit find her a satisfactory place to live—that's their problem," Franklin maintains. "Our problem is to make a decision about whether to fix up her place or tear it down." He knows that the house is beyond repair according to the standards employed by the MRA for all other similar projects.

The tension has been rising between Harmon and Franklin and at this point a heated argument breaks out between the two men. You try to calm their tempers and, as they settle back into their seats, you express appreciation for both men's concerns. You assure them that you respect their judgment and indicate that you would like to give the matter some thought and discuss it again later. Harmon and Franklin thank you for hearing them out and then leave your office.

It is not our intention to attempt to resolve the issue of Mrs. Carmichael's house, but to use this case to illustrate some of the concepts just discussed in this chapter and indicate ways of clarifying the situation that will be helpful in arriving at a decision.

First, you consider the facts concerning your objective responsibility. You know, for example:

1. The laws related to this redevelopment project clearly authorize the condemnation and demolition of substandard structures. If the owner cannot, or will not, make the necessary repairs, the building may be torn down.
2. A long series of court cases have upheld this kind of action.
3. The criteria for determining substandard buildings are well defined in the agency guidelines for such projects and in the Urbopols building and safety code.
4. You are responsible to Bronson, the Victoria Redevelopment Project director, for recommending which buildings should be demolished and which rehabilitated. If it looks as though this case will be a matter of dispute, or if you cannot resolve the issue in your own mind, you may have to discuss it with him.
5. You are not sure what your responsibility for upholding the public interest requires of you in this case. You need to ascertain how the public, at least in the Victoria area, feels about it.

Then you review in your mind what you know about Mrs. Carmichael's case, and what essential information you need to obtain. You feel reasonably confident about the following:

1. From Harmon's description of her house, it probably falls into the demolition category. Harmon did not try to soften the hard realities of its condition, and Franklin concurred.
2. Since the house is in such bad shape it will not qualify for a federal grant or loan large enough to do the work required to avoid condemnation.
3. Mrs. Carmichael could not qualify for a loan from a private lending institution, and she would be unable to make the payments if she did.
4. If demolition takes place, Mrs. Carmichael could not afford to rebuild on the present site.
5. If the agency condemns the house for demolition, Mrs. Carmichael will receive market value for it.

You feel much less certain about several other aspects of the case. You believe that you need to clarify the following:

1. How does she feel about the situation? Harmon is deeply concerned about saving Mrs. Carmichael's house, but not once in his presentation of the problem did he report *her* viewpoint. It would be a good idea to stop by and hear her reactions first-hand. Maybe she would like to move into a place that she could manage better.

2. Can she handle a change in residence? What are her mental, emotional, and physical states? Is she in reasonably good health? You know that Harmon is right about the serious negative impact on some older people, but probably not all.

3. What are some options if her house is demolished? Will she have enough money from the agency's purchase of her house to buy another house elsewhere, or perhaps a condominium? Maybe she could invest the proceeds and produce enough additional income to afford a nice apartment?

4. Is Mrs. Carmichael truly an exceptional case? Are there other elderly people in project area one who face the same threat? Maybe they should be considered as a group.

5. How do people in the community feel about Mrs. Carmichael's case? Without violating her privacy, is it possible to assess how others believe their interests might be served or subverted by the way her case is handled?

Finally, you reflect on your own personal inclinations. You attempt to clarify in your own mind what your subjective responsibility is with respect to Mrs. Carmichael. After mulling over it for a while, you realize:

1. Your general *attitude* toward older people is one of deep respect. Since your boyhood days with your grandparents you have felt almost a reverence for those who have survived the vicissitudes of the modern world. They evoke within you a deferential feeling.

2. This attitude is composed of a number of *beliefs.* You view them as having "paid their dues," as having worked hard and deserving our esteem for having done so. You believe young people often do not recognize the valuable knowledge and experience that older people have accumulated. You believe that

the elderly are often ignored and mistreated. They generally do not receive what is coming to them.

3. Behind these beliefs are some *values* you have long recognized within yourself. Wisdom about life in the world, based on knowledge and experience, is important to you. Getting the most out of the time allotted to you is something about which you feel deeply. Perseverance in the face of hardship is a significant virtue in your value system. Fairness, or equity, is one of the most essential principles of all. Sensitivity to the feelings of others is another of your values.

On the basis of these reflections you conclude that your strongest sense of subjective responsibility leads you in the direction of trying to resolve the problem without harming Mrs. Carmichael in any way. You do not want to disturb her life.

However, you do have other obligations, also. You are the administrator responsible for making a recommendation about Mrs. Carmichael's house. You are paid to do that by MRA and you made a commitment to carry out that responsibility when you accepted the job. It is your objective responsibility, and as long as you hold this position you may not ignore it.

Also, you have other subjective responsibilities associated with your administrative role. You feel responsible for maintaining morale and a cooperative team spirit among staff members. You value efficiency, and you believe these qualities are essential for an efficient organization. You also feel responsible for avoiding conflict with the residents of Victoria, both because that would upset the orderly schedule of work and lead to reduced efficiency, and because you value the esteem of others. You want the residents to feel that you have been fair with them. Furthermore, you feel responsible to Bronson, the Victoria Project director, and Markham, the executive director of MRA, for maintaining the image of the agency. Loyalty to the organization is important to you.

In determining the best course of action you may simply respond to the strongest and most definitive sources of objective responsibility—perhaps your superior, the law, or both, if they coalesce. On the other hand, you may allow deep-seated feelings to function as the decisive factors.

The perspective outlined in Chapter One assumes that if we want to make ethical decisions in a more intentional and rational manner, we must be more systematic. Working through the steps of the process outlined there is a way of accomplishing this task. As we consider alternative courses of action, their probable consequences, and how each might be defended, we are seeking an acceptable fit among the facts of a situation, our values, and our external obligations. Resolution is achieved when we are able to imagine an alternative that satisfies the need for consistency in our fundamental self-image. This allows us to maintain our sense of integrity, a feeling of being an identifiable whole, someone whom we and others will recognize as the person we imagine ourselves to be. Needless to say, this self-image and sense of integrity should be shaped to a large extent by a normative public administrative identity, by an internalized public service ethic.

Fulfilling our responsibilities is a stressful, complex task in modern society. As should be obvious from this chapter, the management of the administrative role with its dual components is a difficult task in itself. Any reader with administrative experience will realize by this point that, in actual fact, it is much more complicated than is suggested here. If we begin to consider, for example, the multiplicity of roles that must be maintained by an individual in the urban world of today, the thought and energy required can be overwhelming. Conflict among responsibilities related to a single role, compounded by conflicts among several roles, is a regular, even daily experience for public administrators. In the next chapter we examine these conflicts.

Chapter Four

Conflicts of Responsibility: The Ethical Dilemma

Confronting conflicting responsibilities is the most typical way public administrators experience ethical dilemmas. We may feel torn between two sets of expectation or inclination, neither of which is without significant costs. "Damned if you do, damned if you don't" is a common way of expressing this feeling of being caught between incompatible alternatives. Frequently we do not identify this dilemma as an ethical issue, only as a practical problem. However, at base these situations involve ordering our values and principles, consciously or otherwise. They are, therefore, problems of ethics, as well as practical problems. They are occasions in which we run the risk of violating one or more of what Banton calls "the social bargains which underlie cooperation." He argues that they involve "moral as well as legal customary requirements" (1965, p. 2).

It is not surprising that conflicts of responsibility are so common when we look at the nature of roles in modern society, reviewed in Chapter Two, and at the dual meanings of administrative responsibility discussed in Chapter Three. Since the administrative role is only one among a whole repertoire of roles we might occupy in modern society, the possibility of role conflict is always present. Furthermore, since the role of public administrator is sometimes in tension with the citizenship role, there is the potential for recurring conflict among these two in particular.

Also, the fiduciary character of public-service employment, involving responsibility to act on behalf of the citizenry, and the fact that it occurs within organizational settings establish the possibility of two types of conflict: conflict among interests (personal interests, those of the organization, and those of the public) and conflict among various sources of authority (organizational superiors, political officials, and laws).

Before we examine each type, it might be useful to remind ourselves that in this book we are dealing with administrative responsibility and so our attention is focused on the conduct of an administrator within an employing organization. Thus, we will not examine here activities of family, community, and voluntary associations unless they directly relate to the administrative role within the organization. However, we should not be oblivious to the ways those other sources of responsibility affect administrative conduct. Even though roles such as mother, spouse, or investor are not enacted within the organization, nevertheless these sources of obligation and interest are carried with the person who functions as an administrator during working hours.

It is important to emphasize that the different kinds of conflict that will be discussed here are not classified according to some universally accepted categories that are inherent in the nature of things. Instead, they are simply ways of perceiving and experiencing a conflict that have emerged from our previous experience and peculiar cognitive style.

Three ways of the most common ways of experiencing conflicts of administrative responsibility are conflicts of authority, role conflicts, and conflicts of interest. We will consider each of these and illustrate the first two with cases. Since conflict of interest includes a number of legally defined types, it will not be possible to provide a single extended case illustration; brief examples must suffice for that category.

Conflicts of Authority

In the previous chapter we discussed the difference between objective and subjective responsibility. However, here we are examining conflicts between two or more objective responsibilities imposed upon us by two or more sources of authority, such as the law, organizational superiors, elected officials, and the public. In these situations we feel torn between two sources of authority that demand incompatible actions from us. The law mandates one course of action, but the boss orders you to do something else; or the boss instructs you to move in one direction, while an elected official tells you otherwise; or your superior gives you an order that conflicts with one you have received from her boss. Let us look at a case in which this kind of ethical dilemma is confronted.

"The Major, the Captain, and Corporal Montague"

You are a first lieutenant in a military organization responsible for maintaining and providing a wide range of supplies for the larger unit of which you are a part. You report to a captain who reports to a major. You have been in your current job for about a year and have developed positive working relationships with both these senior officers.

An office manager position, involving the supervision of two secretaries and three clerks, opens up in your office. Both the captain and the major come to you independently and encourage you to request that a particular woman, Corporal Montague, be transferred from her present post to fill your open position. They both acknowledge that although this position would normally be filled by someone at the rank of sergeant, they believe she is very competent and would serve your office well.

You do not know Corporal Montague, but after reviewing her personnel records and conducting an interview, you are not impressed. She has performed adequately as a senior secretary, but there is no indication of the level of excellence reported by the captain and the major. Your interview left you feeling that she seems unmotivated and somewhat lacking in the communication and interpersonal skills needed for a supervisory position.

After thinking it over, you decide to put in a request for Corporal Montague. Although you see no evidence of a level of competence that would justify hiring a corporal for this job, you decide to trust your two superiors, who have always demonstrated good judgment in the past, especially concerning personnel matters.

After Corporal Montague has been on the job for a month, it is clear to you that your own judgment was correct and your two superiors were wrong. Her productivity is adequate but certainly not exceptional. The quality of her work is generally acceptable but very uneven. Although she is now developing better supervisorial skills, at the beginning she precipitated some problems in the office by her inept treatment of the clerks and secretaries under her supervision and the atmosphere is still a bit chilly. You see her as someone who was promoted too soon but who can now probably develop her skills, given some time in the position, some coaching, and formal in-service training.

However, the situation has become extremely complicated in some unexpected ways. Soon after the corporal came to work in your office you received some alarming information. Corporal Montague had been having simultaneous affairs with the captain and the major, but neither knew of the other's involvement with her. To make matters worse, during the last month you learned that Corporal Montague and your immediate boss, the captain, have had a lovers' quarrel and have broken up. However, she is still seeing the major.

Even more disturbing, the captain and the major are now sending you conflicting signals. The captain recently has commented that Corporal Montague does not seem to be working out in her new job after all, and strongly suggests that you review her performance early and transfer her out. However, the major has several times urged you to write an early, highly positive, performance evaluation for Corporal Montague. This would, according to the major, provide a basis for then applying for a promotion to the rank of sergeant for her. It seems likely to you that Corporal Montague has been encouraging her remaining lover, the major, to offer this suggestion on her behalf. Finally, since you have not yet acted on their "suggestions," both senior officers have issued oral orders to get on with Corporal Montague's evaluation and then to take the action they recommended.

As with other cases we have considered, the point here is not to arrive at a solution but to stimulate thought about the nature of one kind of conflict of responsibility. We are attempting to cultivate a way of thinking about the conflict of authority that this case represents.

When you begin to reflect on your dilemma over Corporal Montague, you realize that you are faced with a conflict among three authorities: your boss, his boss, and the personnel regulations. The regulations provide for a performance evaluation at the end of the first three months in a new position, but Corporal Montague has been in your office for only one month. Furthermore, the regulations require you to provide regular evaluative comments and constructive advice during the probationary period and objectively evaluate her performance on the various aspects of her work specified in the job description at the end of the period. If she is to be retained, you are to recommend steps to improve her skills wherever necessary. If you comply with the requirements of this source of authority, you will undertake an evenhanded review of Corporal Montague's performance two months from now, not now, as your superiors are urging.

Hiring Corporal Montague was a mistake, but you want to try to redeem the error. You hope that, with your counsel and guidance, her skills will have developed significantly by the time of the scheduled review and that her motivation will have improved as she feels more competent in the position. You anticipate a report that will find her acceptable for the job but needing training in supervisorial skills, time management, and advanced training in the use of computers.

However, you know that compliance with the personnel regulations will place you in conflict with the authority of your two superior officers. Generally speaking, you are required by basic military rules to carry out the orders of superiors, but in this case if you obey one you will be disobeying the orders of the other. And if you follow the orders of either the captain or the major, you will be violating the personnel regulations, since neither wants to wait out the probationary period and neither wants an objective evaluation.

As you consider possible courses of action, you define these alternatives:

1. Discuss this problem with the personnel officer and ask her to intervene.
2. Confront the captain with your knowledge and try to get him to withdraw his order.
3. Confront the major with your knowledge and try to get him to withdraw his order.
4. Inform Corporal Montague of your knowledge, explain the problem, and ask her to request a transfer.
5. Go to the colonel, who is the next highest officer up the chain of command, and ask him to intervene.
6. Ask both the captain and the major to put their orders in writing.
7. Simply refuse, in writing, the orders of both superior officers, with references to Corporal Montague's performance, progress, and promise, and to appropriate sections of the personnel regulations and procedures.

You are painfully aware that each alternative will almost certainly produce intense conflict, with potentially dire consequences for your future.

Faced with this kind of conflict of authorities, which reflect objective responsibilities, you realize that you must clarify your own subjective responsibility and consider any broader or more fundamental objective responsibilities. Since you cannot escape conflict in this situation, you must first turn to your own beliefs, values, and principles to decide which conflict to engage, which course of action would be best, and how you could justify your conduct.

As you do so, it is clear that although you are accountable to your superior officers, you do not feel responsible to follow the orders of either of them. The sources of that feeling require some reflection, which leads you to thoughts about your deep sense of loyalty to the military service, to the nation, and more concretely to the Constitution. You recall taking an oath to uphold and defend the Constitution. To you, taking that oath meant more than simply meeting a legal requirement to join the military service. It was an overt manifestation of the value of public service you had grown up with. Your parents had always involved themselves in service activities for the community, and had encouraged you to do so.

Taking that oath not only reflected your commitment to serve the nation, but also your belief in the fundamental importance of the rule of law. The Constitution is the basic law of the land, and anyone who vows to uphold it must also uphold specific laws that proceed from it and are consistent with it. It is true, on the other hand, that you believe that there are some rare circumstances when specific laws must be broken in order to challenge their consistency with the Constitution and fundamental ethical principles. However, that does not seem to be the case here; the personnel regulations seem fair and consistent with constitutional values like due process and equal protection under the law, as well as with basic ethical principles like justice.

As you consider your devotion to the rule of law, it occurs to you that the legal structure of the nation, including military laws, rules, and regulations, represents a source of authority and objective responsibility that supercedes the authority of your superior officers. In fact, no member of the military is required legally to obey an illegal order; the authority of law is higher than the authority of any military officer.

You reflect on the importance of being fair with your subordinates. You recall your military academy training: one of your instructors in leadership stressed the cardinal importance of officers "taking care of their troops." He used to argue passionately that the authority delegated to an officer must not be abused by using it to exploit and manipulate subordinates for the officer's own ends.

Also, you think about what is best for your organization. Since its management is your responsibility, you feel the need to do that which will make it function most effectively. That is what gives you professional satisfaction and meaning. If Corporal Montague is transferred for other than job-related reasons, or unjustifiably promoted before she has earned it, will that serve the organization's best interests, or will it have destructive consequences? On the other hand, what if you keep her for the full three months and she does not improve, or even becomes increasingly destructive?

Through this kind of assessment of your subjective responsibility, and identification of more fundamental objective responsibilities, you attempt to move toward an alternative that will fulfill *both* objective and subjective responsibility. Following the line of reasoning developed here, this will necessarily require subordinating, although not abandoning, some objective responsibilities to others—probably your responsibility to superiors to your responsibility to the regulations. Also, it will likely require subordinating your objective responsibility to your superiors to your subjective responsibilities rooted in your long-standing beliefs.

You may resolve the ethical conflict through this process, but it should be clear that ethical resolution does not resolve the practical problems. It only helps you identify your primary obligations and establish a basis for explaining your behavior to yourself and others. In other words, it is a way of establishing a perspective on the problem, a place to stand in dealing with the captain, the major, Corporal Montague, or other higher authorities in the government.

In situations such as this you are likely to suffer in one way or another, but it is still important to be clear about what you will suffer for, and why. It is important to have a means for maintaining accountability for yourself in the midst of intense and hazardous conflict. In the most basic sense it is through this kind of analytical and normative reflection that we create an operational ethic, develop integrity, and maintain responsible behavior.

Role Conflicts

The key attribute with this type of conflict in responsibility is the concept of *role*. Values associated with particular roles are experienced as incompatible or mutually exclusive in a given situation. Generally, however, we do not simply experience the values themselves. Rather, we feel the collision of roles governed by those values. We may be confronted with an expectation in our work that we believe to be inconsistent with being a good mother, a good Catholic, or a good member of the American Society of Public Administration. In these cases the conflict is between the administrative role and one or more of our roles outside the work organization.

Sometimes we may also feel that we are being asked to do something as a fiscal manager that does violence to our ability to function effectively as a supervisor, or asked to behave as a subordinate in a way that jeopardizes our ability to be a good fiscal manager. These are examples of conflict among our roles within the organization. To be more precise, we might refer to these as conflicts among subroles of the larger administrative role, or conflicts among components of the administrative role.

Inside Roles Versus Outside Roles—"Politics and Toilets"

Imagine that you are the public health officer for the municipal health department of the city of Micro. Your professional training was in public health, but you have been in administrative positions for the last ten years. You are now at the second level of the department, reporting directly to the director. You supervise eight professionals and an office staff of six. Most of your unit's work involves inspecting restaurants, food markets, food processing plants, and sanitary facilities for large public buildings.

The city of Micro has been experiencing severe financial pressure. Some traditional sources of revenue have been lost recently and the city council is having to cut the budget wherever possible, as well as search for new revenue. One of the more progressive members of the council observes that rock concerts often attract large crowds willing to pay high prices for well-known entertainers. He argues persuasively that Micro might be able to raise much of its lost revenue by sponsoring one big event of this kind each year. After lengthy debate, extended over several council sessions, a coalition of citizens forms to support this proposal. For the most part they are consumers of services threatened by the loss of revenue and property owners who fear new taxes such as garbage collection and sewer fees.

The council finally approves the idea and signs a contract with a concert promoter. He arrives in town and begins meeting with appropriate city officials to make the necessary arrangements. He contacts you to discuss the requirements for public health services: toilet facilities, water, food vendors, and emergency medical care. Since the concert is to take place in a city-owned field on the edge of town and there are no utilities of any kind at the site, temporary, portable equipment must be provided. Also, since there are no existing city or state laws establishing public health standards for events of this type, you have been given the responsibility for determining what should be required.

When you meet with Ripley, the promoter, you are astonished to learn that he expects a crowd of about five hundred thousand people for a fourteen-hour concert. As you begin to talk with him about the necessary public health services for such a large number of people, it soon becomes clear that your standards are much higher than he expected. In the absence of legal requirements you have resorted to the recommendations for large outdoor events approved by the National Public Health Association (NPHA) some years ago. After Woodstock and two attempts at imitating it, the NPHA had appointed a committee, of which you were a member, to study public health conditions at these events and propose a set of guidelines. These included sanitation, water, food, safety, and medical standards.

The further you go in discussing the plans, the more incensed Ripley becomes. He argues loudly that one toilet for every 50 people is absurd and impossible. He insists that if he provided ten thousand portable toilets for the anticipated half million people, the rental costs would be prohibitive and space for paid attendees would be reduced. The ratio he had in mind was more like one toilet per three hundred people. Ripley's reaction is much the same for the number of medical tents and personnel, the amount of food, and "all of those damned tank trucks full of water." He finally refuses to comply with your standards, informs you that he will take the matter up with the city council, and storms out of your office.

Later that same day your boss, Harley, the director of the city health department, asks you to come to his office. It seems that he has received a call from the president of the city council informing him of the financial exigency faced by the city of Micro. He had suggested that Harley have a chat with you about the importance of the rock concert, and then send you over to meet with two members of the council the next morning. The council president had expressed confidence that reasonable requirements could be worked out to the satisfaction of all parties involved. Finally, he had observed that "it would be detrimental to all of us if we frightened Mr. Ripley away."

After relating this conversation, Harley urges you to be cooperative and to acknowledge the practicalities of the situation. There are no legally prescribed standards, and this is only a one-day event, which should make it possible for you to live with less stringent requirements. Harley reminds you that there is a lot of support for the concert among the citizens of Micro and that anyone, or any agency, that complicates the success of this important event might "feel the wrath of an unforgiving public." He assures you that as a member in good standing of the NPHA he is concerned about maintaining public health standards, and he believes in supporting the recommendations of the association. "However," argues Harley, "we mustn't be rigid or foolish about such things."

He assures you that he will not resolve the matter bureaucratically by exercising his authority as your superior, but he hopes you will keep uppermost in your thinking what is best for the department and the city of Micro. He respects your professional judgment and autonomy, but he reminds you that your responsibility as an employee of the health department and the city is to support the efforts to solve the serious fiscal problems.

You leave the boss's office and return to your own. You are uncertain about your responsibility in this matter and need to think it through.

First, you are accountable to Harley, your superior in the chain of command. Ultimately, he is to be held accountable by the city council for accomplishing the mission of the department. However, he is not threatening you with his authority as your superior; he has indicated his willingness to let you do what you feel must be done. But he has requested you to cooperate with Ripley and the council by relaxing the standards for this brief and unusual affair. And you know from five years of association with Harley that he has both personal and professional integrity. He has backed you on some tough cases. There was the market chain with the filthy meat department; a council member was a partner in the corporation that ran that chain. Harley withstood a lot of heat on that one.

Furthermore, Harley is right about the standards; they are not required by law. Their only authority comes from the professional prestige of the NPHA. Maybe the most important consideration is the long-term effectiveness of the department and your position within it. If you insist on maintaining the standards, the council may hold a formal hearing on the issue and inflame the public. You, Harley, and the department could get hurt if that happened. You might be fired, or eased into a dead-end job. Your reputation might be irreparably damaged if they made you the butt of a joke about ten thousand toilets. The headlines would be brutal. Besides, you might, at least, be able to negotiate Ripley down from his position of one toilet per three hundred persons if you are willing to be flexible. But if you are discredited, or fired, the council will probably give Ripley a free rein to do as he pleases.

Even if you are not attacked, the department could lose the support of the public and the good will of the council. The next budget cycle begins soon, there is enormous financial pressure, and the department is requesting approval for a bond issue to expand its facilities. Does not the daily routine work of the department contribute far more to enhancing public health than this transient issue over a rock concert?

Your role within the City of Micro Health Department gives rise to these concerns. Loyalty to Harley, based on your professional esteem for him personally as well as on his position, has created a bond with him. The way he carries out his job provides a model that gives definition and integrity to your role as a member of the department. Another factor is trust in his good judgment and sense of proportion. Furthermore, you value the well-being of the people of Micro; your role is to protect and enhance their health. Also, the department has an instrumental value in serving that goal; its long-term effectiveness and continuity are important to you. As an administrator you have learned to value the efficient operation of your unit. One aspect of your role is to seek more efficient ways of fulfilling your mission, particularly with the recent decreases in revenue. These are some of the values that constitute your internal code, or subjective responsibility, for your role inside the organization.

On the other hand, your role as a member of NPHA is influenced by a different cluster of values. Since you have been involved in that organization for about fourteen years, and recently served as a member of the national executive board for four years, you are well known as an active leader within its ranks. You greatly value the respect and esteem of your NPHA colleagues. Since you were a member of the committee that developed the guidelines for these unusual large outdoors events, and argued for their approval at the annual meeting, you are particularly concerned about how you will be perceived by the members of NPHA. Your professional integrity is at stake.

Also, you have taken unpopular positions on issues before the NPHA in the past and insisted that courage and commitment to high standards for the health of society are essential for public health professionals. There was the time a large fast-food chain violated a number of generally accepted requirements for sanitary food handling. Some of your colleagues were reluctant to openly support a resolution calling for action against this company, for fear of political repercussions. You told them that an effective public administrator "can never bend to political pressure on things that count."

Now how will you look if you do not uphold the association's guidelines that you helped write? What if you give in to the pressure from the city council and there is an outbreak of botulism? Or influenza? Or some other contagious disease among five hundred thousand people? What if there is a riot and hundreds of people require emergency medical care in a remote area such as this?

Ripley dismissed such spectres as the "fantasies of an all too fertile imagination." He pointed out repeatedly that this is a one-day event, and asked rhetorically, "What is likely to happen in one lousy day?" But you now realize that it is not really a one-day event. The police department has estimated that it will take a full twenty-four hours just to park the cars for that many people. They indicate that you can expect arrivals during the three days before the concert, and hangers-on who will be around for a day or two after it formally concludes. That amounts to a five-day span during which concert goers will pose a public health concern for the city of Micro. You must provide for very large numbers of people for approximately three of the five days. A lot can happen in that amount of time.

If this thing blows up in your face and it gets into the press, will you ever be effective again in calling for progressive action by NPHA? You have always felt that it was important to be an agent for change within any organization, and you have especially valued that image of yourself in the association. What will happen to that

image? Will anyone take your crusades seriously in the future? Will
you?

Your role within NPHA has been shaped and defined by
these values. Your colleagues in NPHA have come to expect you to
behave in certain ways. They know you value your personal integrity and the respect it evokes. They think of you as one of the
courageous administrators in the public health profession. Whenever the question of public health standards arises, they know they
can count on you to push for the most. Similarly, they expect you
to be one of those people in the association who is never willing to
stay with the status quo just because "it has always been done that
way"; they look to you to make the case for shaking things up and
experimenting with new ideas, techniques, and procedures. The
members of NPHA expect you to be this kind of person, but it is
not they alone who have cast you in this role. You have cultivated
these expectations. You have carved out this kind of role for yourself
because you have wanted to be this kind of person. These are some
of the elements that constitute your inner code, or subjective responsibility, for your role as a member of the NPHA.

This is an extreme case of tension between a role inside the
public organization for which you work and an outside role; in this
case, between two kinds of subjective responsibility. The values that
shape and direct the enactment of each role are pulling you in two
different directions, motivating you toward two mutually exclusive
alternatives. You are confronted with one kind of ethical dilemma
rooted in the roles we occupy. Let us now look at a case in which
you experience the other common kind of role conflict.

Inside Roles Versus Inside Roles— "Raising Salaries or Raising Hell?"

The Rancor County sheriff's department is a large law enforcement
agency with about three thousand sworn deputies. You are the lieutenant in charge of the research and planning unit (RPU); you were
appointed to the position three months ago, after two years of service within this particular organization. You previously have
worked alongside four of the five deputies in the unit and know
them well; in fact you have often socialized with them. You do not

know well the new woman who was just assigned to RPU as a replacement, nor are you well acquainted with the new civilian statistician whom you have just hired.

You are in the midst of your first salary review process as supervisor of the unit. All the supervisors meet with Assistant Sheriff Dutton, who is in charge of the personnel and training division. Dutton briefs the group on departmental procedure, the required forms, and the time schedule for completing the process. The department, along with all other departments in Rancor County, conducts merit reviews for step increases and promotions at the same time each year that the across-the-board cost-of-living increase is negotiated with the county board of supervisors. Dutton reminds you that your role in the process has to do only with the merit review. The cost-of-living raise will be discussed and negotiated by the sheriff and his staff; it is "a given" over which you have no control.

Someone asks Dutton what the across-the-board percentage is likely to be for the coming year; the department grapevine is beginning to float rumors about a low figure. He is evasive at first, but finally admits that it is likely to be lower than recent years— probably about 2 percent. Before the scattered mumbles can erupt into disorder, Dutton rushes on to explain.

Several members of the board of supervisors are running for reelection and are facing stiff opposition from a slate of "cut the fat out of government" candidates. They realize that any new tax measures adopted this year to fund the county budget would be extremely risky for their futures. After consultation with the county administrative officer, the board members have indicated they will not support across-the-board wage increases of more than 2 percent. Merit raises must come from department funds already budgeted for that purpose.

After hearing this, a captain from the juvenile division asks how the board can get away with only 2 percent when there is a clause in the county charter establishing pay levels for law enforcement and fire service employees comparable to those paid to the state troopers and other counties of similar size. The captain points out that a study conducted by the local unit of the Law Enforcement Professional Association (LEPA) concluded that 5 percent would be necessary to meet that charter requirement. Dutton's response is that "statistics are easy to manipulate." He firmly suggests that all of you stay out of this matter and pay attention to your particular duties. When a lieutenant asks how to handle any complaints from the rank and file, Dutton reminds him that he is to support the sheriff and demonstrate loyalty to his position at all times. He terminates the discussion by saying, "Some of you are going to have to absorb a little flak over this, so be prepared to put some iron in your spines."

You leave the meeting feeling perplexed. There have already been several bull sessions around the RPU offices about the salary situation. You know the people on your staff are expecting more than 2 percent and have been expressing their feelings about the "gutless brass in this department" who they fear will not stand up to the politicians. Two of them have been members of LEPA for a year now; you know it is not a docile professional association but a militant police union. If the department gets stuck with a low percentage for salaries, LEPA will gain a few more recruits from your unit. You realize the sheriff pays attention to units in the department where LEPA is growing in power. He tends to view increases in union membership in a unit as a sign of weak or inept management.

The merit review process will not help this highly volatile situation. You recall your own feelings about the small 2 or 3 percent raises for good performance. When the blanket cost-of-living increase was decent, the merit raise evoked a feeling of satisfaction, even though it was not very large. However, it seemed to have the opposite effect when the basic increase was inadequate. You tended to resent something called a "merit increase" when in fact the total amount hardly met the rise in the cost of living. With only 2 percent across-the-board this time, you anticipate some bitter feelings from deputies in RPU who have a higher level of education than the median for the department and view themselves as generally underpaid.

You feel caught between your staff and the departmental hierarchy. Because you are new to the supervisory position, you are still establishing your credibility as an administrator. The members of RPU still feel that you are one of them, but you have sensed a degree of benign suspicion about how long you will remain so. You are attempting to overcome those feelings while at the same time redefining your role. You do not want them to stop trusting you or feeling friendly with you, but your duties have changed. You want to be accepted as the supervisor of the unit, but you do not want to create a gulf between yourself and the staff.

On the other hand, you need the trust and support of the sheriff and his staff. At the time of your promotion Dutton expressed concern about your ability to meet the demands of the administrative role after having worked so closely with four of the five members of RPU. He feared that this might create problems both for you and the RPU staff. The sheriff had discussed this potential pitfall with you and encouraged you to pay attention to it. He had told you that he expected loyalty to the chain of command, and had reminded you that as the supervisor of RPU you would become a member of the management team, accountable for carrying out the policies of the department.

You are still being watched and sized up. You do want to support the sheriff. He is the boss and his negotiations with the board of supervisors are too sensitive to tolerate dissension in the ranks. He will expect you to exercise your authority, as he will exercise his. You have to trust his judgment about what can be gained in the short run over against the long-term future of the department. He is the only one with the information and position to deal with that kind of decision.

And yet you feel the need to let the department brass know how it looks from your vantage point. The county charter provision does seem to call for more than a 2 percent raise. If the raise is not larger, the department may wind up with far more members in a very tough union. Can you present these concerns without appearing to abandon your management responsibilities? Will this confirm the suspicion that you could not make the transition from rank and file to supervisor?

You feel caught because this salary issue could destroy your relationship with both your staff and the hierarchy of the department. This is not just a practical management problem. It is also an ethical dilemma involving a conflict between objective and subjective responsibilities. You are experiencing conflict between the subjective responsibility of your role as the supervisor of a unit on the one hand, and both the objective and subjective responsibilities of your role as a member of the sheriff's management team on the other. Each role evokes feelings of obligation rooted in sets of values (subjective responsibilities) that influence your behavior, and you are formally held accountable (objective responsibility) by the sheriff for fulfilling your obligation to stand behind his decisions.

If we examine your role as the supervisor of RPU we see that you are viewed by your staff as their channel to the hierarchy. They expect you to take care of their interests and to look out for their needs. They cannot hold you formally accountable, but in a tight chain of command, such as in a law enforcement agency, the implicit bargain is acceptance of the hierarchy as the means for communicating with the organization in exchange for an acceptance of responsibility by the hierarchy for those below. The members of your unit see you as their spokesperson, their voice, to those above. They expect you to stand up for them when their interests are at stake. They project these expectations on you, and your role as supervisor within the unit is partially structured by them. You empathize readily with these expectations since you recall having shared them so recently.

A set of values emerges in response to these role demands. These values are internalizations of expectations. You find yourself valuing the loyalty and trust of your staff because both are necessary for your function as their spokesperson. If they do not feel bound to express their concerns to you, believing that you will not take them seriously, your role will be truncated. You will be severed from your subordinates. This creates pressure from your staff to value the narrow interests of the unit above those of the whole department. Loyalty to RPU means to them that you support their needs and preferences above those of others.

Furthermore, you value being perceived as a fair person by your staff, one who will hear them out and speak on their behalf in an honest, even-handed fashion. You also value credibility as a spokesperson. You want to be viewed as one who conveys their views accurately to those above. Another related value is integrity. Your staff expects you to behave with consistency and with some degree of independence and courage in dealing with management. Responsiveness is another value that you draw from their expectations. They not only want you to listen, but they also expect you to do something consistent with their wishes.

Those above you in the chain of command give primary definition to your other role as an administrator. In your capacity as a member of the management team, they expect you to communicate the wishes of top-level management to your staff. More important, they expect you to gain compliance from the members of your unit and they hold you accountable for doing so (objective responsibility). Behind these expectations there are also values that you must internalize in order to conduct your managerial role (subjective responsibility). Cooperativeness, for example, is likely to be a significant value for this role. Those above you in the chain of command expect that you will generally go along with their decisions. In other words, they expect compliance from you in the same way that you expect it from your staff. In response to this expectation you are likely to value being perceived as a cooperative person.

Primary identification with the management team is probably viewed as a necessary concommitant of cooperativeness. Cooperation is strengthened and enhanced when people internalize a belief in the importance of management solidarity. You are encouraged to see your interests as identical with those of the departmental hierarchy.

Maintenance of authority is, in all probability, another value associated with this role. Your ability to direct and, ultimately, to command is apt to be highly valued. Being cooperative and viewing yourself as a member of management will come to naught if you are unable to control the behavior of those in your unit. This requires the ability to exercise authority in its various manifestations.

Comprehensiveness is another management value. You are expected to take into account the needs and interests of the entire organization, not just those of your unit alone. You learn to value the well-being of the whole rather than that of a part. You value the larger perspective of the organization and learn to place your unit's needs within that perspective.

The value subsystems associated with these two roles are not always in conflict. In fact, values such as trust, credibility, and responsiveness are generally viewed as necessary attributes of an effective manager by those above as well as those below in the hierarchy. However, in specific situations, such as this matter of salary increases, there may be conflict. In this case you are torn between loyalty to staff and solidarity with management, between responsiveness to staff and the authority of management, between the interests of the RPU and the interests of the department as a whole. The impending conflict between employees and management creates tension between two of your organizational roles, which are structured around responsibility to one of these groups and responsibility for the other. You face the risk of neglecting one role for the sake of the other, or failing in an attempt to serve both.

The members of your unit will not be satisfied when you explain that the matter is out of your hands. They will want you to be loyal to them; they will appeal to your ability to identify with their point of view. Your staff will expect you to respond to their interests and stand up to the sheriff and Assistant Sheriff Dutton. They will want you to insist on more than a 2 percent raise.

On the other hand, it is clear that Dutton expects you to represent management, to support the position adopted by the sheriff. He will expect you to exercise your authority in dealing with the dissension of your staff. Dutton will want you to defend the interests of the organization as a whole and not capitulate to those short-range immediate needs for a larger raise. Furthermore, he will evaluate your performance, and your retention in the role of supervisor, accordingly. He will quite specifically hold you accountable for maintaining that role.

We experience ethical dilemmas in ways portrayed in these two cases—as conflicts between the roles that present us with formal obligations (objective responsibilities) and the underlying values (subjective responsibilities) that tend to motivate us in incompatible directions. Barnard (1964) argues that these conflicts become more frequent as our array of inner codes, or subjective responsibilities, increases. The more of these "codes" we have to respond to, the more likely that situations will occur in which two of them pull us in different directions. Furthermore, he notes, we are likely to have more of these unwritten inner codes if we are associated with many organizations.

Another way of explaining the same phenomenon is to suggest that value subsystems emerge around our roles and, therefore, the more roles we adopt, the more value subsystems we need to maintain. Since the multiplication of roles is inherent in modernity, so is the management of multiple value subsystems. According to Banton (1965), people in modern urban society are far more likely to experience conflicting inner codes than those who live in traditional settings.

This perspective is helpful in understanding Barnard's claim that executive positions involve a complex morality. It is the role complexity of high-level executive positions that leads to a complex interaction of often conflicting values. As we move up the organizational ladder it becomes increasingly difficult to behave responsibly, to respond consistently and dependably to the multifarious demands of the many roles involved.

In the face of such conflicts, what do we do? Barnard (1964, pp. 271-272) suggests several possible consequences:

1. General moral deterioration as manifested in frustration and inability to make decisions
2. A diminution of the sense of responsibility demonstrated by a tendency to allow incidental or external pressures and chance determinants to make decisions for us
3. Withdrawal from active involvement in the arena of decision making, such as resignation, a leave of absence, or retirement
4. Development of an ability to avoid responsibility by steering clear of conflict situations that may require difficult decisions
5. Development of the ability to construct alternative measures that satisfy immediate desires or requirements without violating any codes

It is clear that Barnard prefers the fifth alternative. He believes that any of the others involves a neglect or sacrifice of one or more codes. This would amount not only to dereliction of duty, but a degradation of character. A failure to respond positively to a role and its value subsystem would weaken both. Their power to determine behavior in the future, therefore, would be diminished. Behavior would become less consistent with espoused values, less dependable, less responsible. Since Barnard regards responsibility as essential to effective executive leadership, he views its erosion as a serious matter indeed.

Although Barnard does not dwell at length on how we acquire the ability to develop alternatives that do not violate any of our codes, it seems certain that he had in mind a quality called "moral creativity," something he experienced in himself and others but does not discuss in any detail. Moral creativeness is understandably difficult to explain or teach, but one of the assumptions of this book is that, like any other acquired skill, it can be cultivated. The thesis here is that moral creativity requires:

1. A clear understanding of the obtainable facts relevant to the situation.
2. An understanding of the roles involved, including the codes, or value subsystems, that guide their enactment.
3. A consideration of all the possible alternatives.
4. A projection of the consequences of each alternative, as imaginatively as possible. How would your role and the roles of others be affected?
5. An attempt to anticipate how you would feel about yourself if you adopted each alternative.
6. A consideration of how you would justify each alternative to a broad public audience. On what moral rules and principles would you base a choice of each alternative and its consequences?

As we pursue this reflective process involving moral imagination, sometimes it is possible to conceive of ways of inventing what Barnard (1964, p. 279) calls a "moral basis for the solution of moral conflicts." This may involve redefining the values that govern a role's enactment; it may call for renegotiating the expectations and obligations that give it structure; or it may necessitate "a bargaining process which decides how much attention" will be given to any one role (Banton, 1965, p. 209).

For example, in the case of the city of Micro and the rock concert, you might decide to adopt a more flexible attitude that would permit you to negotiate arrangements that are as close to NPHA guidelines as possible. One of the conditions for such flexibility might be a formal written agreement with the city council that would phase in the NPHA standards through a series of city ordinances during the following two years. Since there is no such legislation at present, this would be a chance to initiate it. Also, the council would be given enough advance notice about the requirements to determine whether to continue holding such events in the future.

Using this strategy you would not subvert your role as a progressive public health professional, but neither would you maintain a position that would jeopardize your role with the Micro municipal health department. You would have an opportunity to test the effectiveness and practicality of NPHA's guidelines, which you might consider writing up for the association's journal. You might be able to recommend changes that would improve the association's guidelines and offer suggestions about the politics of implementing them. A critical case study of your own efforts would be a way of maintaining your bargain with NPHA.

In the Rancor County sheriff's department case you might need to take this opportunity to further define your role—for your staff, your superiors, and yourself. Meeting with your staff to clarify the limits of your role as their representative to the hierarchy might be in order. Perhaps you would want to assure them of your willingness to go to bat for them in situations where you believe they had a legitimate case and when you had a chance to influence decisions on their behalf. You may want to be sure that they understand, however, that you had no intentions of going down in flames over battles you could not win. The 2 percent salary increment for the cost-of-living raise appears to be one of those instances. In dealing with your staff in this way, you reenforce your role with them and add to it the necessity for some degree of autonomy in dealing with the hierarchy.

As to the department, you may want to prepare a well-thought-out memorandum assuring the sheriff and Assistant Sheriff Dutton of your loyalty but suggesting a broader definition of loyal behavior. You might indicate that your understanding of loyalty includes the obligation to inform your superiors of the impact of certain decisions. You might feel obligated to express your concern about the effects of a small raise on the unionization of the department. You might also include your own analysis of the LEPA study of the comparable salaries included in the county charter provision.

The kinds of responses suggested here are attempts to rationally and actively maintain responsible conduct in conflicting role situations. They are efforts to confirm and preserve the values associated with these roles. Sometimes you will be successful and at other times you will fail miserably, but being aware of the dynamics involved and dealing with them intentionally and systematically is likely to enhance your overall administrative responsibility.

It is difficult enough to manage your own role conflicts in this way, but the administrative role often calls for more. Barnard (1964, p. 279) observed that those with executive positions are expected to assist others with their ethical dilemmas. Borrowing language from jurisprudence, he described this as the "judicial function," "the appellate function," or "handling the exceptional cases." One of the tasks of management is this "inventing of a moral basis for the solution of moral conflicts."

When one of your subordinates is faced with a decision that seems right from one perspective but wrong from another, instead of dismissing his or her concern as only a moral issue that is irrelevant to the business at hand, you should take the matter with the utmost seriousness. The employee wants to maintain congruence between values and conduct—to maintain a high level of responsibility. That impulse should be reenforced. Help the person clarify the objective conditions and seek alternative courses of action. You may even need to redefine the code to account for special circumstances. According to Barnard (1964, pp. 281–282) this creative judicial function is the "highest exemplification of responsibility" and "the essence of leadership." He explains, "It is the highest test of executive responsibility because it requires for successful accomplishment that element of 'conviction' that means identification of personal codes and organization codes in the view of the leader. This is the coalescence that carries 'conviction' to the personnel of organization, to that informal organization underlying all formal organization that senses nothing more quickly than insincerity. Without it all organization is dying, because it is the indispensable element in creating that desire for adherence—for which no incentive is a substitute—on the part of those whose efforts willingly contributed constitute organization."

Dealing with these conflicting role demands and the values associated with them is a matter of ethics that, if not justified by our philosophical or religious views, is most certainly essential to maintaining an effective organization. Orders, edicts, rewards, human relations training, and organization development strategies are not likely to accomplish much if we do not encourage and systematically develop responsibility by addressing ethical dilemmas that arise from role conflicts. It is unfortunate, but true, that many members of public organizations have never learned to understand these conflicts and cope with them effectively, while others have become so inured to the pressure to be practical and political that they no longer think about these experiences very seriously.

Conflicts of Interest

Another way we experience conflicts in responsibility involves situations where our own personal interests are at odds with our obligations as a public official. They may involve combinations of conflicting roles and tensions between sources of authority, but more typically these occasions simply present us with an opportunity to use our public office for the sake of private gain. They represent conflicts between the public role and self-interests, between objective responsibility and the possibility of personal gain or advantage.

As we shall see in more detail later, here we are dealing with something broader than the legal definition of conflict of interest. In this sense "interest" includes, as Michael Davis (1982, p. 23) suggests, "all those influences, loyalties, concerns, emotions, or the like" that can make competent judgment "less reliable than it might otherwise be." Conflicts of interest involve collisions between these various kinds of influences and the interests of the public we serve.

The ethical problem presented by these conflicts is that our fiduciary relationship as trustees of the public interest may be jeopardized by a loss of trust in our professional judgment. If some private personal interest is able to influence our reason and conduct, we may serve it rather than the interests of the citizenry, or at least we may be perceived as doing so. Our judgment may be impaired in this way, or may appear to be, and either will call into question our trustworthiness as representatives of the public interest.

Tussman (1960, p. 17) locates the roots of these conflicts in the Western "spirit of individualism." With the emergence of the individual as the locus of political and social rights and obligations, comes a tendency to see him "chiefly as a complex of values, desires, drives, or interests." Given this perspective, it seems quite natural for individuals to pursue their own interests. Satisfying personal desires and enhancing one's own life are viewed as legitimate forms of conduct. Tussman points out that acknowledging the right to behave in this way is generally what we mean by the phrase "respect for the individual."

On the other hand, as Tussman hastens to observe, we do seek to impose duties to serve the collective interests of the public on these legitimately self-seeking individuals. Certain individuals assume extensive duties as public agents on behalf of the citizenry, generally as employees (elected or appointed) of a public jurisdiction. However, the role of citizen is the most universal form of this collective obligation. Citizenship requires all self-interested individuals who are members of the polity to act, in their public role, on behalf of the public good.

These claims of the collectivity on the individual are acknowledged, but with reluctance and ambivalence. Our Western liberal heritage causes us to view any constraints on individual self-realization with suspicion and uneasiness. Nevertheless, the fact that we do ultimately support these public claims is "evidenced by the indignation we feel when a public trust is betrayed by self-interest. The public agent," asserts Tussman, "is expected to do his duty" (1960, p. 18).

In the problem of conflicts of interests we are, at base, confronting this "inescapable tension between interest and duty, between the inclinations of the private life and the obligations of the public role" (Tussman, 1960, p. 18). This tension is inescapable, not only because individualism dominates in the Western world but also because it is inherent in the structure and dynamics of modern society. Modernization places this exalted individual into a network of complex interrelationships and interdependencies that constantly impose collective demands. Urban industrial society thus intensifies the tension that Tussman identifies. It is not surprising, then, that people employed as public servants, particularly those with elected and administrative roles, experience frequent tension between public and private interests.

Dorothy Emmet (1967) helps us focus on the particular problem for public administrators by noting the discrepancy between two dimensions of modern complex organizations. She contends that an organization must be viewed both as "a community with a common purpose" and "as a field within which people hope to have a career" (p. 196). In our case public organizations are not only collectivities established to serve some public interest, but they are also the arenas within which individuals attempt to realize their self-interests through the development of careers. If this is so, the pluralistic nature of modern society suggests immediately that conflicts will emerge between individual interests and organizational interests.

Presumably, the way this tension is resolved depends to a great extent on the relative values attributed to the private and public spheres of our lives. Richard Sennett (1974) has concluded that the trend over the last two hundred years has been toward devaluing the public sphere for the sake of cultivating the private. He argues that a narcissistic preoccupation with inner feelings as the basis for personal identity in modern society has led us to believe that the impersonal world of public affairs is of secondary importance. If he is correct, we should not be surprised to find a tendency to resolve the tension in favor of personal private interests.

Small (1976), in his survey of the problem of conflict of interest in American government, produced findings that support the conclusion that this tendency has been on the increase in modern society. He writes, "Increasingly, then, in the late Twentieth Century it becomes more and more difficult to separate the simplistic, completely personal interest from the public interest. Because these interests are overlapping and no longer separable, older norms of right and wrong, desirable or undesirable are inadequate" (p. 554). He concludes that it is "part of the human condition" to seek money and power from public sources for the sake of private gain.

If this kind of conduct can be attributed to "the human condition" it may be because the public sphere of life has come to be no different from any other common property resource. If the affairs of government and the common resources of the citizenry are, as Sennett suggests, viewed as having lesser importance than private individual interests, then it seems quite likely that they will be exploited. Garrett Hardin's analysis of the "tragedy of the commons," in an article by that title, may help us to understand why this occurs (Hardin, 1977).

Hardin asks us to imagine a pasture that is open to all the village herdsmen for grazing livestock. Each herdsman quite rationally seeks to maximize his gain; this is the logical consequence of individualism. In attempting to acquire the greatest benefit for himself, the herdsman considers, more or less consciously, what the utility would be of adding one more animal to his herd. Hardin notes that this utility has two components, one positive and one negative. The positive component is a function of adding one more animal; he receives all the proceeds from the sale of this additional animal. The negative component is a function of the overgrazing created by the additional animal. However, since the effects of this overgrazing are borne by all the herdsmen, the negative utility for the herdsman is only a fraction.

The result is that when these positive and negative partial utilities are added together, there is a clear net gain and "the rational herdsman concludes that the only sensible course for him to pursue is to add another animal to his herd. And another. . . ." The problem, of course, is that every other herdsman is drawing the same conclusion. Each one feels compelled to increase his herd without limit until the pasture is overgrazed to the point of being useless for all. Hardin observes from this scenario that "ruin is the destination toward which all men rush, each pursuing his own best interest in a society that believes in the freedom of the commons. Freedom in a commons brings ruin to all" (1977, p. 20).

It may be that the public sphere is a "commons" subject to this kind of abuse. It may have become so secondary to the pursuit of individual interests that we are constantly tempted to "overgraze" it. In the short run we seem to experience personal gain by resolving conflicts between private and public interest in favor of ourselves.

However, the long-term result of that course of conduct by millions of individual citizens and citizen–public servants, each seeking to maximize personal gain, is the ruination of that commons we call government.

Conflict of interest, therefore, is an insidiously difficult problem, but especially so for public administrators. Citizens in public administrative positions have special access to the governmental commons that most ordinary citizens do not. This access presents unusual opportunities and, therefore, temptations to exploit governmental resources for personal gain. Furthermore, administrative responsibilities often include the obligation of supervising, coordinating, and monitoring the conduct of others who are confronted with similar opportunities and temptations. As fiduciaries of the public interest, public administrators are responsible not only for managing their own conflicts of interests, but to some extent those of peers, subordinates, superiors, and private citizens as well.

With this conceptual background in mind, let us now turn to some specific definitions and types of conflict of interest. The extensive study conducted by the Association of the Bar of the City of New York (1960) reflects the apparent tendency of those concerned with the legality of conduct to opt for narrow definitions of conflict of interest. After identifying a continuum of situations, ranging from bribery at one end to policy conflicts at the other, this report limits its concern to conflicts between officials' duties and their personal economic interests. Consequently, bribery, which involves overt payment to influence official action, is identified as the clearest instance of conflict of interest. At the other extreme, differences over public policy, which might be attributable to past or present affiliations, are ruled out of consideration as being too removed from economic interest. This definitional constraint is found also in Lieberman's approach. He identifies "the conflict between a Government employee's official responsibility and his private economic interests" as the generally accepted conflict of interest in public affairs (Lieberman, 1973, p. 206).

The strict definitions in these legal approaches seem, reasonably enough, to grow out of a concern for the most effective legislative remedies. It seems likely that the contribution of the New York study to the passage of the Federal Conflict of Interest Statute of 1962 was due, in large part, to its narrow legal orientation. However, the bar committee report (pp. 17–18) justified its limitation to economic interests on three grounds: "The simplest reason is that it is better to control whatever fraction of improper behavior is attributable to economic motives than to control none. The second reason is that regulatory schemes have to be administered. Restrictions on outside economic affiliations can be written with reasonable particularity and enforced with moderate predictability; no one has yet devised a method for sorting out acquaintances, friends, relations, and lovers for purposes of a rule of permitting official dealings with some and not others." The final reason is that the bar committee conducting the study believed that the major concern of the public is with the economic corruption of government. Since, in its view, public confidence is a primary consideration in the conflict-of-interest problem, economic matters should be the center of attention.

Since the New York bar report, the debate has continued over broader and narrower definitions of conflict of interest. Some understand it quite broadly to involve role conflicts (Margolis, 1979). Others prefer to view it as a conflict between one kind of role—those with fiduciary responsibility for acting on behalf of someone else's interests—and a broad range of personal interests: material, psychological, and moral (Davis, 1982). Still others continue to argue for a restricted definition consistent with legal provisions. They focus on conflicts between the fiduciary role and personal material interests, usually financial (Luebke, 1986).

This strictly delimited scope may be quite appropriate for those whose chief concern is with the most socially manageable types of conflict of interest and who, therefore, need to focus on economic interests as the most treatable by legislation. However, an examination of the *ethics* of conflicting interests must necessarily proceed from a broader perspective. Our concern is with the principled, systematic, and rational exercise of administrative responsibility. Thus, we must take into account in our ethical reckoning the full range of human interests, which may not be controllable by law but nevertheless influence conduct. Economic interest is only one, however powerful, kind of interest. Other significant interests include affection, social status, power, social relatedness, predictability, personal well-being, the well-being of some others, and recognition.

Actions proscribed by law certainly fall within our purview, but our boundaries must be more inclusive. This is because the law may be understood as only a moral minimum established by society based on widely accepted standards of conduct. Ethical considerations go beyond these minimum standards to examine acts that may be acceptable under the law but may not measure up to certain ethical norms and principles. Just because an act is legal does not necessarily make it ethical. Using terms like *nigger, broad,* or *fag* may be legal, but uttering them may provoke the moral censure of society because they are understood as demeaning the dignity of other human beings. Granting some people greater access to administrative decision makers than others may not be illegal, but may well be judged unfair by the citizenry of a community.

Furthermore, in some situations we may challenge the legitimacy of the law on ethical grounds as not meeting the minimal moral standards of a society. This may lead to civil disobedience and the generation of test cases, as occurred during the civil rights movement of the 1960s, and the women's rights and environmental movements of the 1970s and 1980s. Reform movements of these kinds, if successful in achieving broad public support, are able to establish new and higher minimum standards for conduct, although they still do not preempt ethical considerations.

Thus, while much attention about conflicts of interest is focused on economic interest and legal remedies, it is important to remember that there are other important dimensions of this kind of conflict of responsibility. Ethics legislation tends to preempt ethical reflection, as Foster (1981) has noted. Once the moral judgment of the community has been crystallized in the form of law, we tend to narrow our consideration to the question of whether some course of action is legal or not. Legality becomes our fixation; whether it is ethical tends to be forgotten or devalued. It is essential that we resist that tendency. Conflicts of interest are broader than economic ones and require ethical assessment as well as legal regulation.

Some analyses of conflict of interest do adopt a more general definition, or use one similar to the New York bar, but construe "economic interests" in a broader fashion. For example, Beard and

Horn (1975) use the New York bar definition but then identify five types of conduct, some of which exceed the boundaries of the bar study.

A report prepared by Kenneth Kernaghan (1975) for the Institute of Public Administration of Canada seems to offer a definition that is broad enough for our purposes: "Conflict of interest may be defined as a situation in which a public employee has a private or personal interest sufficient to influence or appear to influence the objective exercise of his official duties" (p. 13). Personal interests includes more than economic matters. Kernaghan then identifies seven situations that fall within this definition: influence peddling, financial transactions, outside employment, future employment, dealings with relatives, gifts and entertainment, and bribery. To complete the array of conflict of interest types, we should add an eighth situation borrowed from Beard and Horn— information peddling.

Bribery—the illegal acceptance of money, or other valuable considerations, in exchange for special favors from public servants having to do with their official duties. The critical condition here is that the bribe giver clearly intends to distort the objective, even-handed conduct of the official and the receiver intends to willingly comply. Thus, the official, faced with personal interests, pecuniary or otherwise, in conflict with the laws, policies, and procedures for the conduct of his office, is induced to resolve it in favor of himself. Although bribery usually involves money, it may include other rewards such as sexual favors, promises of favorable publicity, or offers of access to exclusive social circles.

Influence Peddling—a public employee attempts to influence a governmental decision in favor of a third party in which the employee has an interest. Understood in typical legal terms, this might include such cases as policy decisions regulating a business in which the employee holds shares, developing a general plan affecting the value of land owned by the employee, or approving a federal grant to a local school district where his children attend school. This becomes an actual conflict of interest situation whenever the employee stands a high chance of significant gain.

However, beyond the economic motivations for influence peddling, we might include such interests as religious beliefs or racial ideologies. For example, a public administrator whose religion strongly opposed contraception or abortion might use his insider influence to restrict funding for family planning services or subsidized abortion clinics. A public administrator affiliated with a white supremacy organization might use her influence to derail equal employment opportunity legislation.

Information Peddling—officials who are privy to information not available to the general public use it to their own advantage, monetary or otherwise. The key factors are the power of the information and privileged access to it. Actual conflict of interest is present when the information is highly confidential and the official in question is responsible for maintaining the confidence.

For example, suppose a city planner had information about proposed redevelopment plans for an area where a friend's home was located. He was not a member of the planning team for that area, but had access to the changes being considered. As an employee of the city planning department, he was obliged to maintain confidentiality about the plan until it was publicly disclosed to the entire community. However, the friend had offered money in exchange for advance information. If the planner had accepted the money, that would have been information peddling.

Financial Transactions—a public servant has direct or indirect financial interests that directly conflict with the responsible performance of the job. Actual conflict of interest is present to the extent that an official is in direct personal control over a decision that will produce significant personal gain. This differs from influence peddling in that the official in question effectively controls the outcome, for example, a planning director who could influence the location of a new airport near undeveloped land that he owned.

Gifts and Entertainment—seeking or accepting of gifts and hospitality that may influence a public employee's impartial discharge of his or her duties. This category simply amounts to a broadening of our understanding of bribery. It includes such things as discounts on purchases, theater tickets, sex, vacation trips, use of vehicles, lavish meals, recreational equipment, and liquor. Typically, gifts of this kind are given with no specific favors requested, as would be the case with bribery, but are intended to create a generally positive predisposition toward the donor.

Outside Employment—part-time employment, consulting, contractual retainers, and self-employment that may cause a conflict of interest with official duties. Conflict situations include the use of public employment status to enhance a private employer (or oneself), the draining away of effort and energy required for official duties, and the use of government services and equipment in outside work.

Being employed outside does not necessarily create a conflict of interest; the type of employment and the magnitude of the commitment are both critical factors. A captain in the fire department might very well spend a few hours a week at home painting landscapes and selling them without any conflict of interest. However, if he worked with a private consulting group as an expert in fire fighting, with his official status prominently advertised, a definite conflict would exist. His private consulting activities would profit from his status as a captain in a fire department. Or, if his painting became such an obsessive preoccupation that he neglected his official duties, then a definite conflict would also exist.

Future Employment—a public employee intends to seek employment in the future with a firm he or she now transacts official business with. The tendency may be to give favored treatment to this prospective employer in hopes of encouraging a job offer. Also, the government employee may present his inside contacts and knowledge of agency procedure as an attractive package for a firm that does regular business with that public organization. The widespread "in-and-out," or "revolving door" syndrome, particularly problematic in the defense industries, creates some of the most serious conflicts (Beard, 1978). As people move back and forth between public- and private-sector service, intertwined interests resulting from past work and future employment expectations can become extremely complex.

Dealings with Relatives—situations in which a public administrator may be in a position to do favors for a relative. We might think of this form of conflict of interest, sometimes called nepotism, as a special class of influence peddling since the motivation is similar to other such cases discussed above. Essentially, it involves using influence to gain preferential treatment in hiring, promoting, awarding contracts, or other business practices in which a relative will benefit. The public administrator who engages in such practices gains not directly but indirectly, by reinforcing family bonds and mutual support.

This kind of conflict of interest might well be rooted in noneconomic interests. A case similar to the information-peddling example was presented by a planner in an urban redevelopment agency, except in her case it was her aging parents' home that was affected. As a member of the planning group she discovered at an early stage that their home was to be replaced with commercial development. It was not fear of financial loss that worried her, but the disturbance in continuity and stability of their lives. Their home, which they loved and from which they derived a great sense of security, would be bought by right of eminent domain and demolished if the plan were adopted. Her affection for her parents and concern for their well-being, deep and powerful human interests, were in conflict with her obligations as a public servant for objectivity and equal treatment of all residents. She felt strongly inclined to encourage her fellow planners in the department to change the plan to exempt her parents' home.

Each of these situational types represents a potential conflict of interest. Whether it becomes an actual conflict depends on the extent to which a public servant yields to the temptation. However, as the New York Bar Association report strongly emphasized, being in a potential conflict of interest situation is almost as serious as an actual conflict. Since maintaining the public trust is a crucial aspect of administrative responsibility, the appearance of conflict of interest may be sufficient to jeopardize faith in the integrity of government.

The implication of this risk from only the appearances of evil is well summarized by a report of the National Academy of Public Administration after Watergate. The academy observed that many of the officials involved did not understand that "their obligations to the public as a whole entail an additional and more rigorous set of standards and constraints associated with the concept of public trust. Many practices which are permissible, even normal, in the private sector are, or should be, forbidden in government" (Small, 1976, p. 561). As we face situations that are ethically problematic, we must consider possible public perceptions of our actions as well as the acts themselves. The reflective process of imagining alternatives, projecting the consequences of each, considering the justification for our conduct, and attempting to anticipate how we will feel about ourselves in retrospect is particularly demanding in these cases. It is also necessary to imagine whether objectively honorable behavior is likely to be perceived otherwise.

The mentality that public servants need to cultivate as a guide to this reflection is one that counterbalances the tendencies toward an overweening individualism inherent in Western culture. Weisband and Franck (1975, pp. 187-188) argue that what is required is a "higher consciousness of one's wider responsibility," which is "the apex of personal maturity" and essential "to the collective survival of an interdependent world." They refer to the work of Lawrence Kohlberg, which indicates that the highest stage of moral development "comes when life decisions and actions are rooted in an autonomous, principled judgment of right and wrong, in full consciousness of responsibility to the larger social community." This perspective is based on an assumption that the long-term interests of the governmental commons are our interests as well.

Summary

In this chapter we have examined three different types of conflict of responsibility, all of which involve problems of defining subjective or objective responsibility, or both. This typology is not intended to suggest that there are any inherent or fundamental differences in the way an administrator handles these situations. The reflective process outlined in Chapter One is appropriately used as a guide to resolving quandaries arising from all these types of conflict.

Rather the typology is presented to assist in the descriptive task discussed in Chapter One. This entails identifying and understanding the key characteristics of the problems presented by each type of conflict. Thus, the typology helps focus attention on the particular others, and our relationships with them, that must be managed if we are to maintain responsible conduct of our public office.

With conflicts of authority we confront clashes between two different definitions of our objective responsibility presented by two inconsistent sources of authority. These are situations, such as in "The Major, the Captain, and Corporal Montague," where we face serious consequences for ourselves and the organization, but they are episodic in nature. They do not involve a need to redefine our role for all future situations. The task is to act responsibly in the specific instance, recognizing that it is not typical of the routine performance of our role.

To determine whether to respond to one and resist the other authority, or resist both, we need to clarify our own subjective responsibility, to know where we stand in responding to the competing authorities. Thus examining our professional values and ethical principles becomes the prominent considerations in the reflective process here.

In dealing with role conflicts we face the need to examine and redefine our roles within the employing organization, as in the Rancor County sheriff's department case, or one role inside and another outside the department, as in the case of "Politics and Toilets." These are not instances of such intense conflict that we feel pushed into a crisis of our relationship with the organization and the work role, such as we will consider in Chapter Seven. However, they are sufficiently serious, and with sufficient implications for routine performance, to require role clarification and adjustment. These may involve conflicts of subjective responsibility with ongoing future consequences when the key authority (the boss) is supportive and not imposing a particular course of action, as in "Politics and Toilets." Or they may represent conflicts of subjective and objective responsibility in which the authority (the boss) is imposing an objective responsibility that conflicts with your subjective responsibility. However, in either case we confront the need to review, clarify, and redefine our roles, not only for the specific situation but also for the future.

In conflicts of interest, we must deal with legal as well as ethical considerations. Since this particular form of conflict of responsibility has received the major attention of ethics legislators, we need to be cognizant of any laws that apply to the situation at hand. However, that should not take the place of ethical reflection. Usually the law is an adequate guide to the considered ethical judgment of the political community in which we function; it may represent a moral minimum that is sufficient for resolving the immediate quandary. However, to prevent legal thinking from displacing ethical reflection, we must examine how our personal interests weigh in relation to the objective obligations we bear as public servants.

In thinking about possible personal gain from our public service roles, it is crucial that we avoid even appearances of conflict of interest. Public trust in our fiduciary judgment requires not only that we be free of conflicts, but that we also appear to be free. The most typical ways of avoiding a conflict, or dealing with the existence of one, are withdrawing from handling a decision, or disclosing assets and relationships, or divesting ourselves of them. Even if there is no legal requirement to take these actions, we may feel compelled to do so on ethical grounds.

Up to this point we have dealt with public administrative ethics from the perspective of the individual practitioner confronted with ethical dilemmas of various types in the course of making administrative decisions. In the next three chapters, we shift to the perspective of the organizational setting. Chapter Five focuses on administrative ethics from the viewpoint of the manager and addresses the problem of maintaining responsible conduct within a public organization. The central question addressed is "How do I as a manager keep the members of my organization from engaging in unethical conduct?"

Part Two

Ethics in the Organization

Chapter Five

Maintaining Responsible Conduct
in Public Organizations:
Two Approaches

How can a manager of a public organization maintain the responsible conduct of the public's business by subordinates faced with the array of possible conflicts discussed in the previous chapter? That is a crucial question, and must be answered both by individual managers and by organizational policies. The reflective process outlined in Chapter One provides a way of dealing with ethical conflicts concerning individual responsibility. Also, most of the material in Chapters Two and Three has been developed from an individual perspective. However, the organizational management and policy dimensions must not be neglected. While we are attempting to help individual public administrators cultivate an awareness of ethical dilemmas, develop ways of conceptualizing them, and practice ways of thinking about their resolution, we must consider also the larger organizational arena within which this reflection occurs.

Conflicts of responsibility that people experience within public organizations should not be resolved in an idiosyncratic fashion. If public administrators are to be responsive to the wishes of a democratic citizenry, their general course of conduct toward serving the public interest must be guided by established policies, and these policies should enforce and reinforce prescribed public-service values. That is, they should support the basic principles of the particular polity involved, and oppose the tendencies of individuals and organizations to become self-serving.

There must be limits to loyalty and conformity to particular organizational hierarchies, and these will be dealt with in Chapter Seven. However, it seems reasonable to expect someone who accepts employment in a public fiduciary role to act generally in accordance with the values of the citizenry, as expressed through a political system and direct citizen participation. Otherwise, democratic government would be subverted by an aggregation of individuals employed by the public, but functioning only according to their personal individual values. In a democracy the public has a right to expect some degree of consistency and predictability in the actions of its employees. It is entitled to a public service that can be held accountable for carrying out the designated mission. It should be able to expect its administrative corps to conduct itself in accordance with the explicit and implicit role obligations of a position.

Two Approaches

There are two general approaches to maintaining responsible conduct within public organizations: internal and external controls. The most typical American response to the discovery of breaches of ethical conduct is to adopt new legislation, make new rules, or issue new regulations. And perhaps the second most common recourse is to rearrange the organizational structure, or create new organizations, to establish more careful monitoring. Both approaches are forms of external control, attempts to impose on the conduct of individual public servants constraints that originate from outside themselves.

For example, after Watergate president Jimmy Carter urged, and Congress subsequently adopted, an ethics legislation package— the 1978 Ethics in Government Act. It provided for new and more stringent rules about disclosure of income and employment practices following federal government service. It also established the first U.S. Office of Government Ethics to implement these new strictures. Similarly, President Bush, after scandals during the Reagan administration, called for certain amendments to the 1978 act that extend and strengthen its controls. These were adopted by the Congress as the Government Ethics Reform Act of 1989. External controls of these kinds assume that individual judgment and professional standards cannot be counted on to maintain ethical conduct.

On the other hand, we sometimes, although less often, witness a different response to ethics scandals—an attempt to cultivate and strengthen the professional values and standards of people in public service through training and professional socialization. For example, a treatment of professional values and ethical decision making is being included in an increasing number of criminal justice system preservice and in-service training programs. Police academies are including units on ethical standards and ethical problem solving, and command training programs are devoting blocks of time to the ethical dimensions of leadership. Professional associations related to public service are placing ethics discussions on the agendas of their national and local meetings. The annual conference of the American Society for Public Administration (ASPA) typically offers a dozen panel discussions dealing with ethics in public service and frequently presents preconference workshops on administrative ethics. ASPA conducted its first national conference on government ethics in November 1989.

All these efforts are attempts to develop internal controls as means to maintain ethical conduct in public organizations. These controls are "internal" in that they consist of values and ethical standards cultivated within each public servant and are intended to encourage ethical conduct in the absence of rules and monitoring systems.

These two policy perspectives—internal and external controls—are often associated historically with Carl Friedrich and Herman Finer, but the fundamental viewpoints expressed forty years ago in the debate between these men are very much alive today among both practitioners and scholars. Friedrich asserted the importance of internal controls; Finer insisted on the essential nature of external political and institutional controls. In recent times the advocates of the New Public Administration (see later discussion in this chapter) have tended to support an approach like Friedrich's, while others such as Victor Thompson have opted for a position more like Finer's.

It should be clear at the outset that seldom is this argument, in its serious forms, developed dichotomously, as though a final triumph of one or two antithetical approaches were at stake. When pressed, most participants in this debate will acknowledge that it is not a matter of resorting exclusively to one or the other. Usually advocates will admit that the critical issue is one of emphasis. As we confront problems of behavior that are not consistent with the mandates of the citizenry, the question is usually whether we should pay more attention to passing laws, improving management controls, and tightening performance evaluation procedures, or whether we should be more concerned with counseling, education, training, and the professional socialization process.

Nevertheless, in spite of such qualifications, differences in emphasis do tend to move to the forefront in the heat of debate and sometimes begin to sound absolute: those on one side seem ready to dismiss legislation, rules, sanctions, and hierarchies as devoid of merit; others seem to be proposing that administrators be dealt with as robots whose inner controls are useless. Drawing battle lines in this sharp, unyielding fashion may be interesting as a scholarly exercise to force proponents to test the validity of definition, concepts, and supporting evidence, but the realities of life in modern public organizations force us beyond dichotomies. The real issue is almost always how these two approaches can best be integrated to approximate responsible conduct. But first it may be helpful to delineate the two perspectives.

"Much Ado About Something"

The department of education of a populous state in the heartland of the nation has come under severe public criticism. For several years stories have cropped up in the news from time to time suggesting that all is not well in the organization. A few months ago the state chapter of the association of parents passed a resolution harshly criticizing the superintendent of instruction for his poor management of the agency. After several members of the state board of education followed suit, he resigned. A new superintendent has just been hired, but Grassroots, the largest public interest advocacy group in the state, has issued a scathing report entitled "Much Ado About Something: Maladministration in the State Department of Education."

Grassroots charges that the agency has become "a playpen" for the middle- and upper-level administrators, to the neglect of the educational mission for which it was established, and for which it is funded "with millions of taxpayers' dollars every year." The Grassroots investigation turned up numerous cases of administrators in the department engaged in questionable activities:

- Two unit supervisors have been receiving substantial profits from royalties generated by textbooks that they had authored and then recommended for statewide adoption. In each case coauthors not employed by the agency had taken the visible lead in proposing the adoption of the texts and appearing before the board.
- One of the personnel administrators is living with the president of a teachers' union local.
- The associate director for curriculum development is involved in extensive consulting for companies supplying educational materials and equipment.
- A new school is being constructed, with state assistance, adjacent to a proposed residential development in which the director of facilities planning holds a significant share. The new school will reduce the travel time for students who live in this development.
- Two administrators in the department have been actively subverting the new director's policies through speeches before citizen's groups, conversations with state board members, and anonymously through leaks to the press.
- One area supervisor is a member of an aggressive fundamentalist sect who always opens student assemblies and teachers' meetings with prayer.
- There are twelve cases at various levels of appeal in which two

administrators are alleged to have grossly manipulated the fair employment practices policy adopted by the department.

You have been retained as a management consultant by the new superintendent to assess the situation and make recommendations. In his briefing session with you he indicates that while he wants you to look into the particular cases mentioned in the Grassroots report, his overriding concern is with raising the level of responsibility throughout the organization. He wants the department to become more accountable for its public mission. You accept the assignment and begin to think about your basic strategy.

With this case in mind, let us review the two major perspectives mentioned briefly at the beginning of this chapter. Since the arguments for internal and external controls have not been spelled out more clearly and precisely than in the Friedrich-Finer debate, we will review their opposing viewpoints as they developed them some time ago.

External Controls

In 1936, in an article entitled "Better Government Personnel," Herman Finer argued: "though the codes of ethics, interior discipline, and all the arrangements to make these effective, offer the guarantees of inventiveness, agility and fruitful administration, *nothing is more important in our own day than the fundamentality of political control, or political responsibility*" (p. 583).

Finer was moved to this assertion by the suggestions of Carl J. Friedrich a year before, in "Responsible Government Service under the American Constitution," that there is a "psychological factor which supplements 'objective' responsibility" (1935, p. 38). Against Friedrich's acknowledgment of subjective sources of responsibility, Finer insisted that only the set of legal and institutional controls that rest in the hands of the governed can be viewed as producing responsible conduct.

It should be noted parenthetically at this point that there was a degree of ambiguity about the status of codes of ethics in Finer's argument. For example, in the quotation above, "codes of ethics" is followed by "interior discipline," which might suggest that they were viewed similarly. However, a careful reading of his other works, such as "Administrative Responsibility in Democratic Government," indicates that "codes of ethics" were likely considered a form of external control while "professional standards" referred to the internalized values of the profession. Finer, of course, found both inadequate to maintain responsible conduct. He favored external controls, which were necessary expressions of political accountability. However, for the purposes of this book the full array of internal and external controls will be considered. Codes of ethics here will be understood as forms of external control, since they represent values collectively imposed on individuals by organizations, professional associations, or political jurisdictions.

In 1941 Finer reasserted his general position by arguing the necessity of viewing responsibility "as an arrangement of correction and punishment even up to dismissal both of politicians and officials" ([1941], 1972, p. 327). Finer was, once again, responding to Friedrich in language that echoed the earlier philosophy of Max Weber. It reflected a belief that "the servants of the public are not to decide their own course," but rather "they are to be responsible to the elected representatives of the public, and these are to determine the course of action of the public servants to the most minute degree that is technically feasible" (p. 328).

In this same work Finer argued that this view of the administrative role in government rests on three doctrines of democratic government:

1. The mastership of the public requires that both politicians and public employees work for what the public wants, rather than their perception of what the public needs.
2. This mastership needs institutions with a centrally located elected organ.
3. Public mastership includes not only the ability to inform government of its wants, but also the power to exact obedience to orders. [(1941), 1972, p. 329]

From Finer's perspective, the responsible administrator is subject to the external political controls implied by these doctrines. Government exercises a monopoly that can be held accountable to the public in no other fashion. Reliance on the administrator's conscience, or subjective moral sense of responsibility, will always result in the abuses of power we have come to expect from any monopoly. According to Finer, without "external punitive controls" employees of the public will inevitably resort to "nonfeasance," "malfeasance," or "overfeasance."

Finer grants, in his 1941 piece, that education, sensitivity to public opinion, and the technical standards espoused by professional associations all have roles to play as "auxiliaries" to legal sanctions, but they are only that, and nothing more. The basic problem with all these auxiliary approaches is that they rely for their effectiveness on informing the exercise of discretion by officials; they have no power to compel and control conduct. Reflecting on this fact, Finer observes: "My qualm is that the official is very likely to give himself the benefit of the doubt where the information he elicits admits of doubt, whereas when the legislative assembly asserts an opinion it also asserts a command" (p. 334). Thus, these internal controls may serve a supplemental function, but they should not receive primary attention.

Rather, our first concern, according to Finer, should be with improving legislative controls over public servants, along with the devices of legal responsibility. Beyond that, we should consider the more effective use of intradepartmental discipline through the hierarchical structure. We should pay more attention to such levers as career prospects, pay raises, promotions, recognition of distinction, and retirement pensions.

In arguing for the primacy of external legal and political sanctions to govern the actions of public administrators, Finer was reaffirming the traditional perspective of the administrative role that had its roots in Max Weber ("Politics as a Vocation," 1946). In Weber's eyes the administrator must be "conditioned to obedience towards these masters who claim to be the bearers of legitimate power" (p. 80). Administrative responsibility involves refraining from making substantive judgments about what the public should receive. Administrators deal only with instrumental judgments about how to deliver most efficiently what has been decided by the politicians. They are to carry out their duties "without scorn or bias" (p. 99) in an impartial fashion.

Weber insisted, "The honor of the civil servant is vested in his ability to execute conscientiously the order of the superior authorities, exactly as if the order agreed with his own conviction. This holds even if the order appears wrong to him and if, despite the civil servant's remonstrances, the authority insists on the order" (p. 99). This subservient conduct is maintained by organized political domination, with a monopoly on the use of force and control of material resources. As with Finer, control of administrative behavior is founded on concrete external sanctions such as the power to grant and withhold wages, or to give and take away a position.

This traditional Weberian perspective, which is evident in Finer's approach, is also clearly discernible in Victor Thompson's *Without Sympathy or Enthusiasm: The Problem of Administrative Compassion* (1975). Similar to Finer's emphasis on the "mastership" of the public is Thompson's argument that the public is the "owner" of public organizations. These organizations are "machinelike instruments" of an "external power"—the public. They are artificial systems of prescribed roles and rules. Bureaucrats, then, are to be viewed as "tools" of the organization who are under a contractual obligation to achieve the "owner's" goals.

The problem of maintaining responsible administrative conduct, Thompson admits, is that these "tools" are people and, therefore, have tendencies toward autonomy and goal formation. They have a strong propensity for developing their own unplanned spontaneous "natural systems," which parallel the artificial organizational system and distort its functions. The inclination to make informal decisions about the goals and ends of the organization, which characterizes these natural systems, is tantamount to a "theft" of the public's property.

Public administrators, from Thompson's viewpoint, are to deal only in "functional rationality"—the rational application of means to prescribed ends—and to leave "substantive rationality"— the evaluation of ends themselves—to the politicians. How to control bureaucrats through suppressing their substantive rationality is viewed by many students of administration, according to Thompson, as the number one problem in sustaining a high level of administrative responsibility.

Unquestionably, Thompson's view of public organizations

and the role of public administrators within them is highly dependent on the external controls represented by law, legislative oversight, and bureaucratic hierarchical structure. "Tools" must be manipulated and used within the "machinelike" ranks of an organization. Any other approach is too susceptible to unpredictable idiosyncratic behavior at variance with the wishes of the public.

"Much Ado" and External Controls

Advocates of external controls would approach your management consulting job with the state department of education from the perspective generally typified by Weber, Finer, and Thompson. They would probably focus their attention on laws, or organizational policies and the effectiveness of the hierarchy of the department.

They would want to know, for example, whether there are either laws, codes of ethics, or departmental rules that regulate consulting activity and potential conflict of interest situations. Are the two unit supervisors violating any existing ethical codes or regulations in the handling of their texts? Is the personnel administrator guilty of any violation through her relationship with someone in a potentially adversarial role? Is the associate director for curriculum development breaking any rules or violating any laws? What about the director of facilities planning?

In the absence of rules and legislation, if you were a believer in external controls you would likely want to propose that some be developed and adopted. You would recommend that these regulations be spelled out in detail, along with clear and significant sanctions. Also, you would want to give serious attention to the means for enforcing them effectively.

Beyond rules, professional codes of ethics, and regulations you would probably want to examine the supervisorial arrangements in the department. You would want to know how clear the lines of authority are and you would look at the span of control at every level. Reporting procedures and systems of accountability would also receive your attention. You would likely want to know how supervisors monitor the activities of their subordinates. How are subordinates informed of improper, undesirable, or ineffective

behavior? How is overall performance evaluated? Is good performance rewarded and poor performance punished? How? Are the
problems with the "subversive" administrators and the "praying"
area supervisor a result of structural and procedural deficiencies, or
simply the irresponsibility of particular individuals?

The essential point here is that advocates of external controls
tend to think about changing the organization and the regulations
or the laws that govern its operation, rather than turning to ways
of changing the subjective states of the people within it. Responsible conduct is sought through establishing limits, requirements,
boundaries, standards, and sanctions instead of persuasion, education and sensitizing. Two typical forms of external control used by
the general public, interest groups, and reformers within government are laws (so-called ethics legislation) and codes of ethics.

Ethics Legislation. It might be argued that coupling "ethics" and
"legislation" is inappropriate; that once legislated, a matter is no
longer a question of ethics, but of law. Since individuals can no
longer freely apply their values to a given situation, but are coerced
by the sanctions of the state into certain types of conduct, any activity covered by law, as the argument goes, has been removed from
the realm of ethics. People need not waste time reflecting on their
obligations in these cases because personal discretion has been cir-
cumscribed. The law defines obligations.

This argument has merit, but only in a limited sense. It is
true that the binding and punitive attributes of the law are intended
to preempt the decision-making process of individuals to some degree. However, it is possible to view the legislative act as a collective
ethical judgment, as a moral minimum established by the political
community. The basis for proscribing certain forms of behavior by
law is still ultimately an ethical one, even though political and
economic considerations may be involved also. The ordering of
principles is as crucial to legislative decisions as it is to decisions
of individuals. The collective nature of the decision process creates
far more complexity in arriving at priorities, but the dynamics are
essentially similar.

Furthermore, there is an element of ethical reflection and
decision making in our decision to accept or reject the law as bind-

ing for our conduct. We regularly engage in acts of law breaking—jaywalking, violating the speed limit, disturbing the peace with our stereo systems late at night, cheating on our income tax, refusing the selective service draft, committing perjury in court. Ethics legislation does attempt to preempt the decision-making field for everyone within its jurisdiction, but we still engage in ethical assessments of the law as it applies to specific cases before us. These assessments vary considerably in seriousness, sophistication, and legitimacy, but they are our means for retaining some measure of ethical autonomy.

Legislation dealing with the ethical conduct of public officials first emerged in the United States in the post-Jacksonian era of the mid-nineteenth century. In 1829, with the inauguration of President Andrew Jackson, the "common men" of Jackson's campaign replaced what they viewed as the entrenched vested interests in the federal government (Small, 1976). In the absence of any concept of the "public servant," or a professional perspective on government employment, the jobs they claimed were regarded as "the legitimate rewards for service to the party"—the "spoils" of victory (Association of the Bar of the City of New York, 1960, p. 29). It is not surprising then that influence peddling, selling information, and the use of public funds for personal gain were commonplace. Consequently, the first conflict of interest laws were passed during the 1853–1864 period to deal with these abuses. Resorting to legislation as a means of dealing with ethical problems has a substantial history of more than 150 years in the United States.

According to the Association of the Bar of the City of New York (1960) there have been several other significant pieces of ethics legislation at the federal level during this century and a half since the first congressional responses to the "spoils system." They are also primarily focused on the problems of conflict of interest and have dealt with postemployment conduct, outside compensation, and reporting financial interests. The Civil Post-Employment Statute of 1872 forbade employees of executive departments to serve as counsel, attorney, or agent during the two years following their federal employment in the prosecution of any claims pending in the department while they were in office. This was followed by legislation in 1919, 1944, and 1948 to extend the coverage to all agencies of the United States, since it had been determined during World War II that the army was not included under the 1862 act. Also, a criminal penalty was established for violating the act's provisions.

The New York Bar further reports that in 1917 an outside compensation act was passed by Congress forbidding federal employees from receiving any "salary in connection with their services as such" from any nongovernmental source. Also, it prohibits anyone outside the federal government from making any contribution to or supplementing the salary of a government employee "for the services performed by the government" (1960, p. 55).

The first major comprehensive review and appraisal of existing ethics legislation at the federal level was undertaken by the Association of the Bar of the City of New York in 1955. This five-year study, published in 1960, revealed the following: "In the overwhelming majority of instances it appears that, where the statutes are recognized and considered at all, government appointees and their lawyers lean over backwards in an effort to comply. But the crude style of the ancient conflict of interest statutes is an inducement to artifice, and there will always be a minority ready to pursue every advantage. When compliance with the law becomes mainly a matter of form, the law is made to appear ludicrous, legal administration is undermined, the underlying policy of the law may be subverted, and the most conscientious bear the heaviest burden. And it is usually a sign that the law is out of touch with reality" (p. 71). The study concluded with a set of detailed policy recommendations for a more effective approach to conflict of interest legislation and a proposed Executive Conflict of Interest Act. One year later President Kennedy appointed a three-person Advisory Panel on Ethics and Conflict of Interest in Government. This panel's proposals were melded by the Congress with those of the New York Bar in a new ethics act (87-849), which became effective on January 21, 1963 (Small, 1976).

President Lyndon Johnson issued Executive Order 11222, Presidential Order on Federal Ethics, in 1965; it prohibited government officials from holding "direct or indirect financial interests that conflict substantially with their responsibilities and duties as federal employees." It also attempted to control outside income in a more specific manner and required that financial statements be filed with the heads of agencies or other designated persons.

In spite of these efforts to close loopholes, smooth out inconsistencies, and extend the coverage of federal ethics legislation, problems in effectiveness continued to exist. Common Cause issued a "Conflict of Interest Report" in 1976, an analysis of the findings of an investigation by the General Accounting Office. The report concluded that violations of the conflict of interest legislation in existence at that time were infrequently prosecuted, the financial reporting process was inadequate, and postemployment conduct was insufficiently regulated (Beard, 1978; Kneier, 1976).

A further attempt at rationalizing, specifying, and extending federal ethics legislation was undertaken by President Carter and Congress in 1978. On October 26 of that year, the president signed into law the Ethics in Government Act of 1978 (95-521), which covers all three branches of the federal government. The act established more detailed financial disclosure provisions and postemployment regulations, with substantial penalties ($10,000 fine, two years in prison, or both for violating postemployment restrictions). However, it had two major innovations: it created an Office of Government Ethics located in the Office of Personnel Management, with responsibilities for implementing the provisions of the act and recommending changes in ethics legislation, rules, and policies; and it established mechanisms for appointing an independent counsel to investigate charges of criminal activity by high-ranking officials in the executive branch.

The Ethics in Government Act of 1978 was amended twice in 1979 (96-19, 96-28) and again in 1982 (97-409), 1983 (98-150), and 1988 (100-598). The 1988 amendments separated the Office of Government Ethics from the Office of Personnel Management, established it as an independent executive agency, and extended the director's responsibility for ensuring that each executive agency in the federal government develops systematic formal procedures for collecting and reviewing financial disclosure information. Appropriate authority, including the power to conduct investigations, was also granted to the director.

In 1989 additional legislation at the federal level was passed by the Congress and signed into law by President George Bush as the Government Ethics Reform Act of 1989 (101-194). Its provisions include a tightening of restrictions on representing private parties before government agencies in which one was previously employed, including specific references to federal personnel who had participated in foreign trade and treaty negotiations. Some of these provisions were extended to cover more people in the executive branch, including certain White House staff members, and members of the legislative branch. The act also included restrictions on gifts of $75 or more to members of the Congress. Furthermore, members of the Senate were specifically prohibited from accepting gifts "from any one source with a direct interest in legislation that aggregate over $100 in any one year and from any other source that aggregate over $300 in one year." House members and executive-branch employees were prohibited from accepting honoraria; Senators were specifically exempted from this provision.

In addition to federal ethics legislation, most of the fifty states of the union have been actively involved in adopting similar legislation. Although these are too numerous and diverse to summarize and analyze here, it is clear that conflict of interest restrictions, financial disclosure requirements, and postemployment prohibitions are the common concerns there as well. Many states also have established ethics boards and commissions to administer these laws. The reports prepared each year by R. Roth Judd, executive director of the Wisconsin Ethics Board, for the Council on Governmental Ethics Laws, summarizing legislative and judicial action on ethics laws state by state, provide up-to-date information.

Codes of Ethics. Codes of professional ethics are the other major form of external control. They usually lack the specific concrete sanctions of legislation and are much broader in the types of conduct covered. Codes vary considerably in their sanctioning power and mechanism for enforcement. Many carry only the authority of professional peer esteem and have no formal means for enforcing their prescriptions.

For example, the Law Enforcement Code of Ethics of the International Association of Chiefs of Police is a 300-word statement that acknowledges the highest obligations of police officers to the law and the public. This brief statement is accompanied by Canons of Police Ethics, including eleven articles of a more specific nature— limitations of authority, cooperation with public officials, conduct toward the public, arresting and dealing with violators of the law, handling of gifts and favors, and presentation of evidence. The code has been adopted by all major police associations and agencies in the nation, but King (1976, p. 381) observes that "there is no system yet for the profession to discipline its members on a national basis." At the departmental level the seriousness with which the code is applied appears to be quite variable. According to King, California requires by law that it "be administered as an oath to all police recruits training in the forty-five police academies certified by the State Commission on Peace Officer Standards" (1976, p. 381). However, in most other cases the code is referred to in training, but has not been adopted as a department policy statement.

The American Public Works Association's code of ethics is similar in scope to the law enforcement code without the eleven articles of the canon. It is approximately 350 words long, expresses support for the public interest, attempts to distinguish the political role from the technical-administrative function, prohibits gifts or favors, cautions against several forms of conflict of interest, and rejects outside employment. However, again there is no formal enforcement machinery. Also, those who are employed in public works may tend to look more to the American Society of Civil Engineers, and the licensing procedures for the civil engineering profession, for the definition of their professional obligations. Loss of membership in the American Public Works Association would not effectively bar them from professional employment. Adherence to the code is purely voluntary, with no apparent strong incentives to do so.

George Graham has prepared a document entitled "Ethical Guidelines for Public Administrators: Observations on Rules of the Game" for the National Academy of Public Administration; it bears similarities to a code, but is not purported to be one. These "guidelines" deal largely with the concept of administrative due process in decision making within a public organization. The responsibility of a public administrator "to be informed, to be fair, to be rational, and to be reasonable" is stressed. No authority is claimed for the provisions of the document "except to the extent that they may reflect a consensus, or at least preponderant opinion" (n.d., p. 2).

The Code of Ethics for Government Service was passed as a joint resolution of the 85th Congress during its second session (House Concurrent Resolution 175) for all government employees and office holders. It does not have the binding force of law, nor is it administered as an oath of office. This code is lofty in its language but quite general in its prescriptions, hortatory in style and brief in length. The use of this statement is determined by each department of the federal government.

Two professional associations that have taken a more aggressive approach to codes of ethics are the National Educational Association (NEA) and the International City Management Association (ICMA). The NEA code for teachers in public schools is rather long, about 1,200 words. It is organized around four fundamental principles concerning commitment to the student, the public, the profession, and professional employment practices. Adherence to the code is a condition of membership and a committee on professional ethics holds the power to "censure, suspend, or expel any member for violation of the code subject to review by the Executive Committee." Members may appeal the decision of the ethics committee within sixty days.

The ICMA's is, perhaps, the most elaborate and operational of the public-sector codes of ethics. The City Management Code of Ethics itself is not long—about 300 words. However, the accompanying Guidelines for Professional Conduct and General Policy and Rules of Procedure for the Committee on Professional Conduct provide considerable detail both in interpreting and in enforcing the code. Members may be suspended, censured, or expelled from the association if found to be in violation of the code. Explicit rules of procedure for handling such cases and informing the membership of their disposition are spelled out.

The American Society for Public Administration (ASPA) adopted a code of ethics in 1984 and a set of guidelines for its implementation in 1985. The code begins with a preamble statement that sets out the general responsibilities of ASPA members for striving to serve the public in a professional manner according to principles meant to guide administrators "not merely preventing wrong," but "in pursuing right through timely and energetic execution of responsibilities" (ASPA, 1985). It then proceeds to outline these principles in twelve brief articles, ranging from commitment to certain personal attributes such as honesty, fortitude, and integrity, to obligation to improve the legal and constitutional arrangements that "define the relationships among public agencies, employees, clients, and all citizens." The implementation guidelines discuss the more specific meaning and implications of each article for administrative conduct.

Although proposals for establishing enforcement mechanisms have been proposed from time to time, none has been adopted by ASPA. The major reasons seem to be (1) a lack of consensus about the functions and purposes of a professional code, (2) a belief that ASPA's membership is so diverse that enforcement would be difficult at best, and (3) an assumption that ASPA's sanctioning power is extremely weak since it has no ability to impose significant penalties; it exercises no control over whether a violator continues in public service.

The ASPA code has other, more fundamental shortcomings because it was developed with inadequate attention to the fundamental ethical premises on which its specific provisions are based. Consequently, it lacks coherence and depth rooted in an underlying view of the public administrative role in modern American society (Cooper, 1987). Nevertheless, ASPA's code has served a useful purpose in stimulating discussion about the ethical obligations of public administrators, both during the period of its formation and at the annual conferences, where it is not unusual to find panels or specific presentations addressing proposed changes in the code.

One thing is certain. The development of external controls such as ethics legislation and professional codes of ethics has not arrived at perfection. They present us with a very mixed bag of results. In spite of more than a hundred years of passing ethics laws at the federal level, scandals still occur; from time to time men and women in government service continue to violate the trust with which they are endowed. However, on the whole, public service has probably been improved through the establishment of these boundaries for conduct. There are pros and cons to be acknowledged for both ethics legislation and professional codes. We will review them briefly.

Pros and Cons of Ethics Legislation. In the case of ethics legislation the "pros" include the following:

The administration of the public's business must be rooted ultimately in law. Discretion exercised by administrators is necessarily broad in modern government, but it must be generally consistent with the wishes of the citizenry. Judgment exercised in the day-to-day conduct of an agency's affairs requires flexibility and latitude to effectively address specific concrete situations. However, the range of possible decision options should be constrained by the will of the people as expressed by the legislative boundaries established by elected officials. Ethics legislation provides these broad constraints within which the ethical conflicts and dilemmas faced by public administrators are to be resolved, formal statements of the moral minimum for a political community.

Ethics laws also provide sanctions for those public servants caught stepping beyond the limits established by the citizenry. Fines, prison sentences, and administrative penalties for misconduct are ways of establishing the sovereign right of the people to require that their will be done. Legal sanctions confront the whims, greed, and self-assertion of an irresponsible public administrator with a reminder that she or he is employed on the public's behalf, and that this obligation may not be taken lightly.

Finally, although ethics laws are negative in nature—oriented toward catching crooks by establishing a moral minimum for conduct, rather than fostering the highest idealism—they do provide a means for setting negative examples. On those rare occasions when a wayward public servant is publicly dismissed and brought to the bar of justice, a vivid object lesson is provided about what those employed by government must not do. Although inadequate as a way of cultivating the most responsible public service, these examples may discourage a drift toward seriously irresponsible conduct.

When we consider the cons of ethics laws, three points emerge: They are seriously lacking in specific reference to particular situations; they address general conditions. Fritz Morstein Marx once observed that "even though administrative responsibility gains its direction from legislative decisions, neither the statute nor the budget can attempt to outline specifically the path of administrative action. The law never addresses itself to the concrete case" (1940, p. 247). Consequently, the interpretation of the law for particular situations is inherently indeterminate and problematic to some degree, depending on the extensiveness of the precedents established by previous cases and the knowledge of the interpreter. Well-intentioned public administrators may simply misunderstand the law. Also, people inclined to report apparently illegal conduct by government employees may very well feel uncertain about the applicability of the law in a particular instance. As tools for accomplishing Finer's goal of determining the course of action of public servants "to the most minute degree that is technically feasible" ([1941] 1972, p. 328), they are blunt instruments indeed.

Ethics legislation has generally been difficult to enforce. Loopholes in the ethics law, the difficulty in acquiring hard evidence, and the reluctance to report fellow employees suspected of misconduct have resulted in irregular and infrequent prosecution. Also, the inadequacy of governmentwide enforcement machinery has left these laws without the necessary tools for effective implementation. The lack of consistent and effective enforcement of ethics laws can only contribute to the disrespect for law in general and encourage the flouting of these in particular.

On the other hand, a serious attempt to enforce ethics legislation may erode the morale of government employees. The machinery required for more effective administration of these laws may be so enormous and pervasive that an oppressive atmosphere of suspicion and "big brotherism" might result. Creativity and legitimate risk taking might be diminished even further in bureaucratic organizations already burdened with in-fighting, self-protection, and fear.

At the federal level the Office of Government Ethics, established by the Ethics in Government Act of 1978, has now more than a decade of history behind it. As it has grown in resources and authority it has played an increasingly active role in heightening the awareness of ethical considerations in public service. However, it is not clear whether this has created morale problems for the majority of public administrators, and other public servants, who obey the law faithfully.

Pros and Cons of Codes of Ethics. When we turn to codes of ethics, we can identify the following pros:

Codes of ethics can go much further than legislation in projecting ideals, norms, and obligations for particular professional groups. Ethics laws generally focus on conflict of interest and tend to be negative in their prescriptions. They rule out certain types of conduct, but they do not prescribe, in a positive fashion, the highest expectations for performance. Codes, on the other hand, can do this. They can present the loftiest values of a profession in a hortatory fashion that would be inappropriate for legislation. Codes can establish an ethical status to which members of a profession may aspire—the moral optimum rather than the moral minimum established by ethics legislation (Chandler, 1983).

Codes can also be tailored better to the typical situations of a profession. While law tends to be universalistic, or at least more inclusive, codes can be more particularistic in their audience. The NEA code of ethics can address the obligations of teachers to their students, the law enforcement code can deal with proper conduct in arresting suspects, and the code of the ICMA can refer to relationships with the citizens of a municipality.

A code of ethics can provide a mechanism for clarifying and internalizing the values of a professional group. If a code of ethics is not prepared by a few in isolation from the majority, it can be a means of socializing members into the profession. Durkheim (1957) correctly warned against codes that are prepared and imposed by a few rather than evolved through the active participation of many. He suggested that this participatory, ongoing process of defining, refining, and revising a code of ethics is one important way individuals resolve their inherent antagonism with any group. Discussing the code, applying it to concrete problems, and proposing changes in its prescriptions can bind individual interests to group interests. In the case of public administration, it may also offer a way of binding the group's interests to those of the public, toward the enhancement of the political community. To assure that this occurs, public involvement in the formation of the code is essential.

The shortcomings of codes of ethics include the following: Codes are often so vague, abstract, and lofty that they are difficult to apply in specific situations where ethical guidance is needed. For example, when the law enforcement code uses language such as "my fundamental duty is to serve mankind," "I will keep my private life unsullied as an example to all," and "Honest in thought and deed in both my personal and official life," it is far from clear what specific behavior is expected in particular instances. The words are noble but subject to widely differing interpretations. Fortunately, in this case a set of more specific "canons" accompany the code. All too often, however, professional codes of ethics fail to heed the admonition of the Subcommittee of the Senate Committee on Labor and Public Welfare: "The broad moral code, to which members of a society owe allegiance, is not enough. Its principles must also be applied to the professional activities in anticipation of the issues and dilemmas which arise, so that professional obligations can be seen clearly and understood, free from the tensions and temptations which beset a busy professional life" (1951, p. 35). Professional groups are sometimes reluctant to take this step toward concretion and practicality for fear of potential division and conflict in the ranks.

In many cases the code of a professional group carries no means of gaining compliance. Either literally or figuratively, they take the form of elegant plaques that are hung on the office walls and thereafter ignored. They may be quoted on ceremonial occasions, but never taken seriously enough to use in assessing the conduct of individual members. As a form of external control they are generally weak since they seldom have operational enforcement structures and procedures. With respect to public administration, they do not provide the public with "the power to exact obedience to orders" (Finer [1941], 1972, p. 329).

Even when codes of ethics have enforcement mechanisms, and even when they are used, they may still be meaningless. Since most professional associations in the public sector are not the "gatekeepers" for their professions, censure or expulsion may have little effect. They do not license practitioners in their fields, so a wayward member's career is not likely to be significantly affected by the actions of a professional association.

Internal Controls

Herman Finer's assertions in 1936 and 1941 about the primacy of external controls were responses to the views of Carl J. Friedrich. In *Problems of the American Public Service,* published in 1935 by the Commission of Inquiry on Public Service Personnel, Friedrich had suggested that responsibility has a "psychological factor" as well as an objective external accountability dimension (p. 38). He began by identifying a kind of responsibility exemplified by the medieval church as it "sought to make governments responsible to God" (p. 30). It was not responsibility in terms of accountability to some person or body, but a "moral or religious" responsibility, an idealized political responsibility. It was a feeling, a sense, of responsibility to a transcendent ideal.

Five years later in "Public Policy and the Nature of Administrative Responsibility," Friedrich carried this notion further. From an argument that politics and administration are not neatly separated, Friedrich concluded that political accountability is inadequate to ensure responsible administrative conduct. Since public administrators in modern society are regularly involved in making policy, and since the complexity of contemporary governmental activities prevents them from submitting all their actions to elected officials for review, accountability of administrators to politicians must, at best, be partial. Administrators and politicians are not even able to communicate sufficiently to maintain accountability through agreement on policy.

Given this unavoidable limited responsibility to elected officials, Friedrich asked, "But are there any possible arrangements under which the exercise of such discretionary power can be made more responsible?" His general answer was that before considering additional institutional safeguards, we should "elucidate a bit more the actual psychic conditions which might predispose any agent toward responsible conduct" (1935, p. 320). Upon examining those conditions Friedrich concluded that administrative responsibility amounts to responsiveness to two dominant factors: technical knowledge and popular sentiment. "Responsiveness" for Friedrich connoted an inner attitude or disposition to act, even though the two dominant factors refer to sources outside the individual. It is an internalization of "technical knowledge" and a positive sensitivity toward "popular sentiment" that is crucial.

Friedrich viewed technical knowledge as a standard for which public administrators can be held accountable, but only by "fellow-technicians who are capable of judging his policy in terms of the scientific knowledge bearing upon it" (pp. 321–322). As he viewed modern government, Friedrich argued that administrators are increasingly involved in specialized, highly technical decisions that neither the politicians nor the public can effectively monitor and control. However, the administrators' colleagues in a particular field of expertise can scrutinize and evaluate their work.

Friedrich acknowledged that John M. Gaus had developed a similar view several years earlier in "The Responsibility of Public Administrators." Gaus predicted that in the system of government emerging in the mid-1930s in the United States, "one important kind of responsibility will be that which the individual civil servant recognizes as due to the standards and ideals of his profession. This is his 'inner check' " (1936, p. 40). Both men sought to avoid becoming ensnared in what they perceived to be a "literary struggle," or "an argument over words," over whether this new kind of responsibility was "subjective" or "objective." Friedrich suggested that it might be best to eschew such language altogether and instead talk about "technical" or "functional" responsibility on the one hand, and "political" responsibility on the other.

At about the same time Fritz Morstein Marx began to develop a line of thought similar to Friedrich's. Marx had also begun to move away from the notion that administrators have no role in policy making. In *Public Management in the New Democracy* (1940, p. 237), he recognized that statutes must be transformed into "a mass of detailed orders" and that although they "must bear a close relationship to the letter of the law," nevertheless, "their formulation is a creative act, separate from the making of the law itself." Marx concluded, therefore, that external political controls are an inadequate source of responsibility. He argued that legislative control is necessary, but added: "Judicial redress, official liability, and the whole gamut of disciplinary measures are poor substitutes for a sense of duty. No formal device for accountability can give us a clue as to the components of answerable conduct. One cannot commandeer responsibility. One can only cultivate it, safeguard its roots, stimulate its growth, and provide it with favorable climatic conditions" (p. 248).

Returning to Friedrich's argument, the other "dominant factor" in maintaining a responsible exercise of administrative discretion is public sentiment. In a democratic society the public will freely communicate with their government "in the form of inquiries, criticisms, and suggestions" ([1940] 1972, p. 325). Furthermore, the magnitude of legislative work has become so great that citizens will become "more and more accustomed to turn directly to the administrator" (p. 325). Administrators will be required by the public to be responsive to their preferences and demands. Moreover, the administrator will increasingly need to be attuned to changing societal trends: "Instead of administering according to *precedent,* the responsible administrator today works according to *anticipation"* (p. 324, emphasis added). The public relations task of public administrative organizations involves attempting to identify probable resistance by the citizenry to new policies and adapting them to public preferences.

These two factors in administrative responsibility have external dimensions: the public, and the professional community with its technical standards. However, they are referred to here as "internal controls" because the source of their power to shape behavior is ultimately not a matter of external regulations and procedures manipulated by someone else in the form of commands and directives, but a set of internalized attitudes, values, and beliefs. Administrators are not responsive to the professional opinions of colleagues unless they have incorporated the norms and standards of that profession into their value and belief system. Considerable latitude of discretion remains in the application of those professional values. Similarly, responsiveness to public opinion is directly related to the extent to which they have internalized a set of values that attribute high status to the views of citizens.

Having argued for the existence and value of these internal controls, Friedrich acknowledged the continuing importance of the traditional political responsibility of public administrators. In "Public Policy and the Nature of Administrative Responsibility," he acknowledged that "a double standard" is necessary for responsible public policy. Administrative responsibility is never perfectly achieved and "institutional safeguards designed to make public policy thus truly responsible represent approximations, and not very near approximations at that" ([1940] 1972, p. 322). Consequently, political controls must be supplemented with the influences of technical standards and popular opinion.

The New Public Administration. Friedrich's insistence on these internal sources of responsibility, alongside political controls, was given renewed impetus by the so-called New Public Administration movement (Marini, 1971), which had its first organized manifestation at the Minnowbrook Conference in 1968. Although this movement of the late 1960s has exhibited considerable diversity in its effort to redefine the field of public administration, it has generally proceeded with the same basic assumptions expressed by Carl Friedrich thirty years earlier. In attempting to define the nature of administrative responsibility, both began with the observation that the separation of politics and administration is untenable. Public administrators are inescapably involved in policy making, a function previously restricted, in theory, to the province of politics.

From this assumption about the political nature of public administration, adherents of the New Public Administration define responsible administrators as those committed to certain values that guide their conduct. They are not simply neutral instruments of the elected officials, but bring to the policy-making/administrative task a commitment to change. According to Frederickson (1971), the change should be directed toward social equity. However, not only are administrators to view themselves as change agents in specific policy issues, but furthermore, argues Frederickson, they are obligated "to find organizational and political forms which exhibit a capacity for continued flexibility or routinized change" (p. 312). This is tantamount to the fundamental alteration of organizational machinery and processes.

Although organizational change is the fundamental strategy of the New Public Administration, it cannot be separated functionally or philosophically from social equity and good management; all three are inextricably bound together. Good management, insists Frederickson, implies change away from "entrenched, nonresponsible bureaucracies that become greater public problems than the social situations they were originally designed to improve." It also involves using the most effective scientific tools of management, such as modern budgeting and accounting techniques, computer science, policy analysis techniques, and organization development methods, to achieve greater social equity. In a similar fashion, social equity cannot be considered apart from fundamental change in public organizations and policies and the use of the best techniques of management.

An important further implication of this philosophy of administrative responsibility is that the administrator must be "client-oriented." Although this terminology of the New Public Administration, which refers to the people as "clients" rather than as "citizens," smacks of professional elitism, it does suggest that the public and its problems are the focus of concern rather than the institutions of government. Organizations must be reformed to serve the public, not just to become stronger, or to become more efficient but in terms that benefit the citizen-client. Involvement of citizens in the policy process and major attention to the public impact of policies are manifestations of this concern.

Eugene Dvorin and Robert Simmons (1972, p. vii) have provided one example of the New Public Administration's character in a "small volume dealing with big issues" entitled *From Amoral to Humane Bureaucracy*. They argue for "courage," "commitment to humane values," and "integrity" as the most important qualities of the public administrator (p. 48). Without this fundamental commitment to value, "no external check or combination of obstacles is capable of channeling bureaucratic power in the modern state toward humane ends" (p. 46). With "radical humanism" as their basic value orientation, administrators must operate with a "situational ethic" if human dignity is to be preserved for the public. Bureaucratic power must be guided toward achieving human dignity not by the constraint of institutional controls but by an inner moral sensitivity. Bureaucracy "can never in the long run be restrained by external means only" (p. 63).

Michael Harmon (1971) may have carried the argument for internal controls to the most extreme position. Harmon is critical of both Friedrich and Finer for sharing the same premise about human nature. He maintains that they both believe checks of some kind are necessary to prevent administrators from selfish and capricious behavior and thus both hold negative views of human inclinations.

Harmon turns to Abraham Maslow for a more positive appraisal of human potential. He tells us that Maslow "has predicted that the choices of self-actualizing people are more likely to meet the test of 'responsible' behavior than those of less healthy people" (1971, p. 178). It follows, then, that administrators should be encouraged to seek self-actualization. They should seek to develop their own values, assert them openly, and encourage others to do likewise. Harmon acknowledges that there is no guarantee of responsible behavior in this approach, but argues in response that "it is also clear that the opposite assumption—that public administrators will act irresponsibly unless otherwise checked—is similarly devoid of empirical support" (p. 178).

Although he insists that he is not proposing that narrow self-interest become the governing ethic of public administrators, Harmon's commitment to self-actualization would make it difficult for him to identify misconduct. If an existentialist posture is to be adopted for the public administrative role, there are neither universal nor independent normative grounds for evaluating the behavior of anyone occupying it.

In the perspectives of these advocates of the New Public Administration there are significant parallels with Carl Freidrich's positions:

- All recognize that administrators are inevitably involved in politics and policymaking.
- All acknowledge the necessity for some form of political control over the bureaucracy.
- All acknowledge the inadequacy of external political controls to ensure administrative responsibility, and the necessity of internal controls.
- All except Harmon acknowledge the importance of other points of reference that enhance responsible conduct through the internal values they engender: public management techniques, professional standards, democratic government.

It is interesting to note that the importance of internal controls seems to have found a permanent place in the basic assumptions of public administration during the two decades since the emergence of the New Public Administration. The dominant themes of the Minnowbrook II Conference in 1988, commemorating the twentieth anniversary of the original New Public Administration meeting, suggest that values and ethics are now viewed as central to the field. At this session, attended by most of the original participants plus a group of younger scholars reflecting the 1980s, the significance of social equity for administrative practice was no longer seriously questioned, and the "client" orientation of many at the 1968 conference had grown into a broad commitment to the cluster of values associated with democratic political theory. Concern for civic virtue and the responsibilities of citizenship in a democracy typified this perspective (Mayer, 1989, p. 218; Guy, 1989, p. 219; Porter, 1989, p. 223).

The American Society for Public Administration. ASPA, in addition to adopting a code of ethics, a form of external control, has also attempted to encourage the development of internal controls within its members. The most significant means for accomplishing this has been the publication of a booklet entitled *Applying Professional Standards & Ethics in the Eighties: A Workbook Study Guide for Public Administrators* (Mertins and Hennigan, 1982). One of the first major tasks the ASPA Professional Standards and Ethics Committee placed on its agenda, soon after being established in 1976, was to develop a guide to ethical reflection that might be used by practicing public administrators. The consensus at the time was that raising probing questions that might stimulate ASPA members to become more self-conscious about their own professional values and ethical perspectives was more important than writing a code of ethics. The idea was to provide a publication that could be used by individuals or by groups. One might read through it alone for self-assessment and personal professional development, or it might be discussed by groups of administrators in ASPA chapter meetings, in educational and training settings, or among members of a public organization.

The workbook that resulted provides brief background statements on such topics as "Relationship to Law," "Responsibility and Accountability," "Citizenship and Responsibility," "Conflicts of Interest," and "Whistleblowing." These statements are followed by a list of self-diagnostic questions that public administrators ought to be able to answer for themselves, for colleagues, and for the public. The underlying assumption is that this kind of self-reflection and discussion will contribute to the cultivation of internal controls in the form of professional values and ethical standards.

"Much Ado" and Internal Controls. Proponents of the primacy of internal controls would approach your management consulting job with the state department of education with concern for the development of public-service values and sensitivity to the public. They would probably recommend developing ethics training courses at both the point of entry into the organization and in-service programs for those already employed. These courses would deal with the distinctions between private and public interest, and the importance of avoiding even the appearance of conflicts of interest. They might well examine the process of ethical reflection and analyze the cardinal ethical principles inherent in American public service such as equality, freedom, beneficence, respect for individuals, popular sovereignty, and justice.

Pros and Cons of Internal Controls. Let us consider briefly the pros and cons of greater reliance on internal controls as means to enhance administrative responsibility. First, the advantages.

Values that are internalized by an administrator are always present in the decision situation. Even when a supervisor is absent, lax in discipline, or corrupt, the administrator's internal controls still operate. Even when the legislative mandate provides no guidelines for conduct, an administrator can call on those inner guides. External institutional controls are not as immediately experienced in decision making as one's own values. Many of the problems you encountered as a consultant for the department of education could have been prevented if the administrators involved had been deeply ingrained with a set of professional values. Lacking these, you are left with catching crooks and punishing bad guys after the fact.

Internal controls are apt to create a more responsive and creative bureaucracy. Even when uniform external controls actually work, they prevent administrators from addressing the unique dimensions of concrete situations. They encourage the faceless-bureaucrat syndrome: the public servant who is unwilling to respond to the particular needs of citizens for fear of violating the rules and being reprimanded. Cultivating a set of internal value controls provides a sense of self-confidence in exercising judgments, a feeling of structured autonomy in dealing with unanticipated circumstances. Administrators can take risks and depart from the book because they are not acting capriciously, but are governed by a consistent value system.

The problems—the cons—that need to be acknowledged with internal controls include the following:

In a pluralistic society it is difficult to achieve agreement about which values public administrators should adopt. One of the most common criticisms of an emphasis on the inner check is that in modern society values are relative. Whose values will become the norm for the bureaucracy? Will it be Catholic values? Protestant values? Scientific values? Economic values? Who will decide which it shall be? Will all administrators operate with the same professional values?

Internal controls are not completely reliable. If an individual administrator applies her own values to a decision situation we cannot be certain that she will not do so in a manner that is self-serving. Since values are by nature private and hidden from view, there is no possibility for public review of the values that govern a decision. We cannot determine easily whether a public administrator is employing professional values or personal values.

There is a possibility of conflict among competing values. For example, if Friedrich's deference to public opinion and technical standards is viewed as the significant internal controls, is it not likely that these two will be at odds from time to time? Imagine an environmental administrator whose technical standards tell him that air quality will suffer seriously if a new steel mill is constructed, but who is faced with a public that prefers the job opportunities. What or who will guide a public administrator through such conflicts?

Assumptions About Human Nature

Behind the debate over internal versus external controls stand some conscious and unconscious assumptions about what human beings are like in essence. Some of these assumptions lead to an attitude of trusting people to behave in a socially constructive fashion, while others evoke suspicions that, left to their own devices, people will act only in self-interest.

When you think back to your consulting job with the department of education, your experience probably tells you that the people who have been overindulging their self-interests may have behaved quite differently at other times. They may have expended considerable effort in their assigned work; perhaps they do so even now while involved in questionable practices. If you were simply to proceed as though people in the state board of education were totally self-centered and needed to be controlled entirely by external means, you would be ignoring their potential for self-control and self-discipline. However, if you assume, with equal simplicity, that they are all likely to be cooperative and socially oriented, if only allowed to work unimpeded by rules, regulations, and supervision, you would be flying in the face of your own experience and the evidence before you.

The critical task is to develop a balance between internal and external control, as well as congruence between them. That is, there must be enough control from outside the individual to discourage those inclinations toward indulgence of self-interest, but enough internal control to encourage the most socially constructive, idealistic, altruistic, and creative impulses to flourish. This balance of controls is essential for the fully responsible conduct of a public administrator.

However, it is also necessary that the internal and external controls reinforce each other; they must support the same kind of behavior. They must not give conflicting signals. All too often in organizations we set up policies, performance standards, regulations, and supervisory processes that are at odds with the publically espoused values with which public servants are to function.

In the next chapter we will begin to map out a synthesis of internal and external controls; we will attempt to integrate ethics and values with laws, rules, codes, and bureaucratic organization.

Chapter Six

Integrating Ethics
with Organizational Norms
and Structures

This chapter continues the examination of the problem of maintaining responsible conduct from the perspective of the manager. In the managerial role we sometimes feel perplexed about our inability to achieve the desired results from changes in rules, policies, training programs, laws, and organizational arrangements. In spite of our efforts, people in public organizations still do not conduct themselves consistently with the goals we have in mind. They do not always enthusiastically direct their energies and skills toward implementing new policies and abiding by added rules; at other times they clearly behave unethically, even illegally.

Although we tend to think of unethical activities and willfully inadequate work performance as two separate problems, both are forms of irresponsible conduct. Both represent a diverting of the public's resources from the fulfillment of its preferences and demands. Using a public organization's information and access to key people for personal gain, on the one hand, and simply bending the direction of policies and programs away from their mandated objectives, on the other, are both failures to serve the citizenry. They are two faces of irresponsibility.

If a deficiency in basic abilities to undertake the job is not the underlying impediment, both forms of conduct may be the result of insufficient congruence between internal and external controls. A public administrator may behave irresponsibly because his subjective responsibility and the objective responsibility of the position are not well linked. A conflict among internal and external controls is conducive to conduct we might consider unethical and also to conduct we might view as inadequate effort toward accomplishing the organization's designated goals. Let us look at several examples to illuminate these dynamics.

Conflicts Among Internal and External Controls

Gay People in Law Enforcement. The Fair City Police Department conducted a recruitment campaign to hire an experienced police officer on a lateral-entry basis. The department received fifteen applications from officers in other departments throughout the state. All were put through the usual selection process involving written examinations, interviews, medical checks, psychological evaluations, and background investigations. At the conclusion of this process the top candidate was a patrolman named Adam with five years of experience in another department in the county. He had scored substantially higher than his competitors, his previous performance appraisals were strongly positive, and his current supervisors praised his work.

However, just before Adam was sent a written offer of employment, a hitch developed. One of the senior officers in the unit where Adam was to work approached the personnel officer and expressed a "gut feeling" that Adam was gay. This senior officer had participated in the interview process. Although he did not express concern at the time, he subsequently began to feel that something about Adam's mannerisms seemed "suspicious."

The personnel officer agreed that Adam seemed ever so slightly "effeminate," then revised his opinion—"No, not really ef-

feminate, just not as masculine as most cops." However, the personnel officer reminded the senior officer that the city had an equal
employment opportunity ordinance that prohibited discrimination
on the basis of sexual orientation. The senior officer chuckled and
reminded the personnel officer that the police department had a
well-established tradition, which had never been challenged, of not
hiring gays. The personnel officer agreed and admitted that hiring
a gay person would create serious problems within the department.
Most of the officers would refuse to work with Adam if he were gay,
or even if they thought he was, not to mention the harassment they
would subject him to. They would see Adam's presence among them
as somehow eroding the status of their profession and likely to evoke
the ridicule of other police departments in the region. Eventually,
inevitably, they would hound him out of the department.

Both officers agreed that this could be a costly hire in a multitude of ways and that it required special handling. They decided
that their only recourse was to check further on Adam's background
and conduct some surveillance to determine whether their suspicions were well founded. Within a week they had information that
confirmed their initial intuitions. They decided to "adjust" his
scores so that he would not be the number-one candidate. They were
convinced that this was for the good of the department, the city, and
even Adam.

What we see in this case is the impotence of an external
control like a city antidiscrimination ordinance to produce responsible conduct when there is conflict with a powerful internal control
like the norms of the police subculture. The deeply internalized and
longstanding macho values of a male-dominated, action-oriented
occupation like law enforcement represent an enormous barrier to
the effective functioning of external controls like laws and even
departmental regulations. Unless we can devise training and organizational development strategies that reshape these values and beliefs, as well as personnel selection procedures that result in hiring
people with values more consistent with the law, the law is likely
to be flouted.

Natural Death. Another, more complex example of conflict among
internal and external controls concerns a piece of legislation passed

by the legislature of a large western state. An active, well-financed interest group called "Die Free" was deeply and passionately concerned that an increasing number of terminally ill patients were being kept alive artificially by the sheer power of modern medical technology, many in an unconscious vegetative state, or in great pain. Its spokespersons maintained that this was an affront to human dignity and a violation of the human right to control one's own life, including its termination. Keeping people alive who have no hope of recovery, they insisted, deprived them of their freedom and privacy with no benefit for themselves or society. They also argued that it created heavy financial and emotional burdens for the families of the patients. Consequently, they asserted, people should be given the opportunity to anticipate such a situation for themselves and decide in advance how it should be handled.

Die Free was successful ultimately in pushing through the state legislature, and getting the governor to sign, a bill providing for "natural death." This meant that anyone twenty-one or older could sign a declaration stipulating that in the event that she was found to be terminally ill by two physicians at any future date, no efforts were to be made to "artificially prolong the moment of my death" and "that I be permitted to die naturally."

According to the statute, physicians were its key implementers. Doctors were to inform their patients of this new right and offer them the opportunity to sign a declaration and file it with them. The directive would be in effect for five years and then would expire unless renewed.

One year after this statute went into effect, a survey of physicians throughout the state revealed that no evidence could be found that even one declaration had been signed. Shocked that apparently physicians had not done their duty under the law, the leadership of Die Free convened a conference of leading physicians, medical educators, legislators, policy analysts, attorneys, and ethicists to try to discover the root of the problem.

It did not take long to figure out why the new act had had no effect. There was a conflict between significant internal and external controls. If we examine the internal and external controls operating in this case we discover two external controls—the natural-death act and the courts—and one internal control, the ethical norms of physicians. One external control, the natural death act, was in conflict with the other external control, the courts. It also ran counter to the internal control represented by the ethical norms of physicians. The conflict lay in the fact that the new act was attempting to get physicians to do something that was inconsistent with the values and norms they had internalized through medical training and practice, and which would expose them to malpractice litigation in the courts.

Doctors are trained to save and prolong life, not to terminate it, or even to allow it to be terminated if they can effectively intervene. The ancient Hippocratic Oath, although not officially an operative external control over the conduct of physicians today, still reflects a two-thousand-year-old tradition of medical ethics. Central to this tradition is the physician's obligation to avoid providing assistance in the termination of life.

Furthermore, physicians are trained and socialized to jealously protect the doctor-patient relationship from anything that might violate the bond of trust. The idea of suggesting to their patients that they consider signing a termination-of-life declaration and filing it with them was seen as antithetical to this trust relationship. Doctors feared that patients might not understand their motives and might view such advice with suspicion.

In addition to these longstanding and widely held norms of practice, the risk of being sued for malpractice provided a potent external control in further conflict with the new act. Although there were provisions in the act to exempt physicians from such litigation, those present at the conference expressed fear that they were not adequate. The attorneys agreed that this concern was well founded. They indicated that criminal charges and civil suits would likely be filed by survivors against physicians who participated in any way in the declaration and natural-death process.

As the conference deliberation unfolded, it became clear that the new act alone was not a sufficiently powerful external control to overcome the resistance of the very potent controls, one internal and one external, arrayed against its provisions. Its language was imprecise, its protection from litigation was insufficient, and it placed the wrong person, the physician, too squarely in the role of implementer with no attention to reeducation.

In cases such as these two, ethical components of decision making are left unshaped by public policy. The lack of potent external controls with clear sanctions, coupled with internal and external controls that are not congruent with the intent of the new policies, leaves other external controls, personal values, the norms of an organizational subculture, or a professional tradition dominant in the decision-making process rather than those intended by the public's representatives. Unless those values can be reoriented, and made more congruent with those of the policy objectives, there is not likely to be consistently responsible conduct. The wishes of the citizenry, as expressed in the public policy, may not be fulfilled by their servants.

The Components of Responsible Conduct

Ethical conduct cannot be effectively shaped and maintained in isolation. The reflective process discussed in the earlier chapters of this book requires a supportive environment if it is to result in responsible conduct. As Figure 2 indicates, the internal controls represented by individual attributes must be generally consistent with organization structure, organization culture, and societal expectations.

Individual Attributes. These include our skills in making ethical decisions; our virtues, understood as character traits or inner moral qualities; and our professional values. Most attention from scholars and practitioners during the last ten to fifteen years has been devoted to these individual attributes. Within this general category the greatest effort has been directed toward the development of ethical decision-making skills.

In developing these skills the typical approach has involved the use of case studies along the lines suggested in the first chapter of this book. Ethics workshops of this kind have focused on learning to apply decision models to case studies. In these sessions administrators typically are taught a series of steps that will help develop a clear understanding of the ethical problem they are facing, and then how to work toward its resolution in the form of a decision for action. They learn to use these models by applying

Figure 2. Components of Responsible Conduct.

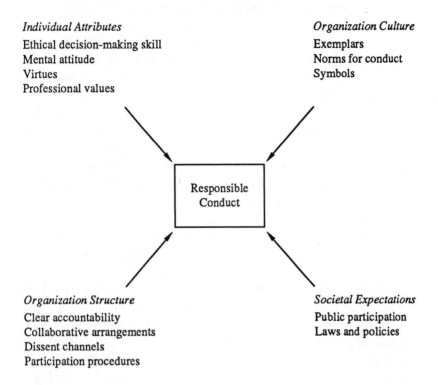

Individual Attributes
Ethical decision-making skill
Mental attitude
Virtues
Professional values

Organization Culture
Exemplars
Norms for conduct
Symbols

Responsible
Conduct

Organization Structure
Clear accountability
Collaborative arrangements
Dissent channels
Participation procedures

Societal Expectations
Public participation
Laws and policies

them to cases, either written by the participants or prepared by the trainer.

Case studies have also been used to cultivate an internalized professional ethic, as suggested also in the first chapter of this book. The assumption here has been that only when ethical standards embodied in codes of ethics are discussed in connection with actual life situations from the experiences of working public administrators, do they achieve relevance as guides for conduct. In in-service training sessions and university classes this often takes the form of analyzing case studies of administrators confronting ethical dilemmas and attempting to relate them to a written code of ethics or significant ethical principles. In this way administrators can develop a sense of what abstract ethical principles or general provisions in a code of ethics mean in terms of their own professional conduct. (Codes of ethics are not listed as a separate component in this chapter since they are relatively weak forms of external control that seem to have their most significant effects on conduct when used not as a form of control, but as an educational tool for inculcating professional values.)

Although most work in administrative ethics during the last ten to fifteen years has been directed toward cultivating applied knowledge of professional ethics and developing ethical decision-making skills, other individual attributes have come to prominence recently. Virtue, or character traits that incline us toward ethical conduct, is also being recognized increasingly as an important personal attribute.

Just because we have internalized a rational understanding of professional ethics and acquired some ethical decision-making skills does not necessarily mean that we will act accordingly. It is also essential that we be predisposed to carry out what we understand to be ethical conduct; that we have a set of attitudes *and* a commitment of will to behave ethically. For example, knowing the course of action that best upholds social justice must be supported by a personal inclination to behave justly, and understanding the truthful alternative for conduct must be supported by a predisposition to tell the truth, if these ethical principles are ultimately to be upheld in an organization.

Although interest in virtue as an essential individual element in administrative ethics has broadened and intensified in recent years, Stephen Bailey in 1965 highlighted the importance of certain inner qualities that might be understood as virtues. He identified three essential "mental attitudes" and three "moral qualities" that are desirable for "all public servants in every branch and at every level of government" (p. 313). He attributed these concepts to Paul Appleby's fragmentary but suggestive treatment of the personal morality of the individual public employee. According to Bailey, the necessary mental attitudes are:

First, a recognition of the moral ambiguity of all people and all public policies. The dual tendencies within all human beings toward self-interest on the one hand and altruism on the other must be acknowledged by those in public service. Public administrators must be mindful, therefore, that human activities in organizations, as well as policies that issue from political and administrative processes, should generally be viewed as "bittersweet"—never all good, or all bad; never completely moral, nor totally evil. This awareness leads to an openness to compromise, which is an essential quality for public administration in a democracy.

Second, a recognition of the contextual forces that condition moral priorities in the public service. Generally consistent with the approach to the ethical process outlined in Chapter One of this book is the notion that values must be reordered as the ethical problem and its context changes. Bailey cautions against abdication to moral relativity and personal opportunism, but acknowledges the necessity for trading off the realization of one or more values in a given situation for the sake of more important ones in another context. It is the larger perspective and the longer-range outcomes that are crucial, not the rigid maintenance of a particular set of principles in each and every situation.

Third, a recognition of the paradoxes of procedures. This attitude acknowledges both the need for standardized procedures and the threat they represent. Order, predictability, efficiency, and equality of treatment all require some kind of established procedure in conducting the public's business. They remove administration from dependence on the changing whims of administrators; they are a buttress against favoritism and the working out of personal biases.

On the other hand, procedures have a way of becoming ends in themselves. The bane of flexible, responsive, expeditious administration is often a preoccupation with abiding by the jot and tittle of the organization's manual of procedures. Taking refuge in procedures can be a way of avoiding discussing the real issues or confronting the merits of the case.

Along with these three attitudes, ethical administrators need a set of what Bailey calls "moral qualities." He identifies three: optimism, courage, and fairness tempered by charity.

First, optimism. This quality should not suggest a kind of Pollyanna euphoria, but rather a tendency to assume that it is possible to achieve positive ends. It is an inclination to believe that true opportunity exists in the world. It is an administrator's tendency to view the business of government as susceptible to constructive intentions and honest, competent effort.

Without optimism of this kind, government all too easily gives up the task of working for the public interest, and private interests tend to become dominant. Cynicism destroys any motivation to search for the collective good; politics becomes instead a struggle among individuals, agencies, and interest groups for power and resources.

Second, courage. The essential meaning of this quality is suggested by the phrase "without fear or favor." The willingness to resist the illegitimate pressures of politicians, the influence of powerful interest groups, and the intimidation of experts and favor-seeking members of the public requires considerable internal strength. A commitment to due process, as prescribed by law and policy, in the face of those who seek to exploit public resources and organizations demands a degree of impersonality that is distinguishable from inhumane or insensitive conduct. This courage extends to dealings with superiors; it includes the fortitude to exercise the kind of "neutral competence" suggested by Heclo (1975), which is willing to "complicate the lives" of those in higher authority.

Third, fairness tempered with charity. Bailey describes this as perhaps the most essential moral quality for public servants. It must be viewed as "the principle above principle." This quality represents the ability to balance courageous commitment to equal standardized treatment of all, with a sensitivity to significant individual difference. If we are obligated to serve the public, we must weigh fairness to all with the needs of individual citizens. A public service that is not prepared to leaven order and justice with compassion will produce the kind of robotlike bureaucracy that alienates people from their own government.

More recently, two seminal works—Alasdair MacIntyre's *After Virtue* (1984) and Edmund L. Pincoffs's *Quandaries and Virtues* (1986)—have stimulated interest in the relevance of virtue for administrative ethics. MacIntyre's work has attracted the interest of public administration scholars because of the way he defines virtue in relationship to complex forms of human activity, which he terms "practices." Practices are organized around certain "internal goods" that cannot be achieved except through the practice. For example, medical practice is organized around certain human goods that have to do with the well-being of the body, which presumably cannot be accomplished otherwise. The practice of architecture is oriented to esthetic goods in the form of physical structures that are assumed to be unobtainable through other means.

A virtue then in this context is "an acquired human quality the possession and exercise of which tends to enable us to achieve those goods which are internal to practices and the lack of which effectively prevents us from achieving any such goods" (MacIntyre, 1984, p. 191). This formulation of the meaning of virtue provides a potentially useful way of understanding the relevance of character traits to various human goods, which are sought through an array of practices. These virtues are predispositions to behave in a way that encourages the pursuit of the internal goods of a practice, and protects them from external goods, such as money, fame, power, and organizational aggrandizement, that constantly threaten to displace the internal goods and become the dominant concern of the practice. This general perspective has offered a way of understanding how virtues relate to the practice of public administration, in which goods like justice, freedom, and equality are being pursued within public organizations that may tend to forsake these values for external goods like turf expansion, larger budgets, and political support. (See Cooper, 1987, for one application of this perspective to public administration.)

Pincoffs's book has caused many who have been addressing the development of public administrative ethics to pause and take stock of their basic assumptions and the focus of their efforts. He acknowledges appreciation for the explosion of interest in professional ethics in recent years, but decries what he views as a misguided preoccupation with ethical theory and its application. He attacks the idea that ethical judgment simply implies skill in using an ethical theory to solve a problem. Pincoffs views this approach as reductive, as simplistic. From his perspective, moral judgment is more crucially linked to moral character—to virtue—than to the application of theories. He maintains that "the primary business of ethics ought to be with qualities of character, with the virtues and the vices" (p. 5). This assertion that virtue should be our central concern is a challenge to reorient the emphases and directions of much of the work that has been done in public administration ethics during the last fifteen years.

Perhaps the earliest recognition of the importance of virtue for public administrative ethics during these years came from David K. Hart. In 1984 he described the "honorable bureaucrat"—one who bears the same obligation as the citizenry to uphold civic virtue, but beyond that to seek honor. In 1985 with George Frederickson he focused on the specific virtue of benevolence as central to the ethical public administrator in a democratic society. In 1989, in the collection of papers published from the Minnowbrook II conference, he set forth his concept of civic humanism, rooting his argument in founding thought.

However, although it seems increasingly clear that virtues are necessary personal attributes if ethical conduct is to be maintained, two things are not so clear yet: (1) how to identify and select virtuous people for the public service, and (2) how to cultivate virtue in those already employed. These problems are among the frontier agenda items for public administrative ethics.

Another kind of individual attribute that has been recognized as significant is the professional value system of the public administrator. As Rokeach (1970) suggests, values are beliefs about conduct and goals; they are more cognitive than character traits, which are predisposition to act in a certain way. These have more to do with cognition—ideas about what is desirable or undesirable.

John Rohr's work is an excellent example of a treatment of values that a public administrator ought to internalize and reflect upon. He suggests (1989) that a course in administrative ethics based on "the values of the American people" be adopted in public-service education. In his earlier work (1976), Rohr suggested that these "regime values" are to be found in the "writings and speeches of outstanding statesmen, in major Supreme Court opinions, in scholarly interpretations of American history and even in the rhetoric of standard Fourth of July oratory" (p. 401). In his later treatment of regime values, Rohr (1989) narrows the focus to the central values found in the U.S. Constitution and its interpretations by the Supreme Court—freedom, equality, and property.

To those who would question prescribing the values of a particular regime, Rohr responds that this approach presupposes that we have previously decided whether the regime in question is "fundamentally just." If we enter the public service of a regime, this more basic issue should be resolved first. However, it should also be clear that Rohr is not proposing "lock-step" indoctrination of bureaucrats, but a thoughtful study of the very complex field of values associated with the history and institutions of the United States.

Taking this general approach, but extending it beyond Rohr's specific focus on the U.S. Constitution, we might note these regime values associated with the American tradition: the beneficial aspects of a pluralism of interests, the creative possibilities in conflict, the sovereignty of the public, the rights of the minority, the importance of citizen participation in government, the societal values of freedom of expression. These are but a few exemplary values that might emerge as important in such a broadened study.

These inner qualities provide continual guidance for the exercise of administrative discretion. Laws and internal organizational policies can never be specific enough to cover all the situations and contingencies encountered by an administrator. Neither can public participation reach into the detail of day-to-day administrative conduct. Nor can supervision monitor more than the broader boundaries of activity. The gaps that remain are significant and extensive. Only a deeply internalized set of individual attributes can maintain congruence with the organization's goals and, beyond that, consistency with the obligations of citizenship in a democracy. These attributes also are essential for the effective functioning of hierarchical organizations. Bailey has observed that although Appleby emphasized the "series of political and organizational devices for promoting ethical choices" (1965, p. 313) that he found in the American governmental system, he also assumed certain inner qualities of a public administrator as essential. He concludes that these internal factors are necessary for the functioning of organizations according to Appleby's ideal.

Organization Structure. Another important set of factors in maintaining ethical conduct in public organizations is associated with the structure of organizations. All too often the focus of concern seems to be the individual administrator, and ways of making him more ethical without also addressing the nature of the organization. Kathryn Denhardt has rightly maintained that "there has been too little emphasis placed on understanding the important dimensions of practicing administrative ethics *in an organizational setting*" (1988, p. viii). However, she further asserts the importance of dealing with individuals and organizational structure simultaneously: "A failure to direct reform efforts toward the individual *at the same time* as one develops reform for the organization can result in a situation in which the new or reformed arrangements serve as substitutes for the individual moral conscience, rather than as a method of encouraging ethical decision making" (p. 133). (See also Burke, 1986, on the importance of organization structure.) The key to responsible conduct seems to be neglecting neither the individual nor the organization structure.

One suspects that beneath the tendency to focus on individual administrators lies our American individualistic orientation with its roots in the liberal tradition. From this perspective the fundamental reality is the individual moral agent who must be set right, or constrained, before social collectivities such as organizations, communities, and nations can function ethically. The co-equal reality of organizations as shapers of character, values, and identity has not been fully assimilated into our world views. However, the recent works of Yankelovich and Bellah, among others, reflect a growing recognition of the inescapable links between individual and social reality (Yankelovich, 1981; Bellah and others, 1985; Berger and Luckman, 1966; Berger and Neuhouse, 1977).

Within the field of public administration we are very conscious of, even preoccupied with, the power of organization. However, it is essential that we firmly link that understanding with our treatment of administrative ethics. The organization structure is an important part of the work environment within which individuals function, and as such it exercises significant influence on their ethical conduct. The problem in focusing exclusively on the attributes of individual administrators is that we may hire virtuous people and do an effective job of training them to understand what is required by professional ethics and to reason their way to a justifiable decision, but they may work within an organizational structure that discourages, or even blocks, acting ethically.

One of the problems identified by some scholars is the tendency of organizations to diffuse individual responsibility. As Dennis Thompson has observed, "In public life, especially organizations, the problem of identifying the moral agents, of finding the persons who are morally responsible for a decision or policy, becomes at least as difficult as the problem of assessing the morality of the decision or policy" (1985, p. 559). He terms this perspective, which views the organization as a whole, as the proper focus of moral judgment, "the ethic of structure" in contrast to an ethic of individual responsibility. Similarly, Robert Jackall, on the basis of one-hundred interviews with managers in the private sector, concludes that bureaucratic organizations are "moral mazes" that separate "substance from appearances, action from responsibility, and language from meaning." Bureaucracy "erodes internal and even external standards of morality, not only in matters of individual success and failure but also in issues that managers face in their daily work" (1983, p. 130).

These characterizations of bureaucracy are somewhat at odds with the normative bureaucratic theory of Paul Appleby summarized in Chapter Three. There is obviously a discrepancy between the "is" and the "ought" in this case. However, the solution is not to conclude that organizations must necessarily be deleterious to responsibility. What is needed to counter the erosion of individual responsibility and minimize the inhibiting influence of organization structure is generally suggested by what Elliott Jaques (1976, p. 2) refers to as "requisite organization."

Contrary to those who have viewed hierarchical organizations as inherently stifling and insensitive to the dynamics of human behavior, Jaques argues that they can "become agents of human feeling, pluralism and community" (p. 2). On the basis of extensive empirical research on bureaucracies in both the public and the private sectors, he maintains that they are "dependent institutions" that "per se are neither centralizing nor localizing powers, neither humanizing nor dehumanizing" (p. 2). In any particular case they may be either, but ideally should be requisite in the sense of encouraging human collaboration.

Jaques begins with the assumption that it is normal for human beings to engage in collaborative interaction. The human species has survived through its ability to establish reciprocal relations among its members, which includes communication, trust, confidence, and love. These qualities are requisite for the maintenance of human existence. Without them, families, communities, the production of goods and services, social activities, artistic enterprises, and political systems would be impossible. To the extent that they are absent, organizations do not function effectively in achieving their goals.

Jaques terms "anti-requisite" the organizations that discourage or impede confidence, trust, and collaboration. These organizations "arouse suspicion, envy, hostile rivalry, and anxiety, and put brakes on social relationships, regardless of how much individual goodwill there might be" (p. 6). This type of "alienating," or "paranoiagenic," organization not only creates a destructive work environment, but also weakens social bonds and increases anxiety throughout a society. It undermines responsible membership both in the organization and in society as a whole. Covert behavior replaces open and honest communication; cooperation gives way to a competitive struggle for personal advantage. No one can trust "the system" to provide means for assuring security, opportunity, and well-being. When this occurs, personal energy and other resources are diverted from the organization's mission and its effectiveness is diminished accordingly. (This perspective is generally supported by Roderic Gorney in *The Human Agenda* [1972].)

Jaques argues that the solution is not to jettison hierarchical organizations, but to manage them differently. If we are to avoid covert conflict, we must clarify the limits of authority and the lines of accountability as precisely as possible. Members of the organization must know who can make various kinds of decisions and there must be means of holding those individuals strictly accountable for their conduct. The formal and informal organizations must be brought into congruence by reducing the need for political maneuvering, which is at odds with the formal decision-making structures, or even the possibility of engaging in such activities.

The key attributes of a requisite hierarchical organization are those of a "constitutional bureaucracy." In such an organization authority is strictly defined at all levels and policy is established through participation by strictly accountable elected representatives of employee groups. Also strata within the organization are justified on the basis of the organization's function. Constitutional bureaucracies permit consultation, negotiation, and the recognition of diverse interests as part of their normal operation, rather than only when crises occur. Conflict is surfaced and systematically resolved as a function of the organization's structure and constitution, instead of being suppressed or ignored.

Basic to this entire approach is a recognition that real power is held by people at the various levels of an organization and not only by those at the top of the bureaucratic pyramid. Those with client-interaction roles can distort or obstruct the organization's mission by the way services are delivered to the public. Also, information can be transformed as it is communicated up the chain of command. Secretaries control work flows and play critical roles in an organization's communication system. Budget analysts and accounting personnel hold the power to interpret and channel expenditures. Every category of employee holds and wields some portion of the organization's power. That power will be exercised overtly, or covertly; it will be directed by political machination behind the scenes, or by generally understood explicit constitutional rules. Therefore, it can be held accountable only if it is recognized, identified, sanctioned, and bounded.

Actual power in the hands of individual employees must be transformed in this way into legitimized and controlled authority to exercise that power, and then made accountable to a manager. Furthermore, all individuals must be specifically accountable for their exercise of authority to a superior at the next highest level. When manager-subordinate relationships span more than one level, they tend to become confused and ineffective.

This entire system of individual authority and accountability should be rooted ultimately in constitutional arrangements for the organization, which include elected representation of all employee groups in the organizational policy process, and decision-making rules to govern that process. It is also essential that authority be linked to accountability. The role of elected representatives to the organization's legislative council must be defined as involving the authority to make specific commitments for their constituents that are legally binding in nature, hence the necessity for strict accountability of representatives to their electorate. Otherwise, representatives may not feel responsible to support the general interests of their constituent groups in the legislative process. This may lead, in turn, to a flouting of collective decisions and the resurgence of informal organizational networks.

Although in government the constitution of an organization may be imposed in part by law, thus constraining the range of discretion of its members, the concepts articulated by Jaques may be adapted to these special circumstances. While the legal mandates with which an agency must comply generally specify the public goals to be addressed, there is typically a considerable amount of latitude as to how the work is to be accomplished. Public organizations might still function as constitutional bureaucracies within these discretionary limits.

Requisite organizations contribute to administrative responsibility in several ways. First, objective responsibility is enhanced at every level through clear and direct specifications of accountability. The organization's expectations for performance are channeled directly to the employee through the one-stratum manager-subordinate relationship. Conduct is also reviewed through this proximate relationship. Thus behavior and feedback are linked in a fashion that reduces both confusion in the communication of wishes and a delay in evaluative response. If there is a lack of clarity about either, the subordinate knows whom to go to for consultation; the person directly above him is authorized to speak for a specific area of the organization's mission and to review the work of her subordinates. There are no obfuscating chains of "coordinators" who have no precise authority and therefore cannot actually hold others accountable.

Second, subjective responsibility is enhanced at every level through the constitutional nature of the organization. Members of the organization are motivated to feel responsible for its effectiveness through representation and participation in the policy-making process. Orders are not simply handed down from some oppressive oligarchy at the top of the organization, but rather they flow from an elected council in which the interests of all constituent groups are acknowledged. Within the limits of the organization's legal mandates, the citizenship of all employees is affirmed; all are members of the public whose needs the organization has been established to serve; all carry responsibility for the fulfillment of its mission. Consequently, working within the organization under the supervision of a manager is not as likely to be experienced as subjection to an alien force. The orders received from above find their legitimacy not only in public law but more proximately in the collective decision-making process of a constitutional bureaucracy.

Finally, heightening both objective and subjective responsibility throughout an organization focuses effort toward achieving its goals. Much of the irresponsible draining off of time and energy into organizational in-fighting among various competing units can be surfaced and dealt with overtly through the constitutional structure. Similarly, individuals cannot as easily distort the organization for the sake of personal goals. Responsibility for the legislatively mandated goals of the organization is reinforced both by the constitutional process and by the arrangement of one-stratum strict accountability with commensurate authority from top to bottom. Objective and subjective responsibility are brought into greater congruence by the integrative effects of these two mechanisms.

Organizational Culture. The third set of factors in maintaining ethical conduct in public organizations concerns the culture of organizations. During recent years the research methods of anthropology have been applied to the study of organizations so that it is now possible to understand better the peculiar culture of organizations, similar to our understanding of the culture of larger societies. Scholars such as Edgar Schein in *Organizational Culture and Leadership* (1985) and Ralph Kilmann in *Beyond the Quick Fix* (1984) have focused our attention on an informal set of rituals, myths, values, and norms that exist alongside the formal structure of an organization. These organizational cultures exercise powerful influence over the conduct of employees apart from, and sometimes in opposition to, the formal rules, regulations, procedures, and role authority of the managers.

The problem presented by organizational cultures is that they may subvert the best efforts of organizational leaders with respect to the first two sets of factors discussed above. We may do a relatively effective job of selecting and training ethical individuals, and the organizational structure may have clear accountability, collaborative arrangements, open dissent channels, and supportive administrative leadership, but the informal culture may powerfully discourage ethical conduct, or even encourage unethical conduct.

This problem is encountered regularly with police organizations where the culture generally includes a "code of silence"—an informal norm among police officers that strongly discourages reporting unethical conduct of a fellow officer. Police administrators face serious problems of dealing with misconduct because rank and file officers will not often report accurately, if at all, what they have observed their fellow officers doing.

Lawrence Sherman (1987) describes the potency of the police subculture in a treatment of how officers actually learn the ethics of their profession. Even in police academies, Sherman asserts, the culture "begins to convey folklore that shows the impossibility of doing things 'by the book' and the frequent necessity of 'bending the rules.'" He explains that "the central method of *moral* instruction" is the "war story." Sherman concludes from his observation of police training that "the war stories not only introduce police work as it is experienced by police officers—rather than as an abstract ideal—they also introduce the ethics of police work as something different from what the public, or at least the law and the press, might expect." This kind of cultural formation of ethical norms continues throughout the socialization process of an officer's career.

On the other hand, the existence of organizational culture offers opportunities for encouraging ethical conduct if it is managed effectively. Schein (1985) has argued that the most powerful influence on the culture of an organization is the conduct of its leaders. In fact, he maintains that "the unique and essential function of leadership is the manipulation of culture" (p. 317). What leaders pay attention to, how they react to critical incidents and organizational crises, the deliberate role modeling they provide, their criteria for allocating rewards and status, and their criteria for recruitment, selection, promotion, retirement, and excommunication are the primary shapers of an organization's culture, including its ethical norms. The implication of these observations is that those who lead hold potentially powerful leverage for developing a culture that is supportive of ethical conduct. Of course the contrary is also true. Leaders may espouse high ethical standards, but by their actions encourage the opposite.

Oriented mainly to the private sector, but useful for public administrators as well, are the findings of Kilmann (1984), and Peters and Waterman (1982). Kilmann eschews the tendency toward "quick fixes" in books on organizational development and management and identifies instead five tracks along which organizational change must be directed. One of these is organization culture, which he engages through a group process intended to identify gaps in the culture between what is desired and what is actually done. Peters and Waterman offer numerous examples of how the culture of an organization can be either constructive or destructive.

As for public-sector examples, the Los Angeles County Sheriff's Department has been conducting an extensive ongoing effort to intervene constructively in its own organizational culture since 1984 (Preimsberger and Block, 1986). This program involves twenty-four street deputies as facilitators of "Career Integrity" workshops with their fellow officers throughout the department. Of the total 7,700 members (regular and reserve), 4,000 to 5,000 have been through at least one round of training.

The name of these workshops suggests the way the culture of the department was engaged from the outset. Instead of calling the program "ethics training," the leadership of the department has presented it as "survival training"—career survival training. Comparisons are drawn between the relatively small number of deputies who are injured or lose their lives in tactical situations, and the much larger number whose careers are "killed" or "wounded" because of ethical misconduct. Thus the ethics workshops were designed to preserve career integrity just as tactical training is to protect the integrity of life and limb. This way of engaging the culture of the department has been effective in heightening interest in the program and avoiding resistance to ethics training.

The workshop sessions are partially structured and partially open and freewheeling. The objective is not to train deputies in ethical decision making, nor to teach them a code of ethics. Rather it is to provide opportunities to examine with their peers what the prevailing norms are, the implications of operating with those norms, and alternative norms that might be more desirable. This is done, in part, through war stories of the negative sort—cases dealing with misconduct that had dire consequences for the deputies involved. The code of ethics, the department manual, and appropriate ethics laws are introduced when relevant as a way of reshaping the norms of the culture. All members of the department participate in these sessions with their own peers, including the command ranks, and there is exchange of information among levels.

This approach to intervening in organizational culture to encourage norms more supportive of ethical conduct has been so successful that it was approved in July 1988 by the Commission on Peace Officer Standards and Training of the State of California for in-service training throughout the state. (Peace Officer Standards and Training Commission, 1988).

The keys to dealing with problems of a resistant or ethically subversive organizational culture seem to be twofold.

First, organizational leaders need to realize and constantly remember that they are the most significant ethical role models within the organization's culture. Consistent with the positions of Schein, Kilmann, and Peters and Waterman, empirical research for several decades (Baumhart, 1961; Brenner and Mollandar, 1977), including recent work by Warren Schmidt and Barry Posner (1983, 1986), indicates clearly that employees take their moral cues from the leaders of the organization.

This means the conduct of the leaders, not just their words. Chester Barnard (1952) maintains that responsible executive leadership requires that leaders act according to the values they espouse and that they do so consistently. Leadership of that kind creates positive organizational norms, creates trust in the leadership, and induces similar conduct in subordinates.

Therefore, if you verbally encourage ethical conduct but make exceptions for yourself, your subordinates will pay attention to the moral exceptions rather than your nice words and the culture of the organization will be shaped accordingly. If you overlook the ethical transgressions of certain members of the organization just because they get the job done, your subordinates will understand that you do not really value ethical conduct.

If you say nice things about being ethical, but do not devote time and resources to ethics training, your subordinates will read that as devaluing ethical conduct. The allocation of time, money, and personnel for training in administrative ethics can be an indicator of the importance you as a leader really attach to ethical conduct. The members of an organization learn to "read" its values and ethical standards not only through the conduct of its upper echelons but also through its budget. When the boss sets aside four full working days for ethics training for all the administrative personnel from middle management up, expresses his expectation that everyone will spend time preparing in advance, and indicates his desire to follow up with a working group and annual refresher courses, then ethics may be perceived as something that is valued by the organization. If the boss also prepares and participates directly in the training, the significance is intensified. On the other hand, if the person at the top herds everyone into a room for a one-hour lecture on ethics, that action is quickly interpreted as perfunctory, not to be taken seriously. It is clear to everyone that lip service is being paid.

Visible significant rewards for ethical conduct may be another method for leaders to engage and shape the culture of their organizations. One difficulty with direct rewards to individuals is the impossibility of measuring systematically how ethically people are conducting themselves under routine conditions. Ethical considerations in day-to-day decision making may be invisible to an observer since they are generally subtle and undramatic. Consequently, the most effective approach may be to reserve rewards for those less frequent, more dramatic, identifiable instances of ethical courage within the organization—for example, when employees take action to rectify corrupt organizational activities at some risk to their own careers, face up to safety or quality problems rather than ignore them or cover them up, or move forthrightly to deal with discriminatory practices. One recent proposal involved giving up to four $25,000 annual cash awards from a fund raised by a philanthropic foundation to encourage ethical conduct in the public service. Promotions, commendations, and salary increases are other alternative rewards.

Although some may consider these kinds of rewards distasteful, since we all ought to pursue the good and the right for their own sake, we need to realize that more is going on in this process than just "paying people to be good." Such action provides dual role modeling; both the executive giving the rewards and those receiving them are providing models of ethical organizational conduct. The recipients exemplify the appropriateness of ethical fortitude in a particular organization; the executive's conduct encourages others to act in this way. This is also one of the ways that organizational culture is shaped. The activities we publicly reward reveal the values of the organization and reaffirm and confirm them for its members. Of course, this entire process is fragile; one instance of an employee experiencing retribution from a resentful boss for engaging in courageous ethical conduct will obliterate ten instances of rewards, and drive the real moral heroes into whistle blowing outside the organization.

Societal Expectations. The final set of components has to do with what a society expects of its public servants. These components are the most difficult to deal with and some are the least susceptible to manipulation by organization leaders. The point here is that a society projects in many ways what it expects from people who work in government: the relative level of remuneration for public servants; the body of law that regulates official conduct; public opinion of public administrators; and their public image as revealed in popular culture including books, plays, political cartoons, and movies. To some extent a society gets from its career government employees the level of ethical conduct it expects. Here we will examine two expressions of societal expectations.

First, let us look at public participation. Carl Friedrich was correct in identifying public sentiment as a dominant factor in administrative responsibility. He rightly predicted that the legislative task would become so enormous and complex that citizens would increasingly turn to the administrator to affect the workings of government. Friedrich saw that administrators, faced with this direct interaction with members of the public, would have to begin anticipating their preferences, demands, and resistances. Administrators would need to be more and more aware of the social trends relevant to their duties.

However, Friedrich did not anticipate the developments of

the late 1960s and early 1970s in the United States. During those years, segments of the public began to feel inadequately represented by their elected legislative representatives, especially at the federal level, and began to insist on greater participation in shaping the goals, objectives, and policies of government. Blacks, Hispanics, students, and women demanded more direct opportunities to express their preferences and needs. Legislators tended to respond to these demands by inserting requirements for public participation into legislation providing public goods and services. As I have argued elsewhere, in effect this amounted to passing along to public administrators the responsibility for responding to direct public expressions of need, preference, and demand (Cooper, 1979).

Although Friedrich believed that the public in a democracy would freely communicate with its government, he did not foresee the legislative mandates that are now included in many important pieces of legislation, nor apparently did he anticipate the proactive role that would be required of administrators. Given the diversity of publics in modern society and the increasing complexity of public programs, it is not sufficient for administrators to passively await the voices of the citizenry. Administrative initiative is often required by law, but more important it is essential if useful information is to be generated from the public, and if participation costs for citizens are not to be prohibitive.

Opportunities for participation must be carefully planned and systematically structured, using a variety of techniques to elicit the views of the public. The unstructured expression of public sentiment seldom gives direction to administrators. Instead, it tends to reinforce the notion among some administrators that the public does not know what it wants, and it further heightens the frustration of citizens who attempt to have their opinions heard by government.

In achieving and maintaining administrative responsibility, public participation serves two major purposes. For one thing, it maintains an awareness of the public in the minds of public administrators. Although all appointed and elected public officials are obligated to serve the public interest, it is easy to lose sight of the human reality involved. The demands of functioning within large bureaucratic organizations can cause administrators to become isolated from the public whose interests they are to serve. Negotiating "turf" and resources with other agencies, or with other units of their own organization, can obscure the difficult task of taking into account the complex and conflicting views of the citizenry. Also, the development of professional expertise within an organization can give rise to assumptions that "we know what is best for the public" in spite of their contrary preferences.

Regularly confronting live human beings who expect things from government is a healthy reminder of our service obligation and the sovereignty of the people in a democracy. It is a potentially constructive counterbalance for the tendency of any organization and its members to become self-serving and omniscient. Engaging the public directly may be anxiety-producing, frustrating, time-consuming, and at times embarrassing, but for administrators it serves a purpose similar to one of the benefits of election campaigning for elected officials: It maintains the people of a government as a primary point of reference; it is an enactment of the accountability of the administrator.

Public participation also can assist in clarifying and specifying the intent of laws and policies. When diverse public preferences and demands are aggregated in the policy-making process, much detail is, of necessity, either never considered or lost. The scale for which laws are written generally does not permit the inclusion of specific implementation promises and alternatives. Translating broad legal mandates into specific programs, regulations, and standards has become largely a matter of administrative discretion.

This exercise of discretion by administrators must be informed by particular publics in particular places if laws and policies are to be congruent with the will of those publics. To serve effectively the public will of a pluralistic society, after diverse perspectives have been aggregated into law at a large scale they must be disaggregated again in the implementation process. Of course, we might well go further and agree with public-choice theorists such as Ostrom (1974) that the scale of governance itself needs to be reduced to the boundaries of these pluralistic preferences and demands, thus avoiding the need to aggregate them in the first place. However, whenever that has not been done, as is the case generally in the United States, administrators carry a heavy responsibility for refocusing and reparticularizing governmental activities in the implementation process.

Well-designed public participation efforts are an essential means toward that end. They can provide feedback from the environment that makes possible an open and adaptive governmental system. If the full range of citizen participation techniques is used appropriately, it can generate information about values and attitudes as well as the local conditions to which a policy should be fitted.

However, the responsibility lies with public administrators to develop their knowledge of participation methods beyond the all-too-common practice of holding a public hearing or appointing a citizens advisory board. Survey research, iterative techniques such as Delphi, structured group interaction, charettes, and workshops are only a few of the citizen participation methods that have been underused by public agencies. Acquaintance with these participation tools, and either the skills to employ them or access to people with those skills, are essential for responsible public administration. Rosener (1977) has developed a type-function matrix that should be helpful. Also, Arthur D. Little has published a catalogue of techniques entitled *Effective Citizen Participation in Transportation Planning* that provides a good survey of the available options.

Next, let us turn to laws and policies. While it is necessary to particularize and adapt the activities of government to specific publics, this needs to be undertaken within a broad framework of laws and public policies that represent a more general and continuous expression of public will. Cohesion, order, stability, and predictability are maintained in a society as conflicting interests confront each other and resolution is sought through the policy process. This is especially important for a large-scale heterogeneous society like the United States. The centrifugal forces of pluralism must be offset, to some extent, by the centripetal influences of laws and policies. The task in such a society is to arrive at a calculus of these opposing tendencies that maintains the necessary degree of cohesion and order, with the greatest opportunity for the expression of diversity.

In administrative responsibility, laws and policies serve two significant functions. First, they provide external constraints on the

conduct of the administrator, which identify the broadest boundaries of administrative discretion. This is at the opposite purpose
from that served by citizen participation. Here we are not concerned
about informing the specific decisions of administrators, but rather
with establishing the limits of their professional activities.

Through the legislative process, the people of a jurisdiction,
through their elected representatives, and usually with input from
administrators, determine the general courses of action and major
goals they consider desirable. Then they hold administrators accountable for working within that framework. Conduct that clearly
falls outside these established boundaries is deemed irresponsible
and formal sanctions may be applied. Although strict enforcement
of the laws within which public administrators carry out their duties may be irregular and infrequent, the occasional identification
of flagrant violators serves as a reminder that public servants are
ultimately governed by law and have a responsibility to be aware
of its prescriptions.

In turn, public organizations further define the boundaries
of administrative effort and activity through the establishment of
policies pursuant to the law. Typically, these policies provide
standards, procedures, and regulations for implementing the legislative intent.

Laws and policies link administrative responsibility to the
legislative, executive, and judicial offices of government. The discussion in Chapter Two concerning the fallacy of the politics-
administration dichotomy notwithstanding, the constitutional authority of elected officials ultimately must be maintained. It is not
the political versus nonpolitical attributes of the two roles that is
crucial, but the final authority of constitutionally ordained officials
to speak for the citizenry. Popular sovereignty is subverted if executive, legislative, and judicial officers do not have the formal power
to override administrative judgments, even if they are cloaked in
experience, expertise, concerns for efficiency, and warnings about
risks for an agency's survival.

The law, and policies pursuant to the law, are both symbolic
and actual connecting links between the administrative branch and
the constitutional officers of the citizenry. Even though bureaucratic power has grown significantly during the last half century,

it is always finally dependent on legislative mandate and interpretation. The very fact that administrators seek to engage and manipulate the legislative process is a reminder that at least the boundaries of bureaucratic power are defined ultimately in that arena.

The Key Relationships. These four major components must be taken into account and managed to some degree if responsible administration is to be achieved. The most fundamental relationships in a democratic polity are those between societal expectations and each of the other three components. In this way the democratic values and processes are supported and the primacy of the citizenry is recognized. Individual attributes of public administrators must be supportive of responsiveness to a democratic public through commitment to citizen participation and respect for law, organizational structure must provide channels for public access, and organizational culture must be built on norms that incline members of public organizations to obey the law and engage the public in the governance process.

"Much Ado About Something"—Revisited

Let us now return to the department of education that has hired you as a management consultant (see Chapter Five). If we approach the problems of this organization using the four components outlined above, we will be opting for neither Finer's external controls nor Friedrich's internal controls, but rather seeking to develop the implicit connections among them.

For example, the requisite characteristics of the department might be improved by establishing an internal policy-making body composed of elected representatives of all significant groups within the organization based on strict accountability to their constituents. Several public members elected from relevant interest groups might also be included. This policy council might be asked to begin work on three major efforts: developing an operational code of ethics, identifying all key decision points at which public input should be solicited, and initiating training programs in values and ethics for various levels of employees from the top of the department to the bottom.

The code of ethics might be drafted by a subcommittee after representatives have had an opportunity to discuss the issues with their constitutents. The first draft could include both an attempt to outline the ideas of the members of the department, and a summary of existing legislation applying to the conduct of public employees. After refinement in the policy council and further comments from the organizational constituents, some form of broad public input might be sought out before the code is finally adopted. This might involve public hearings, survey research (maybe a Delphi exercise), or meetings with key interest groups such as parent associations, public interests organizations, professional associations, and unions.

In defining the appropriate points for public participation, each organizational constituent group might be asked to review its functions with this concern in mind. Each group might attempt to identify areas of administrative discretion where there are likely to be multiple preferences and demands from the citizenry. Grassroots, the organization that prepared the allegations against the department, along with the state chapter of the association of parents, could be invited to participate in this review process. The goals for this effort might be a citizen participation plan for the department and the development of expertise in conducting public participation.

Training programs in values and ethics might be designed differently for the various levels of the department, but all of them would probably include some conceptual material on the values of the American democratic heritage, as well as skill-building exercises in the ethical process using actual cases experienced by the participants. Public representatives might also be invited to participate in these sessions as a means of heightening awareness of public expectations. The policy council and the top echelons of management should probably receive the most extensive training since they are role models and those most crucial in the maintenance of accountability. Developing the code of ethics would be, in essence, the beginning of the training process for everyone.

In addition to these three projects, the departmental management might work with you on an assessment of the organizational structure to determine the points at which strict accountability is attentuated by multiple layers without clear accountability for performance at each level, or by confusing cross relationships among units. A reorganization plan might be prepared for presentation to the policy council.

This, of course, is a very brief hypothetical discussion and may be impracticable in various ways. There might, for example, be statutory requirements concerning departmental structures that would keep the reorganization from being as consistent or thorough as desired, or would require approval by an elected body. However, these proposals will suffice to indicate general courses of action.

An optimal situation for responsible public administration is one in which all four components of responsible administration support ethical conduct. It is an environment in which each of these elements is fine tuned to maximize the reinforcing effects of each upon the other in a balanced fashion. Within such a network of interacting forces, a public administrator will not only be motivated to engage in systematic ethical reflections, but will be in a better position to consider alternative courses of action, imagine the consequences of each, and anticipate self-approval or disapproval.

Let us honestly acknowledge, however, that what has been presented here is an ideal type. It is offered as a model that may be used for diagnostic purposes in assessing the conditions within an organization. Seldom can we control these four components sufficiently to even approximate a fine tuning of the relationships among them. Nevertheless, it is essential that we identify the deficiencies of public organizations and address them as much as we are able. Lamenting the ethics of public administrators and deploring irresponsible conduct when it occurs are rhetorical gestures not likely to improve the operations of government. Systematic and complex analysis of these problems, and a willingness to devote time and effort to their resolution, are more likely to bear fruit. Occasional tinkering with ethics laws, promulgating codes of ethics, or sporadic training programs in ethical conduct will not produce responsible public administration. We must undertake a multifaceted, systemic approach directed toward developing the four components of responsible administration. Nothing less will do.

In the next chapter we deal with the opposite perspective—
the individual public administrator confronting superiors who are
attempting to discourage ethical conduct. The key question there
will be "How do I maintain ethical autonomy in a corrupt organization with unethical superiors?"

Chapter Seven

Safeguarding Ethical Autonomy
in Organizations:
Dealing with Unethical
Superiors and Organizations

As we discussed briefly in Chapter Three, administrative responsibility in its objective form has two major organizational dimensions: responsibility *to* superiors and responsibility *for* subordinates. The maintenance of responsible conduct was approached in the previous chapter from the latter perspective—management concerned with maintaining responsible conduct in public organizations; management exercising its responsibility for holding subordinates accountable. Most fundamentally, this calls for techniques for bounding and directing the discretion of subordinates. Management of the four components outlined there is essential to prevent or discourage the irresponsible exercise of discretion through the pursuit of private interests and to encourage a consistent effort to serve the public interest.

The validity of this perspective rests, of course, on an assumption that organizational goals are congruent with the expectations and interests of the citizenry; that the manager is acting responsibly as a fiduciary of the people. However, that is not always the case; organizations and their managers sometimes deviate from their public mandate and become self-serving. When that occurs, individual administrators may find it necessary to define the limits of their responsibility to the organization in order to maintain their ultimate responsibility to the citizenry. It may even become necessary to resist or oppose the organization and its leaders in order to keep faith with the public. This final chapter addresses these sensitive and complex situations.

Responsibility to Superiors

Discerning the limits of our objective responsibility to our superiors is most often experienced as a problem of loyalty. Typically, it is a matter of conflict between our formal obligation to those with a higher level of responsibility and authority within the organization on the one hand, and our fiduciary relationship to the public on the other. Objectively, public administrators are accountable both to their superiors and to the citizenry—proximately and routinely to the former, but ultimately and more importantly to the latter. It is not surprising, then, that situations emerge in which these dual obligations come into conflict, thus giving rise to conflicts in administrators' subjective responsibility.

Cases of Conflicting Loyalties. Conflicting feelings of loyalty require assessing the limits of accountability to superiors. Our ultimate obligation to the public may call for actions that breach our loyalty to the organizational hierarchy—in other words, whistle blowing. Several cases from recent history may serve to illustrate situations of this type.

A commitment to ethical conduct can be lonely and costly. The tragic story of A. Ernest Fitzgerald is widely known and often cited as an example of the price a public servant must be willing to pay for maintaining responsible conduct (Nader, Perkas, and Blackwell, 1972). As deputy for management systems in the Office of the Assistant Secretary for Financial Management in the Defense Department during the late 1960s, Fitzgerald was responsible for cost control. For almost three years, he reported to his superiors cost overruns of 100 percent and more in the development of the Lockheed C-5A cargo plane. In spite of his outstanding professional record and recognized expertise in cost analysis, Fitzgerald's efforts were at first ignored and then blocked. Feeling that he had no recourse within his department, Fitzgerald testified to Senator Proxmire's Joint Economic Subcommittee in November 1968 that the C-5A project had experienced a $2 billion cost overrun and that the Air Force had known about it for two years.

The harassment, scheming, social ostracism, and dismissal by Air Force officials that followed Fitzgerald's congressional testimony is a record of shame for American public administration. Fitzgerald, although rehired in a less prestigious position after prolonged and expensive litigation, is a living witness to the risks and hazards one faces at the limits of administrative loyalty. Fitzgerald arrived at those limits and decided to cross them for the sake of higher loyalties. He has been one of the more conspicuous public servants to make that decision in recent years, but by no means the only one. In Fitzgerald's own words, "The only thing that makes me unique at all is that I have not gone away quietly, whereas most of the others have" (Nader, Perkas, and Blackwell, 1972, p. 40).

No doubt there have been many who have "gone away quietly" leaving us unaware of the crisis they faced. However, there have been other public servants who have openly breached their loyalty to organizational superiors and have "gone public." In a report on whistle blowing prepared for the Committee on Governmental Affairs of the U.S. Senate, Senator Patrick J. Leahy (1978) of Vermont indicates that his office was able to identify seventy federal employees who spoke out about corruption, waste, and unethical conduct in government and suffered serious retaliation. After seven months of reviewing these cases and interviewing the key parties involved, Senator Leahy's staff compiled a detailed report on fifteen, which represent typical examples. This report vividly portrays the plight of the honest civil servant who attempts to maintain ethical practices in government.

For example, one of the most astonishing cases concerned John Coplin, a U.S. Department of Agriculture (USDA) meat grading supervisor. After nine years of distinguished service at USDA, Coplin was appointed supervisor of the Philadelphia office, where he discovered widespread large-scale corruption. Several wholesale meatpacking houses were falsely upgrading the quality of their meat from "good" to "choice," which would get a higher price from retailers. This routine practice was being overlooked by USDA inspectors in exchange for the opportunity to purchase meat for five cents a pound. Coplin's assistant supervisor was even running a meat shuttle service between these packing houses and the national headquarters of the USDA Meat Grading Service in Washington, D.C.

When Coplin became aware of this situation, he ordered his assistant to stop the delivery service and moved to reestablish legitimate meat-grading standards. Almost immediately his relationship with officials at the national headquarters began to deteriorate. Coplin was soon transferred to Chicago, where he discovered similar irregularities and, working with the FBI, fired or forced the resignation of over 70 percent of the meat graders in that region for corrupt activities.

Although Coplin's meritorious service has been widely recognized, the upper echelons of his department have not been among his admirers. Coplin has not been fired, but he has set a record for the longest tenure in the Meat Grading Service without a promotion—over twenty-six years at the time of Senator Leahy's investigation. Beyond this passive opposition to his insistence on ethical practices, Coplin has experienced a common form of active harassment: His unit has been kept in a permanently short-staffed condition. The Leahy report indicated that "he has had 20–25 different assistant supervisors over the last twenty-five years. By the time he finished training one to the degree that he or she can be of real assistance, transfer orders come in and the process starts again." The report concludes that Coplin "has spent more time showing new assistants the ropes than having them help him run a smooth operation" (p. 161).

Consequences for Whistle Blowing. Refusing to be bound by loyalty to the administrative hierarchy when unethical or illegal activity appears to be condoned is clearly risky. Public administrators who ultimately choose to uphold their obligations as citizens in the face of organizational corruption and irresponsible conduct may seriously jeopardize their livelihood, career, reputation, and personal resources. They will, in all probability, become the object of informal harassment such as reassignment to obscure, uninteresting, menial duties; being overloaded with extraordinary amounts of work and unexpected demands; exclusion from the organizational "grapevine" of informal communication; and frequent transfers of staff members. "Disloyal" civil servants may also become the object of formal techniques for applying pressure and making their lives generally miserable, such as suspension without pay, unsatisfactory job performance ratings, letters of reprimand, letters of admonition, or termination.

In these instances, the external controls of the organization, which are experienced most directly, consistently, and with the most immediate consequences, are directed *against* responsible conduct. Hierarchical authority and power are set in conflict with the internal controls of ethical administrators whose commitment is to the well-being of the public, and also to other external controls such as laws and codes of ethics. These cases seem to demonstrate, as discussed in Chapter Six, that it is extremely difficult to maintain responsible conduct only by cultivating the right individual attributes, *or* by intervening in the culture, *or* passing ethics legislation. Often public-interest values, norms, and laws are present and operative, but are overwhelmed by the force of contrary organizational pressures. Some extraordinary public administrators, such as those described here, do resist intimidation, but at unreasonable personal costs. Jos, Tompkins, and Hays (1989), in a study of 161 whistle blowers, found that 62 percent lost their jobs, 11 percent had their salaries reduced, and 18 percent experienced harassment or transfers. Over half indicated that their actions embroiled them in controversy for more than two years, costing them an average of $28,166 of their own funds to defend themselves.

Sources of Organizational Pressure: The Team-Play Ethic

Where do they come from, these organizational pressures on those who expose corruption, waste and abuses of power?

Political Pressure

Sometimes, such as during Richard Nixon's second term of office, partisan political interests give rise to systematic and ruthless efforts to intimidate outspoken members of the bureaucracy. The notorious "Malek Manual" (*Federal Personnel Manual*), with its explicit prescriptions for harassing and removing, by devious means, certain "uncooperative" members of the U.S. Civil Service, epitomizes the unscrupulous use of political power to exact obedience and compliance.

The Team-Play Ethic

However, more often the pressure to conform comes from within bureaucratic organizations. The Leahy report (1978, p. 12) identifies the underlying problem as the "team play" ethic. "The needs of any particular federal agency are best met if its employees remain 'team players'." The needs in this case are for total loyalty to the organization and to ensure that "the agency will continue to run smoothly and prosper." Consequently, any employee who attempts to exercise ethical autonomy by placing loyalty to the greater public good above the orderly operation of his or her agency is viewed as a serious threat that must be dealt with severely. As Caiden and Truelson (1988, p. 120) conclude, "The weight of organizational loyalty and conformity" is used "to intimidate and destroy the credibility of whistleblowers and probably their spirit too." One learns very quickly, Leahy's report found, that "the key to success in the bureaucracy is to be quiet, to do competent work, and to move slowly up the hierarchy" (pp. 11–12).

Organizational needs for stability, order, and respectable image are allowed to supercede the kind of obligation embodied in statements of public-service principles, such as the lofty phrases of the Code of Ethics for Government Services:

> Put loyalty to the highest moral principles and to country above loyalty to persons, party, or Government department. Uphold the Constitution, laws, and legal regulations of the

United States and all governments therein and never be a party to their evasion.

Expose corruption wherever discovered.

Uphold these principles, ever conscious that public office is a public trust.

Public servants who take these admonitions seriously and act accordingly soon discover that those above them in the bureaucracy do not necessarily do likewise. The team ethic is often the dominant guide for conduct, not an ethic of responsibility to the public.

What are the roots of this team ethic? We turn next to an examination of four reasons for its existence.

The Nature of Public Organizations. The Leahy investigation locates the source of the problem in the unique nature of public organizations. From this perspective it is the lack of the profit motive, and the incentives it creates, that give rise to the "don't rock the boat" attitude that prevails in the bureaucracy. Survival in business and industry, so goes the argument, requires that mismanagement, waste, inefficiency, and corruption be rooted out. The fundamental incentive to maintain and increase profits is said to overcome the defensive and self-protective tendencies of organizational hierarchies in the private sector. In the absence of a concern for profitability, public organizations become preoccupied with appearances; looking good is viewed as the way to survive. "Impression management" in relation to elected officials, the media, and the public assumes primary importance.

No doubt there is truth in this line of analysis. A. W. Carney, a former tax auditor for the Internal Revenue Service (IRS), offers partial support for this point of view. He notes that the IRS operates with a quota system for auditing income tax returns; a certain number of cases are to be closed each week. Carney argues that the agency has become preoccupied with meeting or exceeding the quota, to the exclusion of the quality and effectiveness of the audits. He attributes this phenomenon to a concern for presenting an impression of good performance to the House and Senate appropriations committees. Carney, quoted in the *Los Angeles Times* ("Appearance of Success Is

Key to Tax Audit System," 1979), concludes that ineffectiveness and inefficiency are allowed to continue because "both Congress and the IRS have been primarily concerned with the *appearance of success,* rather than with success itself" [emphasis added].

However, the situation seems to be more complex than the Leahy report suggests. Weisband and Franck, in *Resignation in Protest* (1975), present an analysis that is somewhat at odds with the point of view presented there. In a comparative study of resignation behavior among American and British public officials, these two researchers discovered that there is a significant difference in willingness to resign over some ethical issue and publicly protest the wrongdoing. High government officials in the United States who resign for such reasons are much less likely to offer a public explanation for leaving their positions. Typically they give reasons of health, financial exigency, or family pressures rather than divulge the real causes for resignation. In Great Britain, on the other hand, the more typical behavior is to prepare a written statement arguing one's case, give it to one's superiors, and then release it to the press, thereby setting the stage for a public debate of the issues involved.

Of the 389 resignations by American high-level federal officials between 1900 and 1970, 355 (91.3 percent) departed without any form of public protest. Only 34 (8.7 percent) protested in some fashion. In contrast, of the 78 British instances of resignation studied, 42 (53.5 percent) made some public declaration of protest against a government policy. The protest rate of British resigners is more than six times that of Americans.

Furthermore, when the career consequences in each case are compared, it is clear that public protest is far more damaging to Americans than to their British counterparts. In the United States only one person (3 percent) among the 34 protesting resigners was subsequently reappointed to an equivalent or higher post, while 73 (20.6 percent) of those who resigned quietly returned to government later in a position as high, or higher, than the one they left. Only 4 of the 34 (11.8 percent) protesters were subsequently readmitted to either full-time or part-time prestigious posts, while 127 of the 355 (35.8 percent) who left quietly were given positions. However, in the British government 19 of the 42 (45.2 percent) who resigned in protest later returned to equivalent or higher posts, but only 15 of the

36 (41.7 percent) who left quietly were returned later to similar or better positions. From these statistics Weisband and Franck conclude, in the case of the British, that "those who resigned in public protest did marginally better—but in any event no worse—than their more complaisant colleagues" (p. 97). This stands in stark contrast to the American situation, where resignation with public protest is tantamount to closing the door to further service.

Why are those who call attention to corrupt practices, gross inefficiency, and abuses of power and then resign in protest so consistently harassed and banished from government in the United States? Clearly the answer cannot be so simple as the one provided by the Leahy committee. It is not just a difference between public organizations and those in the private sector, as that committee's study suggests. If it were only a matter of government organizations not being required to turn a profit and therefore becoming preoccupied with image management, why is this not true of Great Britain? Furthermore, the Senate committee report assumes a significantly stronger concern for rooting out corruption, mismanagement, and inefficiency in business and industry than seems justified.

Private-Sector Norms. Both Weisband and Franck (1975) and the Leahy committee (1978) conclude that a team-player ethic is dominant in the United States, but they disagree about its source. While the Senate committee identifies this ethic with an absence of private-sector incentives and demands, the authors of *Resignation in Protest* argue the opposite—that the team ethic has its origins in business, industry, and the legal profession and is carried into government by officials from these areas of the private sector. They maintain that the ethical standards of law and big business have come to permeate the upper echelons of government where the norms for the entire system are established. According to their research, 289 (76.9 percent) of the 389 American resigners were either big-business executives or attorneys, or both, before entering government. They conclude that the "boardroom ethic" of corporate loyalty, and the tendency of attorneys to view their government employer as a client, both militate against speaking out about an organization's "dirty linen." Thus the Leahy committee laments the lack of private-sector influence in government, while Weisband and Franck lay the blame on its presence.

In addition to the operative values of business and the legal profession, Weisband and Franck also identify two other sources of the team-player ethic.

Antitattling. In addition to the operative values of business and the legal profession, Weisband and Franck also identify two sources of the team-player ethic: the more pervasive antitattling conditioning which most Americans experience from a very early age, together with the bureaucratic code of subservience to the hierarchy. In the former case, Piaget's studies of child development are cited as evidence for a socialization process that discourages tattle-telling. Moral maturity is equated with maintaining peer group solidarity over against adult authority; the tattler who ingratiates himself with authority figures is viewed as not only immature but also deserving of ostracism from the group. While this rejection of dependence on adult authority may be a healthy requirement for reciprocal peer-group relations among children, these authors argue that it tends to be maintained inappropriately into adulthood.

Bureaucratic Norms. The final source of the team ethic discussed by Weisband and Franck is the bureaucratic code of subservience to the organizational hierarchy. As public employees move up the career ladder, the norm of deference to those higher up tends to be internalized and reinforced through the bureaucratic socialization process. However, what begins as an appropriate civil service ethic of acknowledging legally constituted authority can become so ingrained and dominant that some who rise through the ranks over a period of years to a position of considerable responsibility have difficulty acting against the illegal, improper, or abusive exercise of authority from above.

The Agentic Shift

While the civil servant's tendency to be overly deferential to superiors may be intensified through the socialization process, there is evidence that this may be a far more pervasive problem in our society. Stanley Milgram's research (1974) indicates that a large percentage of the American population may be inclined to obey authority, even when doing so involves actions that are apparently dangerous to others. Milgram conducted a series of experiments designed to test Americans' willingness to obey authority, with a broad range of occupations included in each experiment.

The basic design of these investigations involved naive subjects who believed they were participating in experiments on the effectiveness of punishment in the learning process. These subjects, in the role of "teacher," were instructed to read a list of paired words to a "learner" whose task was to memorize them. Whenever the learner answered incorrectly, the teacher was instructed to administer a progressively intense electrical shock. After each wrong answer the teacher pushed the next in a series of switches, which were labeled from 15 to 450 volts in strength, with verbal designations ranging from "Slight Shock" to "Danger—Severe Shock." The learner, who was in fact an actor hired to participate in the project, was not actually receiving the shock. Concealed behind a screen, he would play tapes with groans of discomfort, followed by loud protests against continuing the procedure, expressions of fear about a possible heart attack and agonizing screams as the electrical shock reached high voltage levels, and finally complete silence.

The fact that 62 percent of the subjects were willing to administer the most intense level of shock—450 volts—under instruction from the experimenter was surprising to those conducting the study and to a panel of thirty-nine psychiatrists asked to predict the behavior of those involved in this kind of experiment. After hearing a lecture on the experiment, all thirty-nine expected disobedience before the halfway point on the shock scale, 195 volts. Yet almost two-thirds of those ordinary Americans were willing to follow orders obediently, even in the face of unmistakable evidence that another innocent human being was suffering severe pain and terror. A surprising number were even willing to force the learner's hand onto an electrode.

Why were so many so obedient under these circumstances? Milgram identified a number of factors in accounting for this surprising behavior, but the primary dynamic involved is rooted in the nature of hierarchical structures. He refers to it as the "agentic shift" (p. 132).

Individual behavior is limited and controlled, according to Milgram, by internal inhibitors that we sometimes refer to as conscience. However, when individuals are brought together in a hierarchical relationship their actions must be coordinated; external sources of control must be created. Internal inhibitors, then, must yield to some extent to this external source of control: "The inhibitory mechanisms which are vital when the individual element functions by itself become secondary to the need to cede control to the coordinating component" (p. 129). Internal changes that suppress local control for the sake of system coherence must take place. In other words, conscience is diminished when a person enters a hierarchical structure.

Thus, in the organizational society there are two functional modes: the autonomous, self-directed mode, and the systemic or organizational mode. The transition from autonomous to organizational functioning is the "agentic shift." It involves an alteration of attitude; we shift from acting out our own purposes to an attitude of acting as an agent who executes the wishes of another person. When an individual views himself in this agentic state "profound alterations occur in his behavior and his internal functioning" (p. 133). He renders himself open to control by those in authority. Milgram observes that the individual has a degree of freedom to choose whether he defines himself as being in an agentic state, but once he does so "the individual no longer views himself as responsible for his own actions but defines himself as an instrument for carrying out the wishes of others" (p. 134). The extent to which any given individual is willing to make the agentic shift depends largely on socialization through experiences of obedience to authority in family life and organizational participation from the earliest years. In modern society this process is intensified by the way individuals are taught to obey *impersonal* authorities based on "abstract rank, indicated by an insignia, uniform, or title" (p. 137).

Milgram's conclusion is particularly relevant to the concerns of this book: "The most far reaching consequence of the agentic shift is that a man feels responsible *to* the authority directing him but feels no responsibility *for* the content of the actions that the authority prescribes" (pp. 145–146). An alteration in personal sub-jective responsibility occurs, which brings it into congruence with the objective responsibility defined and projected by someone in authority. "Morality," Milgram explains, "does not disappear, but acquires a radically different focus: the subordinate person feels shame or pride depending on how adequately he has performed the actions called for by the authority" (p. 146). The definition of a moral act becomes reduced to obedience to authority. Responsibility for the consequences of our actions is thus destroyed; we believe that the authority chose the act, not us; the person in authority is per-ceived to be responsible.

This displacement of personal responsibility is clearly evi-dent in the legal defense presented for Colonel General Alfred Jodl at the Nuremberg trials of Nazi war criminals in 1945 (French, 1972). His counsel, Dr. Exner, argued:

> Whether or not to wage a war is a political question and is the politician's concern. The question of how to wage war is the only question concerning the Armed Forces [p. 197].

> But if he [the military officer] plans and carries out the plan of a possible war, that is, in case the political leadership de-cides on war, he does nothing but his evident duty [p. 198].

> One would object that it is not his affair, not an affair of his conscience to examine the admissibility of the war, but that this is the duty of the responsible state authorities [p. 198].

The separation of politics from administration, the strict mainte-nance of monocratic hierarchical relationships of authority and re-sponsibility, and a firm distinction between substantive and instrumental reasoning combine to exculpate the agent.

Adolf Eichmann, the Nazi S.S. architect of Hitler's "final solution" of the "Jewish problem," epitomized this shift in attitude and behavior. Feeling no sense of personal responsibility for the extermination of millions of Jews, Eichmann freely admitted his deeds when he was captured by Israeli commandos in Argentina, again under interrogation in Israel, and once again during his trial (Arendt, 1963; Harel, 1975). He repeatedly insisted that he was only carrying out the orders of his superiors and, therefore, was guilty only of "aiding and abetting" in these acts (Arendt, 1963). In an attempt to deflect culpability from himself, Eichmann argued that he did not personally carry out those heinous acts of murder and torture, nor did he act out of any personal feelings of hatred for Jews in his organizational and administrative duties (Arendt, 1963).

In her study of Eichmann, Hannah Arendt (1963) concluded that he represented "a new type of criminal" who "commits his crimes under circumstances that make it well-nigh impossible for him to know or feel that he is doing wrong" (p. 253). Viewing himself only as an instrument of a large hierarchical organization, Eichmann was devoid of any sense of a motivation of his own, save that of efficiently carrying out the will of others. Initiative did not lie within himself, but with the Nazi high command. Arendt notes that his very language evidenced a total absorption of the self into a bureaucratic role. Eichmann seemed incapable of speaking anything but "officialese"; his vocabulary consisted of learned "clichés" and "stock phrases which obscured the stark realities of the death camps and the ovens. The longer one listened to him," says Arendt, "the more obvious it became that his inability to speak was closely connected with an inability to think, namely, to think from the standpoint of someone else" (p. 44).

If Arendt's analysis is correct, the agentic shift was almost total in Eichmann; self-deception was nearly complete. Reflective thought issuing from a multifaceted mentality capable of imagining alternatives and viewing one role in the complex perspective of many others had been all but smothered. The surrender to an instrumental role that appeared to obviate personal choice precluded the ability to empathize and to freely respond empathetically. Although certified as normal by half a dozen psychiatrists, Eichmann had apparently managed to so thoroughly become the "agent" that the connection between his conduct and its consequences for others was severed. Only the link between conduct and the will of superiors remained.

This diminution of personal responsibility for the consequences of one's action or inaction in the agentic state ought to be of major concern in a consideration of administrative ethics. If we worry that so few public servants speak out against destructive authority, if loyalty to superiors tends to override individual conscience and obligations to the citizenry, then Milgram's findings should cause us to inquire further into means of modifying the extent to which individuals in public service make the agentic shift.

Organizational Remedies

If fear of reprisal were the only impediment to individual ethical action, schemes to protect legitimate whistle blowers would appear to be the most productive approach. The U.S. Office of Special Counsel under the Merit Systems Protection Board (MSPB), set up to confidentially receive and investigate complaints of improper and illegal activities, seems a reasonable way to provide some degree of protection from hierarchical vindictiveness ("Proposed Civil Service Changes . . .," 1978). Mechanisms such as the Fraud Task Force of the U.S. General Accounting Office (GAO), with a "hotline" for anyone aware of corrupt activities within the federal government, also offer hope for confidential handling of these matters.

It is clear that organizational strategies of this kind cannot provide total confidentiality, nor can they assure public servants that whistle blowing will no longer be a hazardous enterprise. However, they do offer greater security in speaking out than previously existed; the risk level is reduced to some extent. The initial responses of federal employees seem to bear this out. During its first year the Office of Special Counsel reportedly received 1,925 complaints with sufficient basis for opening a case. Whistle blowers constituted 5 percent of the total, or 96 cases; an additional 27 percent, or 520 cases, dealt with complaints of reprisals (*First Annual Report to the Congress*, 1979). This is an astonishing outpouring of grievances and concerns to a new and untried agency with no track record in protecting the anonymity of the complainant, which suggests that the will to maintain ethical conduct is strongly present among some in the public service. Given only *promises* of confidentiality, they will come forward with information.

The GAO Fraud Task Force experienced an even larger response, perhaps owing to its longer history and established credibility. According to Lawrence Sullivan, a member of the Task Force, during its first seven months of operation in 1979 over 6,000 calls were received and, after screening, approximately 4,000 appeared substantive. At a meeting of the ASPA Professional Standards and Ethics Committee (August 30, 1979) Sullivan indicated that although these complaints came both from outside and from within the federal government, 28 percent of the callers were federal employees, blowing the whistle on illegal conduct. Apparently not all public servants make the "agentic shift" so totally as to impair their ability to act independently and exercise personal responsibility on occasion.

Unfortunately, the mechanisms provided by the Office of Special Counsel (OSC) do not seem to have been very effective in protecting whistle blowers from retaliation by their superiors. Caiden and Truelson (1988, p. 122), evaluating these reforms ten years after their establishment, conclude: "In practice, the new legislation has been weakly enforced. Congress, federal employee representatives, and the General Accounting Office (GAO) have all been critical of the Special Counsel for failing to provide adequate protection to whistleblowers, of the MSPB's exacting standards of proof of reprisal action, and of the failure of the Special Counsel to convince the MSPB to take the necessary disciplinary action against victimisers."

Support for this pessimistic assessment comes from a report prepared by the MSPB (1984), which compared data from random samples of federal employees in 1980 (13,078 employees) and 1983 (7,563 employees) concerning whistle blowing in the federal government. In both years approximately 70 percent of those who reported direct knowledge of an illegal or wasteful activity said they did not report it to anyone. In 1980, 20 percent gave fear of reprisal as one reason for taking no action; by 1983 this number had risen to 37 percent. Thus, the number of fearful employees had almost doubled under the protection of the new mechanisms (pp. 5–6). (The most frequently cited reason, given by 53 percent in each year, was belief that reporting the misconduct would not bring about any change for the better.)

Similarly, Jos, Tompkins, and Hays (1989, p. 554), in their study of whistle blowers, 55 percent of whom were from the federal government, found the OSC and the MSPB were rated among the least helpful. On a seven-point helpfulness scale (7 being most helpful) the OSC received an average rating of 1.4 and the MSPB of 1.9. However, these authors do acknowledge that certain flaws built into the original structure and mission of the OSC may have been remedied by a whistle blower protection act signed into law on April 10, 1989 (p. 558). This act "makes the OSC an independent agency, specifies that its mandate includes protecting whistleblowers, and gives the OSC the authority to issue a 45-day stay prohibiting an agency from demoting or firing a worker who has filed a complaint" (p. 558). It also revises the previous burden of proof by making it necessary for a whistle blower only to show that his whistle blowing was a contributing factor in his termination or harassment, instead of a significant or predominant factor.

Beyond these specific devices for easing the burden of whistle blowers, the American Society for Public Administration (1979) adopted a statement entitled "Whistle Blowing, A Time to Listen . . . A Time to Hear," which calls for a more comprehensive organizational approach to the problem. This position paper encourages those in government to obviate the need for whistle blowing by addressing the underlying problems. ASPA emphasizes the importance of establishing and enforcing policies that articulate the ethical standards of public service, regularly communicating these expectations to employees, creating procedures for conducting internal investigation of alleged wrongdoings, providing "dissent channels to permit contrary or alternative views on policy issues to be reviewed at a higher level" (p. 3), and encouraging managers to focus on the substance and merits of an employee's allegations, rather than being preoccupied with "the assumed motivations of dissenters or whistle blowers" (p. 4).

These organizational approaches are necessary to make it possible for public servants to properly define the limits of administrative loyalty and respond responsibly. The organizational components of responsible conduct discussed in Chapter Six, along with these measures specifically oriented toward whistle blowing, are sufficient to suggest the outlines of the organizational requirements.

Individual Responsibility

However, these strategies, while important, are not in themselves sufficient. The more difficult long-run task for those concerned about ethical conduct in public administration involves buttressing ethical autonomy and individual responsibility among those who already possess these attributes in some measure, and extending them to others who may tend to function largely as agents with little clarity about the boundaries of loyalty to an organizational hierarchy. This effort must begin with the reassertion of individual responsibility for one's actions.

The Nuremberg Principle. The Nuremberg Charter, which established the principles and procedures for the trials of the Nazi war criminals following World War II, included these key articles in Section II:

> Article 7. The official position of defendants, whether as Heads of State or responsible officials in Government Departments, shall not be considered as freeing them from responsibility or mitigating punishment.
> Article 8. The fact that the Defendant acted pursuant to an order of his Government or of a superior shall not free him from responsibility, but may be considered in mitigation of punishment if the Tribunal determines that justice so requires [Jackson, 1947, p. 23].

Against the defense offered by Jodl, Eichmann, and others, these articles maintained from the outset that individuals are ultimately responsible for their deeds and must be held accountable before the bar of justice. Neither an official role nor obedience to authority may be used to excuse conduct.

In his opening statement before the Nuremberg Tribunal, Robert H. Jackson, chief of counsel for the United States, argued that the doctrine of individual responsibility for crimes in the international arena had a long history in matters of piracy and brigandage. He insisted, "Only sanctions which reach individuals can peacefully and effectively be enforced." Jackson further maintained: "Crimes always are committed only by persons. While it is quite proper to employ the fiction of responsibility of a state or corporation for the purpose of imposing a collective liability, it is quite intolerable to let such a legalism become the basis of personal immunity" (1947, pp. 88–89).

Jackson continued to advance this principle in his closing address before the tribunal by arguing that all those who sought refuge in the collective responsibility of the Nazi regime, in fact, individually supported that government and never directly challenged its policies: "Nowhere do we find an instance where any one of the defendants stood up against the rest and said: 'This thing is wrong and I will not go along with it'" (pp. 88–89).

Although Hitler's Germany, with its mail-fisted totalitarianism, its bizarre pageantry, and its horrifying slaughter of human life may seem far removed from the mundane ethical problems of contemporary public administrators, nevertheless these Nuremberg principles are relevant and worthy of attention. Under these principles men were indicted and found guilty as "individually responsible for their own acts and for all acts committed by any persons in the execution of such plan or conspiracy" (Jackson, 1946, p. 115). They remind us that although we act as agents for others, we must never view ourselves as only instruments in their hands; though we accept roles that obligate us to act in ways that are not precisely congruent with the choices we would make if acting alone, we are not free to abandon conscience as we consider how to enact those roles, and as we struggle to discern where the boundaries of loyalty lie. We are finally responsible for saying yes or no to superiors, peers, and collectivities in which we participate.

The Final Safeguard. Individual responsibility, insofar as it can be inculcated, is a necessary counterbalance to the agentic shift that bureaucratic organizations tend to require. Wakefield (1976) argues that both a *feeling* of being responsible as an individual, and objectively *being held accountable* by the law and the citizenry for our deeds are the most ultimate buttresses of public-service ethics. Organizational arrangements, designs, and devices are desirable and necessary for the day-to-day routine maintenance of responsibility. However, when organizational goals are seriously diverted from their legal mandate, and the public interest is displaced by private interests, the final safeguards against corruption and subversion of democratic government are a commitment to responsible conduct on the part of individual citizens employed by government, and a public that can exact accountability from them.

This means that although we might not commit misdeeds directly and overtly ourselves, awareness of such conduct by subordinates, peers, or superiors imposes responsibility for rectification, as far as possible. In the judgment of the District Court of Jerusalem against Adolph Eichmann, the judges concluded that with complex crimes involving many people "on various levels and in various modes of activity—the planners, the organizers, and those executing the deeds, according to their various ranks . . . the extent to which any one of the many criminals was close to or remote from the actual killer of the victim means nothing, so far as the measure of his responsibility is concerned. *On the contrary, in general the degree of responsibility increases as we draw further away from the man who uses the fatal instrument with his own hands*" (Arendt, 1963, p. 225, emphasis added). If the impropriety of an act is recognized, distance from its specific overt commission quite likely provides greater perspective for moral judgment and also often implies broader administrative contributions which make that act, and others like it, possible.

Reflecting on the problem of individual versus collective responsibility for the massacre at My Lai during the Vietnam War, Stanley Bates (1972) maintains that although we are often implicated and constrained by our relationships and bonds to others, finally we are morally, if not legally, responsible for what we do or fail to do as individuals. A naive individualism that does not acknowledge the effects of socialization and the power of group identification is to be eschewed; we are not isolated entities free from the encumbrances of association with wrongdoers. Nevertheless, according to Bates, each of us is responsible for the particular things we do as well as the things we omit. We may not have personally engaged in an act, but may have made it possible for someone else to do so. We may not have been directly involved, but may not have done anything to prevent the act. We may not have been able to prevent the act, but may have done nothing to expose the actors, or attempted to mitigate the damage incurred to individual victims or society.

From this perspective a public administrator is individually responsible for avoiding direct or indirect participation in unethical actions, for attempting to prevent such actions by others, for exposing to public view those things that could not be prevented, and for at least attempting to diminish the destructive impacts of wrongdoing. Responsibility in these forms may from time to time confront us with the necessity of defining the limits of loyalty to superiors and clarifying the boundaries of organizational obligation. Dealing with these situations requires a willingness to bracket the claims of the organization we work for or participate in. Maintaining individual responsibility may even ultimately call for resistance to organizational demands and pressures.

Individual Ethical Autonomy in Organizations

The Problem of Organizational Dominance. William H. Whyte, Jr., (1956) outlined the fundamental problem for individual autonomy within organizations in *The Organization Man*. Whyte recognized that the age of organization was upon us and that it embodied an ethic that he variously termed "the social ethic," "an organization ethic," and "a bureaucratic ethic" (p. 6). According to Whyte, the essence of this ethic is a commitment to resolve the tension between individuals and organizations by encouraging a primary identification with the organization, "a belief in belongingness as the ultimate need of the individual." It serves the purpose of making "morally legitimate the pressures of society against the individual" (p. 7).

While Whyte took a dim view of this tendency to absorb individuals into organizational structures and replace their autonomy with collective determination of goals and values, he recognized that the solution was not to be found in a flight from organizational society. Such notions amounted to "misplaced nostalgia," which only confused the issue. Rather, Whyte understood the problem as maintaining "individualism *within* organization life" (p. 11). Organizations, as such, are not inherently evil; organizations "can be changed by man," he insisted (p. 13).

Whyte argued that the evil lies in our unwillingness to acknowledge the conflict that must exist between individuals and collectivities, and our failure to provide for that conflict within organizational life. In fact, not only do we refuse to face this necessary antipathy and divergence of interests, but we actively work at suppressing individual values and behavior that are at odds with those of organizations. From this perspective establishing, reestablishing, and maintaining boundaries between individuals and the organizations they participate in are essential if proper limits are to be established for administrative responsibility.

As is sometimes the case with social critics, Whyte's analysis of the problem was more thorough than his prescriptions for coming to grips with it. Essentially, *The Organization Man* was an exhortation to resist organizational domination of one's values, world view, and conduct. It was a clarion call to fight the organization's seduction into the security and passivity of its all-encompassing web; a cry for resistance to the temptation to abdicate individual responsibility; a reassertion of the primacy of individuality in the face of pressure to conform to the organization's needs and goals.

Recently, this concern for the pervasive subordination of the individual to the organization has been renewed and recommendations have been offered to control the dominance of organizations. William Scott and David K. Hart (1979) have written about the "organizational imperative" that, in their view, has transformed American values. This imperative assumes that "whatever is good for the individual can only come from the modern organization" and "therefore, all behavior must enhance the health of such organizations" (p. 43). Although they basically restate and elaborate the central themes previously explored by Whyte, Scott and Hart attempt to carry the discussion further by offering an analysis of the "role hierarchy" of the modern organization, made up of a few "significant people" at the top, the larger number of "professional people" in the middle, and the mass of "insignificant people" at the bottom.

Scott and Hart conclude, pessimistically, that "totalitarian America" (p. 211) is not far away and it can be turned back only by the "professional people" who can "recognize their historical potential and seize their opportunity to challenge the organizational imperative and reform modern organizations" (pp. 220–221). The villain in the piece, according to Scott and Hart, is current management philosophy, since "the modern organization is value neutral" (p. 223).

In the unlikely event that the professional stratum can and will use its technical scientific leverage, as well as its strategic position, to reestablish the "individual imperative," then modern organizations may be reformed, "totalitarian America" forestalled, and "transcendent America" brought into being. To accomplish this task, new managerial values are needed, which assume that "all individuals have the natural right to the realization of the full potential of every stage of their lives; therefore, all institutions must be predicated upon that right" (p. 226).

Although the overall tone of the argument is colored with an overly dramatic apocalyptic vision of imminent totalitarianism, Scott and Hart have served to remind us again that organizations tend to absorb all individual autonomy into loyalty to the collective goals. However, their reluctant hope that the "professional people" may come riding to our rescue armed with a new philosophy of management is at the same time too hopeful and too pessimistic. Too much may be expected of the professionals and too little from the insignificant people.

Organization Delimitation and Transcendence. A more sophisticated and theoretically complex approach to the all-consuming dominance of organizations is found in the work of Alberto Guerreiro Ramos (1981). He also is concerned with administrative theory, but views its emergence in the context of a more inclusive economic, social, and political system. In a chapter entitled "Theory of Social Systems Delimitation: A Paradigmatic Statement," Ramos views modern administrative perspectives as the product of a "market-dominated social reality" that places primary value on utility maximization. This means that everything individuals do tends to be considered an occasion for achieving the greatest return for available resources. Instrumental rationality dominates thought about the world and our life in it; substantive rationality unconcerned with the achievement of ends tends to be devalued and ignored. Personal actualization is subordinated to economizing.

Thus, Ramos's concern is not limited to organizations, but begins with a comprehensive social analysis that identifies the market mentality as the pervasive and dominant model for political, economic, and social existence. He addresses the problem of organizational theory from this broader theoretical perspective. It is not simply organizations that usurp individuality, but a world view that provides no room for nonmarket activity.

From Ramos's perspective, administrative theory incorrectly assumes that the economizing behavior created by this kind of socialization is synonymous with human nature. The result of this confusion is an attempt to overorganize individuals under the belief that therein lies the path to self-actualization. Human relations experts and organizational development specialists set about the task of integrating individuals into organizations by employing behavioral science and group dynamics technology. The actual consequence of these misplaced efforts, say Ramos, is "the transformation of the entire society into an operationalized universe in which the individual is alway expected to live as an actor with a *prescribed* role" (emphasis added). Hence, the individual is depersonalized and deprived of the conditions for an independent creative personal life: "truly private place and time" (p. 126).

Ramos's approach to dealing with this destructive set of dynamics is one of social systems analysis and design. Briefly, the "paraeconomic" model that evolves from this process includes (1) a view of society as a multiplicity of "enclaves" in which human beings engage in a variety of different but ultimately integrative substantive pursuits, and (2) a societal governance system that can develop policies necessary for optimal transaction among those various enclaves. Market behavior is not viewed as illegitimate, but rather it is bounded and relegated to an incidental, secondary role in individual self-actualization. Utility maximization becomes one form of behavior among many others, instead of the dominant one into which individuals are socialized.

Organization delimitation, then, is essential to this model for social systems design. Market-oriented organizations, which include those public and private systems in which employment occurs, must be bounded, not simply by attempting to manage individual organizations differently, but by managing the whole society with human self-actualization as the goal (Ramos, 1972). "Parenthetical man" must be allowed to replace the "operational man" of a market-dominated society.

"Parenthetical men" are not "integrated" into organizations, but make use of them for certain needs. They "bracket" belief in these ordinary phenomena and "deliberately try to become rootless" in their society in order to establish sufficient distance to understand it. They maintain detachment, and a degree of aloofness, from the surrounding social conditions, including organizations in which they participate, to avoid being captured and totally assimilated to their limited goals and values.

Organization delimitation is already under way in the United States, according to Ramos. A paraeconomy is beginning to manifest itself in the neighborhood movement, "nonviolent guerrilla warfare" within organizations, and in the works of A. K. Bierman, Donald Schön, Ralph Nader, John Gardner, Kenneth Boulding, Barry Commoner, and Robert Townsend.

These perspectives advanced by Whyte, Scott and Hart, and Ramos are introduced in this chapter to suggest the importance of bounding organizational loyalties and commitments in a conscious, active, and systematic fashion if we are to maintain any degree of ethical autonomy. Unless we consistently maintain a larger perspective of other roles, other obligations, other personal needs for self-development, and other legitimate enclaves of human activity, the boundaries of administrative responsibility may become all inclusive. If that occurs, when crises of conscience arise, the limits of administrative loyalty may be impossible to discern because they have become so encompassing that the horizon is too far away to be visible. Worse yet, there may be so little of ourselves remaining beyond the organization's boundaries that these crises are never experienced. This may have been the case with Eichmann, and with some of those involved in Watergate.

All too often I have found myself dealing with practitioners in workshops on administrative ethics who have little ethical autonomy because they allow the organizations that employ them too much importance in the overall pattern of their lives. Work and participation in the organization are their dominant activity and affiliation. Their self-image, self-esteem, and life meaning are tied far too much to the workplace. Consequently, they have difficulty

finding perspectives from which to evaluate the claims of the organization. They lack values and self-understanding from the other
"enclaves" that Ramos considers necessary to prevent being captured by work organizations. Otherwise, when the organization
commands there is only the bureaucratic ethic of obedience to authority and loyalty to the hierarchy to guide ethical judgment.

Organization delimitation means that we make no total commitments to particular collectivities but maintain a certain tenta-
tiveness in dealing with all of them. This degree of detachment
should not suggest a lack of seriousness or a life of superficial dab-
bling. Rather, it represents a recognition of the complexities of
human intelligence and identity, as well as the multiple needs of
self-expression and association. Simply put, life is not all one thing;
to act otherwise is to distort human perception and judgment. It is
to make ourselves ethically a prisoner of those aspects of life to
which time, effort, and identity have been overcommitted.

To develop this approach a bit further, delimiting an organization implies an ability to transcend its boundaries while working within it. The term *transcendence* is used here to suggest the
cultivation of ethical values and principles rooted outside the bureaucratic structure and its inherent norms, the maintenance of
sources of identity beyond the work organization, and the adoption
of a delimiting view of the organization in relation to other aspects
of life.

In order to keep the bureaucratic machine in the service of
the public, rather than of itself or special interests, values and principles essential to democratic political community must provide
constant points of reference from beyond the boundaries of the organization for both the substantive goals and the functional procedures of the organization. At an earlier time, when we assumed the
separability of politics and administration and the possibility of
limiting administrative discretion to functional decisions, this was
the role assigned the political official. The public organization and
its administrators were mere tools in the hands of politicians, who
were the custodians of the values of the political community. Bureaucratic ethics were constrained by political values determined
outside the organization in the legislative process.

However, since we no longer assume that politics and administration can be neatly and clearly understood as discrete processes, we must alter our thinking about how bureaucracy is maintained in the service of the citizenry. Public administrators inside the organization must be understood as bearing an obligation to internalize and cultivate values from the American political community. Their professional values must transcend the limits of the organization and delimit its sway over their professional conduct. The problem, of course, is identifying those values. Addressing it lies beyond the scope of this book, but it is one of the most difficult and important items on the agenda for research and theory development in administrative ethics.

In addition to values drawn from outside the organization, sources of identity beyond its boundaries are also essential. Not only should administrators bring publicly oriented values into the bureaucracy from the political community, but they should also cultivate certain other sources of identity that help to constrain organizational self-service and brake the tendency toward bureaucratic absolutism. As a minimum, public administrators need to develop their professional, political, and community identities.

A professional identity requires continuing professional education and training, involvement in professional associations, regular attention to professional literature, and a sense of responsibility for the public administrative role. Without these a public administrator is cognitively disadvantaged in dealing with organizational definitions of public problems, appropriate administrative conduct, and the purposes of government. In the absence of professional identity the organization's definitions tend to occupy the entire field; vision is narrowed to the organization's interests; responsibility shrinks to the boundaries of the organization; obligation is restricted to the chain of command.

A political identity entails active attention to a broad range of issues on the public agenda. It means more than simple membership in a political party, although that certainly might be included in the development of our political profile. More importantly, public administrators should cultivate independent political judgment on local, state, and national issues. A lively and well-developed sense of personal political position keeps the political process prominently in mind as the larger context within which the organization functions.

Active political involvement keeps alive the public administrator's larger obligation as a citizen of the political community.

A community identity suggests that we are engaged with manifestations of public life that occur close to home at the neighborhood, area, and municipal level. Some might reasonably argue for religious and ethnic identities as well. Attention to neighborhood issues, the efforts of voluntary associations, public school activities, and the affairs of local religious organizations root our mind and self-image in specific human problems and projects. This kind of identity provides a degree of protection from bureaucratic and intellectual abstractions, and vivid points of reference for the aims and purposes of government. Principles such as the public interest, social equity, regime values, and citizenship obligation can be tested in observable social life and personal experience.

A Bill of Rights for the Workplace. A more specific approach to the dilemma of the individual within both public and private organizations is provided by David Ewing's *Freedom Inside the Organization* (1977). Less global than Ramos but consistent with his theoretical perspective, and more thorough and analytical than Scott and Hart, Ewing's concern is that Americans have as citizens enjoyed certain rights that they are required to leave behind when they enter the doors of the organizations in which they work. Freedom of speech, press, and assembly, due process of law, privacy, and freedom of conscience—most Americans are not guaranteed these rights in the workplace.

Ewing argues that "rightlessness" as individuals inside employing organizations is a matter of grave concern since many of them are larger in population than the original thirteen colonies. They are, in fact, "minigovernments" (p. 21) that rule over people's lives for forty or more hours per week. The net effect is that individual rights guaranteed by the U.S. Constitution are abrogated for a large portion of a citizen's working years. Ewing argues that "for all practical purposes, employees are required to be as obedient to their superiors, regardless of ethical and legal considerations, as are workers in totalitarian countries" (p. 21).

Why has this domination of organizations over their employees been allowed to exist? Scott and Hart blame modern management philosophy and organization theory; Ramos identifies the problem with socialization into a market-oriented reality; Ewing finds an additional culprit in the law. The Anglo-Saxon legal principle of freedom of contract has consistently been applied to employer-employee relationships, leading to the view that both enter equally into a voluntary agreement that either can choose to terminate. The employee is free to resign and go elsewhere, just as the employer is free to terminate workers at will. Consequently, the courts have adopted a conservative posture in intervening in these relationships.

Coupled with the law of contracts is an ancient legal tradition that gives the employer the upper hand in determining the conditions of employment. The rights of master and servant, originating in Roman law, were carried over into Anglo-Saxon law as the model of the employment relationship. Thus, modern employer prerogatives in treatment of the worker are rooted in the centuries-old favored status of the master over his servants. According to Ewing, the organizations in which people are employed still retain these prerogatives to a large extent.

In the face of these legal constraints against freedom within organizations, Ewing finds growing inclinations among employees to resist organizational pressures for total loyalty and submission. Far from being an impotent or complacent mass of "insignificant people," Ewing finds mounting rebelliousness, which he explains on the basis of Maslow's hierarchy of needs. Employee demands for greater control over their own lives is a manifestation of a relatively affluent society that has satisfied most of the lower-order survival needs and is now insisting on satisfaction of the higher-level needs for social relationships and self-development.

Ewing's proposals for constraining the power of organizations over individuals reflect his predominantly legal orientation. His essential prescription is organizational constitutionalism, similar to that associated with Elliott Jacques (see Chapter Six), including an enforceable employee bill of rights. If individuals are to be able to carry out both their rights and their obligations as citizens, they must be protected by clearly defined legal constraints on organizational power and effective institutional procedures for ensuring due process. Ewing argues that these measures are necessary to allow individual conscience to assert itself against self-serving organizations.

Components of Individual Autonomy

It appears, then, that three essential ingredients are required if we are to effectively maintain limits on our administrative responsibility and loyalty to an organization. These ingredients are the components of individual autonomy. First, it is necessary to delimit work organizations and cultivate an identity that transcends their boundaries. Second, it is important to establish legal and institutional mechanisms for constraining organizational power and protecting individual rights to exercise ethical autonomy. Finally, self-awareness concerning values, rights, needs, duties, and obligations within and beyond the organization is required if we are to be able to act as individuals in specific situations. It is this third aspect about which more must be said.

The components of responsible conduct discussed in Chapter Six are all potential behavior-control mechanisms; they can be employed for shaping the conduct of individuals within organizations toward certain desired ends. Societal expectations, individual attributes, organizational structure, and a managed organizational culture are all instruments for directing behavior according to the mandated goals of the organization. However, when the organization appears to be deviating from these legitimate goals, or when the preservation of an individual's own integrity conflicts with the organization's demands, the problem becomes one of resisting these behavior controls.

Ethic of Awareness. Perry London (1971) argues that the power to resist behavior controls is to be found ultimately only in human awareness. It is through self-awareness that self-control can be established: "The key to mastery of self is not will, which reduces, even subjectively, to nothing more than our perception of ourselves as struggling, demanding, or insisting. It is awareness, a set of higher processes in the brain with which we recognize ourselves as having self and from which we derive the special human powers of control which animal passions could not supply" (p. 271).

In his call for an "ethic of awareness," London maintains that our attention tends to be directed outward in modern technological society. We become preoccupied with the things around us, to the exclusion of self-awareness. Thus, having no countervailing sense of individual direction and purpose, we become vulnerable to control from sources beyond ourselves, such as organizations. However, he suggests not that we ignore our surroundings and totally withdraw from collective associations, but rather that we focus more on the subjective self in order to expand its contents. If democracy is to be maintained and free society is to prevail, social control must finally be rooted within individuals in the form of a deep awareness of their own values, needs, and aspirations, as well as how they are related to those of others.

When we approach the limits of loyalty to organizational superiors and consider a confrontation or a breach of relations with the organization, this kind of self-knowledge is essential. In fact, it is essential if we are ever to reach that point in the first place. There must be a sense of personal identity that extends well beyond the organization's boundaries, an integrity that is also vested in other roles as well and seeks a larger fulfillment of the self.

Two of Milgram's students, John Sabini and Maury Silver (1982), find this broader identity the essential ingredient in being able to transcend the limited "technical" responsibility of an organization and fulfill "moral" responsibility by questioning its actions. Moral responsibility cannot be confined within institutions and defined by organizational norms alone. One who has the more expansive view afforded by a larger self-identity may perceive the difference between these two kinds of responsibility and be led to question the legitimacy of the organization's authority when it is used unethically; one whose only or primary identity is contained within an organization has no basis for ever recognizing such illegitimacy.

The kind of reflective analysis and ethical imagination discussed in the first chapter of this book is one means for cultivating a sense of the self in its diversity of roles, interest, obligations, and aspirations. Another process that may be helpful when considering the limits of responsibility and loyalty to a particular organization involves an evaluation of the critical role.

Role Evaluation at the Limits of Organizational Loyalty. As we approach crises in our responsibility to the organizations that employ us, we experience the "inescapable tension between interest and duty" that lies at the heart of public life (Tussman, 1960, p. 18). The interests of the self are at odds with the obligations of the organization. Although this potential conflict gives rise to the routine moral dilemmas associated with divergent role demands discussed in Chapters One through Three, when the tension becomes severe we experience a profound crisis. Our selfhood is threatened; our ability to maintain a sense of identity and integrity is challenged. We wonder whether we can still "look ourselves in the eye"; whether we can "live with ourselves" if we comply with certain orders, or fail to oppose particular decisions and activities. These very common clichés reflect the disintegration of the self that we anticipate and fear. Thus, we grope toward the place where the line must be drawn between ourselves as individuals with a larger array of personal interests to be maintained, on the one hand, and the demands of the organization, on the other.

The typical factors involved are certain sources of duty and obligation associated with both arenas. In the administrative role in a public organization, duties and obligations come from laws, a specific government, superiors, peers, subordinates, and the public. Laws mandate certain activities and constrain others. The particular government that employs us projects a set of expectations ranging from the highly formal and explicit to the implicit and informal. Similarly, our organizational superiors prescribe work routines, establish policies, and issue orders that are sometimes broad and general, but at other times specific and detailed. Peers within the organization, as well as professional colleagues beyond its boundaries, create norms, standards, and reciprocal obligations. Supervising and directing the conduct of subordinates toward the goals of the organization imposes another set of responsibilities. Finally, the public, or publics, with an interest in the organization's function generate a further set of demands and expectations.

In a crisis situation, one or more of these external, organizationally related forces seriously conflict with the interests of the self, which include our values, beliefs, and self-images. As indicated in Chapter One, values are beliefs about appropriate behavior and the desirability of end states. "Justice," "honesty," "equal distribution of wealth," and "collaboration" might be examples of values. Beliefs, as used here, would include the general ways of viewing the world:

"Human beings tend to be competitive."
"Life is a constant struggle."
"Good people usually win in the end."
"There is purpose in the cosmos."
"Government is the servant of the people."

Self-image has to do with the particular beliefs we hold about ourselves: "I am fair, trustworthy, sensitive, independent, strong, competent, and outspoken."

Whenever we are hard pressed by role-related duties or obligations to engage in conduct that is highly inconsistent with one or more of these self-interests, we are presented with a problem in maintaining an integrated sense of who we are. It then becomes necessary to (1) resist the demands of the role, (2) alter our values, beliefs, and self-images, or (3) negotiate some kind of compromise. At this point, evaluation of the role may be helpful in identifying the essential problem and determining a course of action.

Role evaluation may be undertaken at three levels (Downie, 1972). Role legitimacy is the level with the most serious potential consequences. The question to be answered here is: "Is this particular organizational role legitimate for *someone* in society to occupy?" More specifically, should there be an environmental impact analyst, or a budget officer, or a prison warden, or a hospital administrator, or a public executioner? Is any one of these a justifiable role? Am I able to condone the ends for which the role in question was established? If I cannot give an affirmative answer to these questions, a breach in my relationship with the organization is highly probable, and may be accompanied by a fundamental challenge to its existence. If the role I have been occupying is found to be illegitimate according to my values, beliefs, and self-images, I may well feel compelled to speak out against its being occupied by *anyone.*

However, if the role is legitimate for someone, the next consideration is its acceptability to me in particular. I might conclude that the role of public executioner is a necessary and justifiable role in society, but find it unacceptable for myself. Perhaps it is consistent with my understanding of justice to execute persons who commit certain types of crimes, but inconsistent with the image I hold of myself as compassionate, sensitive, and forgiving. At this level of role evaluation the consideration is whether to resign if asked to accept that role, but it probably does not call for an attack on the organization. I am unlikely to challenge the organization's maintenance of the role if I find it unacceptable only for myself.

Role enactment is the next level of evaluation and the least serious in its potential consequences. Even if I am able to condone the role of public executioner and to accept the role for myself, there may still be special circumstances when I cannot carry it out. In a particular case I may believe that the accused did not receive a fair trial, or I may find that one whom I am to execute is a member of my own family. In instances of this kind I am likely to seek negotiation with the organization in order to temporarily adjust my role.

An example that may serve to illustrate the distinctions being developed here is the "Saturday Night Massacre" on October 20, 1973, during the events of Watergate. Archibald Cox, the Watergate Special Prosecutor, had subpoenaed the tape recordings of President Nixon's conversations related to matters under investigation. Nixon responded by ordering Attorney General Elliott Richardson to fire Cox immediately. Richardson refused to comply with the order and resigned. William Ruckelshaus, the deputy attorney general and next in succession, also refused to dismiss Cox and was himself fired. Finally, Robert Bork, the solicitor general, was appointed acting attorney general and carried out the order (Jaworski, 1977; Dean, 1976).

It seems plausible to infer from the information available that both Richardson and Ruckelshaus encountered serious difficulty at the level of role enactment. Apparently neither man had concluded that the role of attorney general had lost its legitimacy, nor had they been unwilling to accept the role for themselves under most circumstances. It was carrying out the role in this specific instance that produced an impediment. The presidential order to fire Archibald Cox violated certain self-interests that neither man was willing to sacrifice, so one resigned and the other was fired. Only Bork was willing to accept and enact the role, presumably because his values, beliefs, and self-image were not seriously threatened.

I may run the risk of being fired if I am unable to carry out the orders of my superiors, as happened to Ruckelshaus, but it is more likely that I will only be temporarily reassigned to other duties. Both formal and informal negotiations about the enactment of roles are common modes of organizational behavior. However, if I regularly encounter problems of role enactment, I may need to reevaluate at one or both of the other two levels. Changes in either the way the role is defined by external sources of duty and obligations on the one hand, or in my self-interests on the other, may precipitate an ethical dilemma that calls for such a reevaluation. Self-conscious and systematic management of this process may be helpful in arriving at appropriate modes of action. It is important to be clear about the source of an ethical dilemma: Is it only the circumstances of a specific task? Is the role itself being redefined by the law or superiors so that it is becoming unacceptable? Illegitimate? Are my values, beliefs, or self-image changing in such a way that the role no longer fits me? Am I still able to condone and support the maintenance of the role itself, apart from my own fulfillment of it?

Answers to these questions suggest a range of responses, from negotiating changes in specific tasks on a one-time basis, to seeking more permanent changes in the role, to resignation or transfer to another job, to challenging the legitimacy of the role and ultimately that of the organization itself. Whistle blowing and resignation in protest are appropriate responses at this extreme end of the spectrum, when simply leaving the organization and allowing it to continue on its course undisturbed are unacceptable to our conscience. However, actions of this kind are probably not appropriate if our values, beliefs, and self-image create only infrequent or minor problems in accepting or enacting the role. (Nader, Perkas, and Blackwell, 1972, provide helpful advice on thinking through the possibility of blowing the whistle.)

The limits of organizational loyalty are difficult to identify. Our socialization, the constant organizational pressure to identify with its collective goals and values, and the absence or ineffectiveness of legal and institutional supports for individual autonomy create a murky environment in which it is difficult to discern the boundaries of our obligation. New legislation, new structural arrangements, and a delimiting approach to organizations will help, but without a conscious effort to continuously cultivate self-awareness of the dynamic relationship between the interests of the self and the demands of the role, then laws and organizational safeguards are likely to be of no avail. All three components of individual autonomy are required.

Conclusion

A Model of Responsible
Administration

The vision that emerges from the previous chapters on the meaning of responsible public administration is that of a juggler managing a multitude of competing obligations and interests. The meaning of responsible administrative conduct under these circumstances is problematic indeed. Public administrators find themselves caught between their objective responsibility on the one hand and their subjective responsibility on the other. At times they feel and believe themselves to be responsible for acting in ways that are at odds with what the organizational hierarchy or the law holds them accountable for. These conflicts between objective and subjective responsibility are manifested in three specific types of conflicting responsibility: conflicts of authority, role conflicts, and conflicts of interest. Each confronts public administrators with quandaries about where their ultimate responsibility lies and presents opportunities to engage in unethical conduct.

The argument began in Chapter One with the assertion that administrators' ethical identity emerges incrementally from the pattern of decisions that they make over the course of a career. More often than not this is done without much conscious consideration of the ethical dimensions of these decisions. However, it was suggested that without the guidance of a coherent and widely shared tradition, public administrators, like all other modern people, need to cultivate a process of systematic reflection as ethical dilemmas emerge from these contending interests and obligations. Through "contemplating real moral problems in the abstract where character is formed" (Michener, 1978, p. 1049), we may cultivate a working theory of ethical conduct, a sense of intuitive judgment, and integrity of character that are cumulative over time; in short, an ethical identity.

In Chapter One, four levels at which we reflect and deliberate about ethical issues were identified: the expressive level, where the response is purely emotional; the level of moral rules, where axioms for conduct from the larger culture and that of the organization are presented; the level of ethical analysis, including a systematic examination of the underlying ethical principles; and the postethical level, where our basic assumptions about human nature, the nature of the universe, and what constitutes knowledge and truth are considered. It was argued that it becomes more important to move to levels three and four—moral rules and ethical analysis—as we move higher in organizational responsibility. This enables us to be rationally accountable for our conduct.

A decision-making model was then presented to structure reflection and deliberation at those two levels. It consists initially of linear steps involving defining the ethical problem, describing the context, identifying the range of alternative courses of action, and projecting the probable consequences of each. However, this model also includes a nonlinear process of searching for a fit among several considerations: moral rules, ethical principles, anticipatory self-appraisal, and a rehearsal of defenses. In this final stage of resolving an ethical issue, the fit among these four elements is not a matter of sequential logic leading to an ineluctable conclusion, but more like an esthetic logic or gestalt.

In Chapter Two, two roles in particular, and the tension

between them, were identified as worthy of our sustained attention—public administrator and citizen. Both must be maintained and served if a public administrator is to behave responsibly, but they do not always mesh well with each other. The fact that the public administrator wears these two hats—citizen and employee of the citizenry—at times gives rise to conflicts between obligations to the citizenry and the organization established to serve the citizenry.

From the managerial perspective, we are concerned with maintaining responsible conduct on the part of these doubly bound individuals. Hence, in Chapters Five and Six techniques for shaping the conduct of the members of public organizations toward consistently ethical conduct were discussed—internal and external controls as general approaches in Chapter Five, specific techniques in Chapter Six. If responsible conduct is to be maintained, managers must pay attention to four sets of techniques: individual attributes, organization structure, organization culture, and societal expectations.

But, as discussed in Chapter Seven, we also worry about the self-serving tendencies of large bureaucratic structures. We fear that if public organizations begin to run amuck, our fellow citizens within them may fail to act on our behalf and in our interests, either because they have lost sight of the legitimate goals of these organizations or because they are intimidated into silence by unethical superiors. We are apprehensive that the struggle may not take place at all, with the inherent conflict between individuals and organizations being resolved too decisively in favor of the organizations, or that the struggle may assume a dominant position, consuming the time and resource of the organization. In either case, the public's intended work may never get done.

Thus, in Chapter Seven we considered the elements that are necessary to preserve individual ethical autonomy within public organizations. There organizational remedies were identified for the protection of whistle blowers and assessed as imperfect, but offering some help for those who feel compelled to exercise their conscience about misconduct within their organizations. Individual responsibility was seen as the final protection against organizational corruption. The means of supporting individual responsibility by encouraging autonomy include (1) the conscious delimitation of commitment to an employing organization and the cultivation of identities that transcend its boundaries, (2) legal and institutional protection for individual rights and conscience, and (3) an ethic of awareness. A systematic process for evaluating one's role at the limits of organizational loyalty was outlined as one means for determining a course of action in crises.

It seems then, as Whyte observed a quarter-century ago, that there is an inherent tension between individuals and the organizations in which they are employed. This is certainly true for individuals who attempt to take seriously their ethical responsibility both as citizens and as employees of the citizenry. Some means of managing this conflict, therefore, is in order; some way of preserving a desirable level of individual autonomy while maintaining the collective goals for which public organizations are created. The elements necessary for this kind of balancing of interests have already been identified and discussed. It now remains only to combine these two perspectives.

A Model of Responsible Administration

A general model for responsible administration that acknowledges the necessary and legitimate role duality of the public administrator may be constructed by combining the *components of responsible conduct,* discussed in Chapter Six, and the *components of individual autonomy,* outlined in Chapter Seven. Such a model recognizes the obligations of the organizational and the citizen roles; however, it is assumed here that the priority of the citizen role must ultimately be maintained. When our obligations as a citizen to our fellow citizens are clearly in conflict with the demands of a public organization, the more fundamental duty is to the citizenry.

In the model for responsible administration (see Table 1), it should be clear that the two sets of components, and the actions that follow from them, are not inherently, necessarily, or continuously in opposition. All or some of the components of responsible conduct may be more or less in conflict with all or some of the components of individual ethical autonomy, depending on the extent to which both the organization and any given administrator are responsive to the legally mandated mission of the organization. If an agency deviates from the accomplishment of its mission while an administrator remains committed to it, there will be conflict. On the other hand, if an administrator deviates from an organization's mission either through misconduct or perceived obligations to the public, while the organization remains devoted to the mission, conflict will result. Incongruence between administrative obligation and de facto or de jure organizational goals will produce tension and conflict.

The model proposed, therefore, is not a simple balancing of neatly opposing elements, but rather it identifies elements that together can provide corrective forces if incongruence occurs. It represents a field of forces that can create checks and balances on organizational corruption, self-service, and tyranny, on the one hand, and individual corruption, self-service, and arrogance, on the other.

Since these two sets of components have been dealt with at some length in Chapters Six and Seven, they will not be discussed here. However, it may be useful to comment briefly on each of the juxtaposed pairs of actions.

Acting within current codes of ethics and ethics legislation provides the routine points of reference for what is deemed to be ethical conduct for public administrators. Together these represent the generalized formal judgments of the political and professional communities about acceptable and unacceptable conduct. However, both leave large areas of interpretation and judgment to practicing administrators in concrete situations. This process of interpreting and applying the specifications of ethics legislation and codes of ethics should be informed by the core values that represent the foundations of the political tradition, sometimes referred to as regime values, as well as by the developed conscience of the administrator. These encourage compliance with the spirit of the law and codes rather than merely the letter. Also, internalized political values and developed conscience provide a check on self-protective and self-serving codes, which professional associations have been known to adopt. They also establish a broader point of reference from which to evaluate the legitimacy of any particular piece of ethics legislation.

Maintaining and enhancing knowledge of the professional

Table 1. Model of Responsible Administration.

Components of Responsible Conduct	Components of Individual Ethical Autonomy
• Individual attributes • Organization structure • Organization culture • Societal expectations	• Organization delimitation and transcendence • Legal and institutional mechanism for constraining organizational power • Self-awareness

Responsible Administrative Action

Act within provision of current codes and ethics legislation.	Act within values of the political community and personal conscience
Maintain and enhance the knowledge of the professional field systems.	Maintain and develop current knowledge of the social, political, and economic systems.
Maintain and develop knowledge of the organization, its mission, and policy arena.	Maintain and develop knowledge of own values, beliefs, convictions, world view and life priorities.
Commit energy and time to work of the organization and its purposes.	Maintain and cultivate family, social, and community relationships.
Make decisions consistent with legally mandated mission of the organization.	Offer proposals for legislative change in organizational mission based on public preferences, demands, and interests.
Acknowledge accountability to hierarchical structure of organization.	Question, resist, and challenge orders inconsistent with mission of organization, professional codes, values of the political conscience. Offer proposals for legal and institutional protection from retaliation.
Exercise best technical judgment.	Provide for regular and accessible public participation.
Comply with organization's informal norms and procedures.	Propose changes in norms, rules, regulations, and procedures based on public preferences, demand, and interests; professional judgment; or personal conscience.
Work within specialized structure of the organization.	Encourage collaboration among units with other organizations, elected officials, and the public.

field makes public administrators responsible for having a competent basis from which to perceive a range of alternative courses of action when confronting an ethical issue. It also provides the necessary basis for evaluating the performance of themselves and others. However, that kind of professional knowledge needs to be complemented by a more comprehensive understanding of the social, economic, and political systems. This broader knowledge discourages a narrowly professional perspective and overcommitment to an employing organization. It encourages carrying out public administration as an integral part of the larger political, economic, and social context. It confronts us with obligations to a democratic society with a diverse social fabric and makes us more aware of the economic consequences of our administrative actions.

Maintaining and developing knowledge of the organization, its mission, and its policy arena is essential for adequately carrying out our responsibilities as an employee of a particular public organization. This broader knowledge, broader than our specific job tasks, is the way we move beyond being simple instrumental functionaries and carry a share of responsibility for the overall functioning of the organization and the creative solving of public problems. The necessary complement to this job-related knowledge is our personal values, beliefs, convictions, world view, and life priorities. To appropriately bound the demands and influence of the organization and maintain some degree of ethical autonomy, we must consciously develop self-awareness through regularly reflecting on our position in relationship to job-related issues, as well as where we stand on a broad range of political, social, and philosophical concerns. This is the means by which we develop an identity apart from the employment role.

Commitment of energy and time to the work and purposes of the organization is clearly required of anyone who presumes to accept the role of a fiduciary of the citizenry. This role requires us to set aside private projects and interests, and engage seriously and actively in the work of the public. This includes bringing our best creative insights to bear on public problems. This responsibility includes maintaining physical health, clarity of mind, and focused attention while on the job. However, maintaining family, social, and community relationships is equally essential. Public administrators cannot effectively carry out the role of fiduciary citizen without ongoing experience with, and commitment to, these other enclaves of life. Without these dimensions of life the organization may become too dominant in our thinking; we may lose other points of reference. A citizen administrator must also be a citizen who is consistently involved in private life.

Making decisions congruent with the legally mandated mission of the organization is fundamental to the fulfillment of the employment role and the proper functioning of the hierarchical system of the public organization. This commitment provides a discipline of purpose and a constraint on the personal biases and preferences of the individual administrator and on the tendencies of superiors in the hierarchy to turn public organizations into their own private power fiefdoms. Everyone in the hierarchy must be reminded regularly of what the law adopted by the elected representatives of the citizenry has mandated as the goals and objectives of its work. On the other hand, we should not presume that the law is perfect and simply to be served at any given moment. Public administrators are obligated to offer proposals to their organizational superiors and to the people for changes in the mission of the organization as they learn more about public preferences and the nature of the problems to be solved.

Responsible public administrators generally should acknowledge their accountability to the hierarchical structure of the organization. When functioning properly the hierarchy is, as Appleby suggests, the structure of responsibility; it is the means for managing different levels of responsibility for the mission of the organization and the appropriate delegation of authority. However, being accountable to superiors does not necessarily mean simply following orders that are illegitimate. Administrators are also obligated to question, resist, and challenge orders that are inconsistent with the mission of the organization, established professional codes, the values of the political community, or their own conscience. Ultimately they must maintain accountability to the citizenry, professional colleagues, and their own principles. Superiors who deviate seriously from these touchstones should be confronted with the administrator's best judgment and reasons for believing that orders are not legitimate. This responsibility includes contributing to the development of institutional arrangements that will provide reasonable protection for administrators offering such challenges to superiors. Individual responsibility needs to be buttressed with supportive mechanisms for whistle blowers when such action becomes necessary.

Administrators of the public's business should exercise their best technical judgment when tackling complex problems. Their technical knowledge and skills are tools for which they are being paid; they are the specific justification for the fiduciary role on behalf of the people. However, technical judgment must be complemented with intelligence from the citizenry through regular and effective opportunities for participation. Technical expertise alone does not guarantee that government will be *of* and *by* the people as well as *for* them. Technical efficiency and even effectiveness should be subordinated to the will of the citizenry. In this way professional values are regularly informed by the public. Responsible administrators bring their expertise to bear on problems, do their best to educate the citizenry about the technical considerations in an issue, but ultimately accept the right of the people to influence the decision and action, even the right of the people to be wrong.

Complying with the organization's informal norms, rules, regulations, and procedures is ordinarily required of a responsible public administrator. These are the specific organizational means for structuring and maintaining work that is consistent with the organization's legitimate mission. However, at times these controls may subvert the mission or detract from its achievement, as in goal displacement. A truly responsible administrator will bear an obligation to propose changes when they become problematic for the wishes of the public, inconsistent with professional judgment, or in conflict with personal conscience. It is irresponsible to simply ignore or circumvent inappropriate rules, norms, and procedures, on the one hand, or reluctantly comply with them, on the other.

Public administrators must work within the specialized structure of the employing organization; that is their most immediate obligation and deserves their initial loyalty and effort. That particular piece of the public's property is entrusted to their care and use. Nevertheless, responsible administrators should also bear a larger obligation to encouarge collaboration, rather than competition, with other units, organizations, elected officials, and the public. Suboptimization does not enhance the work of the government as a whole; it wastes resources. Most complex problems require the effective cooperation of various governmental units, as well as the citizenry.

These two sets of components may be used as a template or guide for organizational diagnosis and design. They suggest the essential ingredients that we ought to look for in existing organizations, as well as those that ought to be built into new ones. This model for the sustenance of responsible administrators is an ideal type in the Weberian tradition. It is a construct that will never be fully actualized in any specific, concrete organizational manifestation. Nevertheless, it indicates the complexity of maintaining responsible administration and responsible administrators, and identifies the areas of organizational life to which we should direct our research, analysis, training, and organizational development.

This model is consistent with Ralph Kilmann's admonitions to avoid "quick fixes" (1984). Attention to any one or even several of the essential components will not be adequate to maintain the precarious balance between citizenship and the organization. Only a comprehensive review and treatment of the relevant aspects of an organization's structure, its personnel, training programs, formal rules and policies, prevailing informal norms, relationship to the citizens, and the laws under which it operates will be fully sufficient. A long-term commitment to a plan for organization and personnel development based on such a review will produce far more significant results than sporadic efforts.

However, it is also true that no particular public organization can fully accomplish the task on its own. Elected officials, citizens' organizations, professional associations, and academic institutions will be required to contribute in significant ways as well. Some portion of the work to be done lies beyond both the capacity of public agencies and their perceived interests. Thus, although much can and must be addressed entirely within public organizations, some of the work will entail partnership arrangements, and still other tasks will have to be undertaken outside, and apart from, these public organizations. Responsible administration is not just the task of those who practice public administration, but rather it is the work of all who strive for a democratic society in an administrative state.

References

Aiken, H. D. *Reason and Conduct.* New York: Knopf, 1962.

American Society for Public Administration. "Whistle Blowing, A Time to Listen . . . A Time to Hear." Policy Statement adopted Dec. 2, 1979.

American Society for Public Administration. "Code of Ethics and Implementation Guidelines." Washington, D.C.: American Society for Public Administration, 1985.

"Appearance of Success Is Key to Tax Audit System." *Los Angeles Times,* Dec. 21, 1979.

Appleby, P. H. *Morality and Administration in Democratic Government.* Baton Rouge: Louisiana State University Press, 1952.

Appleby, P. H. "Public Administration and Democracy." In R. C. Martin (ed.), *Public Administration and Democracy: Essays in Honor of Paul Appleby.* Syracuse, N.Y.: Syracuse University Press, 1965.

Arendt, H. *Eichman in Jerusalem.* New York: Viking Penguin, 1963.

Arthur D. Little, Inc. *Effective Citizen Participation in Transportation Planning.* Washington, D.C.: U.S. Department of Transportation, 1976.

Association of the Bar of the City of New York Special Committee on the Federal Conflict of Interest Laws. *Conflict of Interest and Federal Service.* Cambridge, Mass.: Harvard University Press, 1960.

Bailey, S. K. "The Relationship Between Ethics and Public Service." In R. C. Martin (ed.), *Public Administration and Democracy: Essays in Honor of Paul Appleby.* Syracuse, N.Y.: Syracuse University Press, 1965.

Banton, M. *Roles: An Introduction to the Study of Social Relations.* New York: Basic Books, 1965.

Barnard, C. I. "A Definition of Authority." In Robert K. Merton et al. (eds.), *Reader in Bureaucracy.* New York: Free Press, 1952.

Barnard, C. I. *The Functions of the Executive.* Cambridge, Mass.: Harvard University Press, 1964.

Bates, S. "My Lai and Viet Nam: The Issues of Responsibility." In P. A. French (ed.), *Individual and Collective Responsibility: The Massacre at My Lai.* Cambridge, Mass.: Schenkman, 1972.

Baumhart, H. "How Ethical Are Businessmen?" *Harvard Business Review,* 1961, pp. 6–9.

Beard, E. "Conflicts of Interest and Public Service." In J. T. DeGeorge and J. A. Pichler (eds.), *Ethics, Free Enterprise and Public Policy.* New York: Oxford University Press, 1978.

Beard, E., and Horn, S. *Congressional Ethics: The View from the House.* Washington, D.C.: The Brookings Institution, 1975.

Becker, H. "Whose Side Are We On?" In *Annual Editions Readings in Social Problems 1973–74.* Guilford, Conn.: Dushkin, 1973.

Belford, T. S., and Adams, B. "Conflict of Interest Legislation and the Common Cause Model Act." In *The Municipal Year Book.* Washington, D.C.: National League of Cities, 1975.

Bellah, R. N., and others. *Habits of the Heart: Individualism and Commitment in American Life.* Berkeley and Los Angeles: University of California Press, 1985.

Bennis, W. *Beyond Bureaucracy: Essays on the Development and Evolution of Human Organizations.* New York: McGraw-Hill, 1966.

Bentley, A. F. *The Process of Government*. San Antonio, Tex.: Principia, 1949.

Benveniste, G. *The Politics of Expertise*. (2nd ed.) San Francisco: Boyd & Fraser, 1977.

Berger, P., Berger, B., and Kellner, H. *The Homeless Mind: Modernization and Consciousness*. New York: Vintage Books, 1973.

Berger, P., and Luckman, T. *The Social Construction of Reality*. New York: Doubleday, 1966.

Berger, P., and Neuhouse, R. J. *To Empower People: The Role of Mediating Structures in Public Policy*. Washington, D.C.: American Enterprise Institute, 1977.

Brenner, S., and Mollandar, E. "Is the Ethics of Business Changing?" *Harvard Business Review*, 1977, *55* (1), 57–71.

Buchanan, J. M., and Tullock, G. *The Calculus of Consent: Logical Foundations of Constitutional Democracy*. Ann Arbor: University of Michigan Press, 1962.

Burke, J. P. *Bureaucratic Responsibility*. Baltimore, Md.: Johns Hopkins University Press, 1986.

Caiden, G. E., and Truelson, J. A. "Whistleblower Protection in the USA: Lessons Learnt and to Be Learnt." *Australian Journal of Public Administration*, 1988, *47* (2), 119–29.

Calhoun, J. C. *A Disquisition on Government and Selections from the Discourse*. G. Post (ed.). New York: Liberal Arts Press, 1953.

Caro, R. A. *The Power Broker: Robert Moses and the Fall of New York*. New York: Vintage, 1975.

Chandler, R. C. "The Problem of Moral Reasoning in American Public Administration: The Case for a Code of Ethics." *Public Administration Review*, 1983, *43* (1), 32–39.

Chandler, R. C. "The Public Administrator as Representative Citizen: A New Role for the New Century." In H. G. Frederickson and R. C. Chandler, "Citizenship and Public Administration." *Public Administration Review*, 1984, special issue, 196–206.

Cleveland, H. *The Future Executive*. New York: Harper & Row, 1972.

Code of Ethics for Government Service. Joint resolution of the U.S. House of Representatives and the U.S. Senate as: "House Concurrent Resolution 175 in the Second Session of the 85th Congress."

Cooper, T. L. "The Hidden Price Tag: Participation Costs and Health Planning." *American Journal of Public Health,* 1979, *69* (4), 368–74.

Cooper, T. L. "Hierarchy, Virtue, and the Practice of Public Administration: A Perspective for Normative Ethics." *Public Administration Review,* 1987, *47* (4), 320–28.

Cooper, T. L. *An Ethic of Citizenship for Public Administration.* Englewood Cliffs, N.J.: Prentice Hall, 1991.

Crozier, M. *The Stalled Society.* New York: Viking Penguin, 1973.

Davis, K. C. *Discretionary Justice: A Preliminary Inquiry.* Baton Rouge: Louisiana State University Press, 1969.

Davis, M. "Conflict of Interest." *Business and Professional Ethics Journal,* 1982, *1* (4), 17–27.

Dean, J. *Blind Ambition.* New York: Simon & Schuster, 1976.

De Grazia, S. *Of Time, Work and Leisure.* Garden City, N.Y.: Anchor Books, 1964.

Denhardt, K. G. *The Ethics of Public Service.* New York: Greenwood Press, 1988.

Dewey, J. *Human Nature and Conduct.* New York: Holt, Rinehart & Winston, 1922.

Dewey, J. *The Public and Its Problems.* Chicago: Swallow Press, 1927.

Downie, R. S. *Roles and Values: An Introduction to Social Ethics.* London: Methuen, 1971.

Downie, R. S. "Responsibility and Social Roles." In P. A. French, *Individual and Collective Responsibility: The Massacre at My Lai.* Cambridge, Mass.: Schenkman, 1972.

Drews, E. M., and Lipson, L. *Values and Humanity.* New York: St. Martin's Press, 1971.

Durkheim, E. *Professional Ethics and Civic Morals.* C. Brookfield (trans.). Boston: Routledge & Kegan Paul, 1957.

Dvorin, E. P., and Simmons, R. H. *From Amoral to Humane Bureaucracy.* San Francisco: Canfield Press, 1972.

Egger, R. "Responsibility in Administration: An Exploratory Essay." In R. C. Martin (ed.), *Public Administration and Democracy: Essays in Honor of Paul Appleby.* Syracuse, N.Y.: Syracuse University Press, 1965.

Emmet, D. *Rules, Roles and Relations.* New York: St. Martin's Press, 1967.

Ewing, D. *Freedom Inside the Organization: Bringing Civil Liberties to the Work Place.* New York: Dutton, 1977.

Federal Personnel Manual, 1972.

Finer, H. "Administrative Responsibility in Democratic Government." In Rourke, F., *Bureaucratic Power in National Politics.* (2nd ed.) Boston: Little, Brown, 1972. (Originally published 1941.)

Finer, H. "Better Government Personnel." *Political Science Quarterly,* 1936, *51* (4), 569–99.

First Annual Report to the Congress on the Activities of the Office of Special Counsel. Washington, D.C.: U.S. Government Printing Office, 1979.

Fleishman, J. L., Liebman, L., and Moore, M. H. (ed.). *Public Duties: The Moral Obligations of Government Officials.* Cambridge, Mass.: Harvard University Press, 1981.

Foster, G. D. "Law, Morality, and the Public Servant." *Public Administration Review,* 1981, *41* (1), 29–33.

Frederickson, H. G. "Toward a New Public Administration." In F. Marini (ed.), *Toward a New Public Administration: The Minnowbrook Perspective.* Scranton, Penn.: Chandler, 1971.

Frederickson, H. G., and Hart, D. K. "The Public Service and the Patriotism of Benevolence." *Public Administration Review,* 1985, *45* (5), 547–53.

French, P. "Nuremberg Trials: The Jodl Defense." In *Individual and Collective Responsibility: The Massacre at My Lai.* Cambridge, Mass.: Schenkman, 1972.

Friedrich, C. J. "Responsible Government Service under the American Constitution." Monograph No. 7 in C. J. Friedrich and others, *Problems of the American Public Service.* New York: McGraw-Hill, 1935.

Friedrich, C. J. "Some Observations on Weber's Analysis of Bureaucracy." In R. Merton (ed.), *Reader in Bureaucracy.* New York: Free Press, 1952.

Friedrich, C. J. "The Dilemma of Administrative Responsibility." In C. J. Friedrich (ed.), *Responsibility.* New York: Liberal Arts Press, 1960.

Friedrich, C. J. (ed.). *The Public Interest.* New York: Atherton Press, 1962.

Friedrich, C. J. "Public Policy and the Nature of Administrative Responsibility." In F. E. Rourke (ed.), *Bureaucratic Power in National Politics.* (2nd ed.) Boston: Little, Brown, 1972. (Originally published 1940.)

Gaus, J. M. "The Responsibility of Public Administrators." In J. M. Gaus, L. D. White, and M. Dimock (eds.), *The Frontiers of Public Administration.* Chicago: University of Chicago Press, 1936.

Goodnow, F. *Politics and Administration.* New York: Macmillan, 1900.

Gorney, R. *The Human Agenda.* New York: Simon & Schuster, 1972.

Graham, G. A. "Ethical Guidelines for Public Administrators: Observations on Rules of the Game." Washington, D.C.: National Academy of Public Administration, n.d.

Grunebaum, J. O. "What Ought the Representative Represent?" In N. E. Bowie (ed.), *Ethical Issues in Government.* Philadelphia: Temple University Press, 1981.

Gustafson, J. "Notes on Theology and Ethics." In D. Jenkins (ed.), *The Scope of Theology.* Cleveland, Ohio: World Publishing, 1965.

Guy, M. E. "Minnowbrook II: Conclusions." *Public Administration Review,* 1989, *49* (2), 219-20.

Hardin, G. "The Tragedy of the Commons." In G. Hardin and J. Baden, *Managing the Commons.* San Francisco: Freeman, 1977.

Harel, I. *The House on Garibaldi Street.* New York: Bantam Books, 1975.

Harmon, M. "Administrative Policy Formulation and the Public Interest." *Public Administration Review,* 1969, *29* (5), 483-91.

Harmon, M. "Normative Theory." In Frank Marini (ed.), *Toward a New Public Administration: The Minnowbrook Perspective.* Scranton, Penn.: Chandler, 1971.

Hart, D. K. "The Virtuous Citizen, the Honorable Bureaucrat, and 'Public' Administration." *Public Administration Review,* 1984, *44,* Special Issue on Citizenship, 111-20.

Heclo, H. "OMB and the Presidency—The Problem of Neutral Competence." *The Public Interest*, 1975, *38* (2), 80–98.

Hejka-Ekins, A. "Teaching Ethics in Public Administration." *Public Administration Review*, 1988, *48* (5), 885–91.

Held, V. *The Public Interest and Individual Interests*. New York: Basic Books, 1970.

Isenberg, D. J. "How Senior Managers Think." *Harvard Business Review*, Nov.-Dec. 1984, *62*, 81–90.

Jackall, R. "Moral Mazes: Bureaucracy and Managerial Work," *Harvard Business Review*, Sept.-Oct. 1983, pp. 118–30.

Jackson, R. *The Case Against the Nazi War Criminals*. New York: Knopf, 1946.

Jackson, R. *The Nurnberg Case*. New York: Knopf, 1947.

Janis, I. L., and Mann, L. *Decision Making*. New York: Free Press, 1977.

Jaques, E. *A General Theory of Bureaucracy*. New York: Halsted Press, 1976.

Jaworski, L. *The Right and the Power*. New York: Pocketbooks, 1977.

Jones, W. J., Sontag, F., Becker, M. O., and Fogelin, R. *Approaches to Ethics*. (2nd ed.) New York: McGraw-Hill, 1969.

Jos, P. H., Tompkins, M. E., and Hays, S. W. "In Praise of Difficult People: A Portrait of the Committed Whistleblower." *Public Administration Review*, 1989, *49* (6), 552–61.

Judd, R. R. "Ethics Codes and Commissions Legislation and Litigation in [by year]." Available through the Council on Governmental Ethics Legislation, P.O. Box 11910, Iron Works Pike, Lexington, KY 40578-9989.

Kernaghan, K. *Ethical Conduct: Guidelines for Government Employees*. Toronto: Institute of Public Administration of Canada, 1975.

Kilmann, R. H. *Beyond the Quick Fix: Managing Five Tracks to Organizational Success*. San Francisco: Jossey-Bass, 1984.

King, G. D. "Commentary on Codes of Ethics of the International Association of Chiefs of Police." In I. Hill (ed.), *The Ethical Basis of Economic Freedom*. Chapel Hill, N.C.: American Viewpoint, 1976.

Kneier, A. "Ethics in Government Service." In I. Hill (ed.), *The*

Ethical Basis of Economic Freedom. Chapel Hill, N.C.: American Viewpoint, 1976.

Leahy, P. J. *The Whistle Blowers: A Report on Federal Employees Who Disclose Acts of Governmental Waste, Abuse and Corruption*. Prepared for the Committee on Governmental Affairs, United States Senate. Washington, D.C.: U.S. Government Printing Office, 1978.

Lieberman, J. K. *How the Government Breaks the Law*. Baltimore: Viking Penguin Books, 1973.

Lippman, W. *Public Opinion*. San Diego: Harcourt Brace Jovanovich, 1922.

Little, A. D. *Effective Citizen Participation in Transportation Planning*. Washington, D.C.: U.S. Department of Transportation, 1976.

London, P. *Behavior Control*. New York: Harper & Row, 1971.

Lowi, T. J. *The End of Liberalism: The Second Republic of the United States*. (2nd ed.) New York: Norton, 1979.

Luebke, N. R. "Conflict of Interest as a Moral Category." *Business and Professional Ethics Journal*, 1986, *6* (1), 66–81.

MacIntyre, A. *After Virtue*. (2nd ed.) Notre Dame, Ind.: Notre Dame University Press, 1984.

McKeon, R. "The Development and the Significance of the Concept of Responsibility." *Revue Internationale de Philosophie*, 1957, *2* (39), 3–32.

Mayer, R. T. "Minnowbrook II: Conclusions and Reflections." *Public Administration Review*, 1989, *49* (2), 218.

Margolis, J. "Conflict of Interest and Conflicting Interests." In T. L. Beuchamp and N. B. Bowie (eds.), *Ethical Theory and Business*. Englewood Cliffs, N.J.: Prentice-Hall, 1979.

Marini, F. (ed.). *Toward a New Public Administration: The Minnowbrook Perspective*. Scranton, Penn.: Chandler Publishing Company, 1971.

Marx, F. M. *Public Management in the New Democracy*. New York: Harper & Row, 1940.

Mathews, D. "Afterthoughts . . ." *Kettering Review*, Winter 1985, pp. 60–63.

Means, R. *The Ethical Imperative*. New York: Doubleday, 1970.

Meier, K. J. *Politics and the Bureaucracy*. Boston: Duxbury Press, 1979.

Merit Systems Protection Board. *Blowing the Whistle in the Federal Government: A Comparative Analysis of 1980 and 1983 Survey Findings*. Washington, D.C.: U.S. Government Printing Office, October 1984.

Mertins, H. (ed.). *Professional Standards and Ethics: A Workbook for Public Administrators*. Washington, D.C.: American Society for Public Administration, 1979.

Mertins, H., and Hennigan, P. J., (eds.). *Applying Professional Standards and Ethics in the Eighties: A Workbook Study Guide for Public Administrators*. Washington, D.C.: American Society for Public Administration, 1982.

Merton, R. K. "Bureaucratic Structure and Personality." In R. K. Merton (ed.), *Reader on Bureaucracy*. New York: Free Press, 1952.

Michener, J. A. *Chesapeake*. New York: Random House, 1978.

Milgram, S. *Obedience to Authority: An Experimental View*. New York: Harper & Row, 1974.

Mosher, F. *Democracy and the Public Service*. New York: Oxford University Press, 1968.

Nachmias, D., and Rosenbloom, D. H. *Bureaucratic Government USA*. New York: St. Martin's Press, 1980.

Nader, R., Perkas, P. J., and Blackwell, K. *Whistle Blowing*. New York: Grossman, 1972.

Nelson, W. E. *The Roots of American Bureaucracy, 1830–1900*. Cambridge, Mass.: Harvard University Press, 1982.

Ornstein, N. J., and Elder, S. *Interest Groups, Lobbyists and Policymaking*. Washington, D.C.: Congressional Quarterly Press, 1978.

Ostrom, V. *The Intellectual Crisis in American Public Administration*. (2nd ed.) University: University of Alabama Press, 1974.

Parenti, M. "Power and Pluralism: A View from the Bottom." *Journal of Politics*, 1970, *32* (3), 501–30.

Peace Officer Standards and Training Commission of the State of California. "Career Ethics/Integrity Training Approved." *POST Scripts*, 1988, *22* (3), 6.

Perrow, C. *Complex Organizations: A Critical Essay.* Glenview, Ill.: Scott, Foresman, 1972.

Peters, T. J., and Waterman, R. H. *In Search of Excellence: Lessons from America's Best-Run Companies.* New York: Warner, 1982.

Pincoffs, E. L. *Quandaries and Virtues.* Lawrence: University Press of Kansas, 1986.

Porter, D. O. "Minnowbrook II: Conclusions." *Public Administration Review,* 1989, *49* (2), 223.

Pranger, R. *The Eclipse of Citizenship: Power and Participation in Contemporary Politics.* New York: Holt, Rinehart & Winston, 1968.

Preimsberger, D. T., and Block, S. "Values, Standards and Integrity in Law Enforcement: An Emphasis on Job Survival." *Journal of California Law Enforcement,* 1986, *20* (1), 10–13.

"Proposed Civil Service Changes May Encourage Whistle-blowers." *Los Angeles Times,* Jan. 5, 1978.

Ramos, A. G. "Models of Man and Administrative Theory." *Public Administration Review,* 1972, *32* (3), 241–46.

Ramos, A. G. *The New Science of Organizations: A Reconceptualization of the Wealth of Nations.* Toronto: University of Toronto Press, 1981.

Rawls, J. *A Theory of Justice.* Cambridge, Mass.: Belknap Press of Harvard University Press, 1971.

Rescher, N. "What Is Value Change?" In K. Baier and N. Rescher (eds.), *Values and the Future.* New York: Free Press, 1969.

Riesman, D., Glazer, N., and Denney, R. *The Lonely Crowd.* New York: Doubleday, 1955.

Rokeach, M. *Beliefs, Attitudes and Values.* San Francisco: Jossey-Bass, 1970.

Rohr, J. *Ethics for Bureaucrats.* (2nd ed.) New York: Marcel Dekker, 1989.

Rohr, J. "The Study of Ethics in the P. A. Curriculum." *Public Administration Review,* 1976, *36* (4), 398–406.

Rosener, J. B. "Citizen Participation: Tying Strategy to Function." In P. Marshall (ed.), *Citizen Participation for Community Involvement: A Reader on the Citizen Participation Process.* Washington, D.C.: National Association of Housing and Redevelopment Officials, 1977.

Sabini, J., and Silver, M. *Moralities of Everyday Life*. New York: Oxford University Press, 1982.

Schein, E. H. *Organizational Culture and Leadership: A Dynamic View*. San Francisco: Jossey-Bass, 1985.

Schmidt, W., and Posner, B. *Managerial Values in Perspective*. New York: American Management Associations, 1983.

Schmidt, W., and Posner, B. "Values and Expectations of Federal Service Executives." *Public Administration Review*, 1986, *46* (5), 447–54.

Schutz, A. *On Phenomenology and Social Relations*. H. R. Wagner (ed.). Chicago: University of Chicago Press, 1970.

Scott, W. G., and Hart, D. K. *Organizational America*. Boston: Houghton Mifflin, 1979.

Selznick, P. *TVA and the Grass Roots: A Study in the Sociology of Formal Organization*. New York: Harper Torchbooks, 1966.

Sennett, R. *The Fall of Public Man*. New York: Vintage Books, 1974.

Sherman, L. "Learning Police Ethics." *Criminal Justice Ethics*, 1987, *1* (1), 10–19.

Small, J. "Political Ethics: A View of the Leadership." *American Behavioral Scientist*, 1976, *19* (5), 543–66.

Srivastva, S., and Cooperrider, D. L. "The Urgency for Executive Integrity." In S. Srivastva and Associates, *Executive Integrity: The Search for High Human Values in Organizational Life*. San Francisco: Jossey-Bass, 1988.

Stahl, G. O. *Public Personnel Administration*. (7th ed.) New York: Harper & Row, 1976.

Stein, J. *Fiddler on the Roof*. New York: Crown Publishers, 1971.

Subcommittee of the Committee on Labor and Public Welfare, United States Senate. *Ethical Standards in Government*. Washington, D.C.: Government Printing Office, 1951.

Thompson, D. F. *The Democratic Citizen*. New York: Cambridge University Press, 1970.

Thompson, D. F. "The Possibility of Administrative Ethics." *Public Administration Review*, 1985, *45* (5), 555–61.

Thompson, V. A. *Without Sympathy or Enthusiasm: The Problem of Administrative Compassion*. University: University of Alabama Press, 1975.

Thompson, V. A. *Bureaucracy and the Modern World.* Morristown, N.J.: General Learning Press, 1976.

Truman, D. B. *The Governmental Process.* New York: Knopf, 1951.

Tullock, G. *The Politics of Bureaucracy.* Washington, D.C.: Public Affairs Press, 1965.

Tussman, J. *Obligation and the Body Politic.* New York: Oxford University Press, 1960.

Wakefield, S. "Ethics and the Public Service: A Case for Individual Responsibility." *Public Administration Review,* 1976, *36* (6), 661–66.

Waldo, D. *The Administrative State: A Study of the Political Theory of Public Administration.* New York: Ronald Press, 1948.

Waldo, D. "Public Administration and Culture." In R. C. Martin (ed.), *Public Administration and Democracy: Essays in Honor of Paul Appleby.* Syracuse, N.Y.: Syracuse University Press, 1965.

Waldo, D. "Reflections on Public Morality." *Administration and Society,* 1974, *6* (3), 267–82.

Walzer, M. *Obligations: Essays on Disobedience, War and Citizenship.* Cambridge, Mass.: Harvard University Press, 1970.

Wamsley, G. L., and Zald, M. M. *The Political Economy of Public Organizations: A Critique and Approach to the Study of Public Administration.* Bloomington: Indiana University Press, 1973.

Warren, R., and Weschler, L. "The Costs of Citizenship." In R. Warren and L. Weschler, *Governing Urban Space,* 1975 (unpublished).

Watkins, B. T. "Few Colleges Found to Offer Ethics Courses." *The Chronicle of Higher Education,* June 30, 1980.

Weber, M. In H. H. Gerth and C. W. Mills (eds.), *From Max Weber: Essays in Sociology.* New York: Oxford University Press, 1946.

Weisband, E., and Franck, T. M. *Resignation in Protest: Political and Ethical Choices Between Loyalty to Team and Loyalty to Conscience in American Public Life.* New York: Grossman, 1975.

White, L. D. *Introduction to the Study of Public Administration.* New York: Macmillan, 1926.

Whyte, W. H., Jr. *The Organization Man.* New York: Simon & Schuster, 1956.

Wilensky, H. *Organizational Intelligence.* New York: Basic Books, 1967.

Wilson, W. "The Study of Administration." *Political Science Quarterly*, 1887, 2 (1), 197–220.

Winter, G. *Elements for a Social Ethic*. New York: Macmillan, 1966.

Wolin, S. "The Age of Organization and the Sublimation of Politics." In S. Wolin, *Politics and Vision: Continuity and Innovation in Western Political Thought*. Boston: Little, Brown, 1960.

Wright, D. *The Psychology of Moral Behavior*. Baltimore, Md.: Penguin, 1971.

Yankelovich, D. *New Rules: Searching for Self-Fulfillment in a World Turned Upside Down*. New York: Random House, 1981.

Index

A

Administration: generic approach, 45–46; political nature, 35–39; responsible (model), 226–230; and social equity, 47–48; and virtue, 165–166

Administrative ethics. *See* Ethics

Administrators: accountability, 60, 61–62; attitudes, 162–163; citizen role, 40–44; and citizenry, 68–71; conflicts of interest, 109, 111; as diversity managers, 44–48; educational role, 52–55; and elected officials, 53–54, 62–63; fiduciary responsibility, 42; functional rationality, 40–41; implementation role, 56–57; and modernization, 34–48; moral qualities, 163–164; objective responsibility, 59–71; obligation, 60–61; and organizational politics, 38–39; and public par-

ticipation, 180–181; representative role, 50–51; responsiveness, 145–146; roles, 35–36, 38, 40–44, 49–57; subjective responsibility, 71–76; and superiors/subordinates, 63–68, 188–191; values, 166–167

Advisory Panel on Ethics and Conflict of Interest in Government, 135

After Virtue, 164

Agentic shift: defined, 198; Eichmann example, 199–201; and personal responsibility, 198–201, 205

Aiken, H. D., 7

American Public Works Association, 138

American Society of Civil Service Engineers, 138

American Society for Public Administration (ASPA), 25, 73, 90, 125, 139–140, 151–152, 203

"Appearance of Success Is Key to Tax Audit System," 193–194